Crisis at Tiananmen

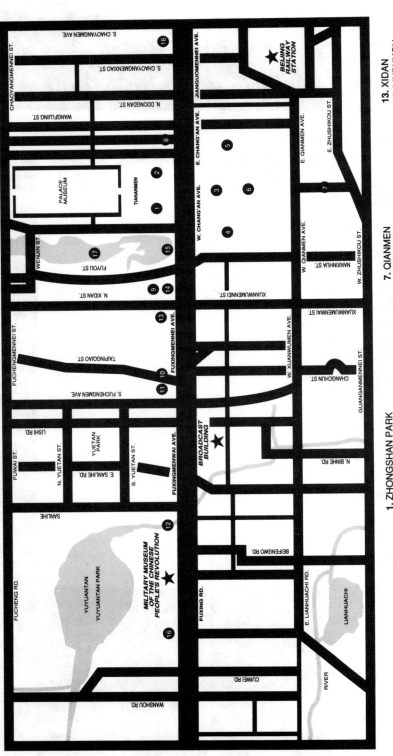

1. ZHONGSHAN PARK
2. WORKING PEOPLE'S CULTURE PALACE
3. THE MONUMENT TO THE PEOPLE'S HEROES
4. GREAT HALL OF THE PEOPLE
5. MUSEUM OF CHINESE REVOLUTION
   MUSEUM OF CHINESE HISTORY
6. CHAIRMAN MAO MEMORIAL HALL

7. QIANMEN
8. BEIJING HOTEL
9. TELEGRAPH BUILDING
10. MINZU (NATIONALITIES) HOTEL
11. LONG-DISTANCE TEL. BUILDING
12. MUXIDI

13. XIDAN
14. LIUBUKOU
15. XINGHUAMEN
16. GONGZHUFEN
17. ZHONGNANHAI
18. JIANGUOMEN

Crisis at Tiananmen

Reform and Reality in Modern China

by Yi Mu and
Mark V. Thompson

CHINA
BOOKS
& Periodicals, Inc.
San Francisco

Cover design by Seventeenth Street Studios
Text design by Dina Redman
Typesetting by Archetype, Berkeley, California
Photographs by Kevin Kraft, Lenore Norrgard,
John Malcolm Stonham and Sean Ramsay
Copyright © 1989 by Yi Mu and Mark V. Thompson.
All rights reserved.
First printing January 1990. Second printing April 1990.

Library of Congress Catalog Card Number: 89-81313
ISBN 0-8351-2290-5

Printed in the United States of America by: CHINA
BOOKS
& Periodicals, Inc.

Contents

Appendix Two: *Eyewitness Accounts*

Photographs (in order of appearance)

Police stand, faced off by citizens; Determined
demonstrators link arms; Faces and flags in the
demonstrations; Trucks carrying sympathetic police
(John Malcolm Stonham)
Demonstrators in the afternoon; Workers from factory
(Sean Ramsay)
Criticism of the press   *(John Malcolm Stonham)*
Monument to the People's Heroes   *(Kevin Kraft)*
The aftermath: tanks near southwest corner of
Tiananmen Square; Students attempted to talk soldiers
out of entering back of People's Congress; Tank at
Tiananmen Square; Helping evacuate Tiananmen
Square; Demonstrators protecting a soldier
(Sean Ramsay)
Soldier who was beaten, burned and hanged;
Burned military vehicles   *(Lenore Norrgard)*
Armored personnel carriers and military trucks burned;
Some of the fifteen dead civilians found in one section
of a hospital   *(Sean Ramsay)*
Staff members of the English Language *China Daily* on
May 17; Veteran professors from Beijing University;
Latest news about the student demonstration
(John Malcolm Stonham)

Preface

THIS BOOK WAS first conceived by the Chinese journalist Yi Mu, who decided that a book for the general reader was necessary to provide the American public a deeper understanding of recent events in China than could be obtained from the mass media. He believed that given China's present and future growing role in world affairs it was absolutely essential for US citizens to have a well-informed grasp of the significance of what transpired in China last spring, as well as its implications for future developments in that giant nation. Given that US-PRC relations are—in terms of formal diplomatic relations between the two states—only a decade old, there was fear that without a better understanding, a reaction to events could seriously damage the relationship between two of the world's most important powers.

Especially crucial was the need to present events from a Chinese perspective and to put the events in the context of recent Chinese history so that Americans could better understand the point of view of both the government and the students.

Mr. Yi Mu asked his American friend Mark V. Thompson to collaborate in the writing, as Yi felt it was vital to have an American to help make Chinese concepts clear to the US readers. Therefore, the book became a joint work, incorporating both American and Chinese points of view, though of course the authors' opinions do not necessarily represent a cross-section of either Chinese or American attitudes.

Because it may very well be years before full documentation and sources are available for a thoroughly in-depth analysis of the April-June 1989 events in China and because this book is intended for a general audience, footnotes and references have been kept to a minimum.

The authors have relied for the most part on newspaper accounts, both official and unofficial, from Chinese language newspapers in Hongkong and China, as well as the American media, and have also used Japanese language and French analysis and media reports of events of those days. They have also relied on many personal discussions with both informed Chinese and foreigners, some of whom were firsthand witnesses to the events in question, as well as official speeches of Chinese government authorities, and declarations and wall posters of the student movement where available and considered relevant. Names of some eyewitnesses have not been used in order to protect them from possible reprisals.

Due to the large role played by the media in communicating the events and the significance of the question of "press freedom" in China (as well as the fact that Yi Mu himself is a working journalist), special emphasis has been placed on the the role of the press. This section has deliberately not been integrated with the rest of the text, despite some possible organizational awkwardness and repetition.

The text makes no pretensions to being an exhaustive analysis of events in the spring of 1989. An entire volume could be written about the movement at Beijing University alone. It is followed by a brief chronology and appended documents. Sources are listed in the text itself rather than in footnotes.

The authors of course accept sole responsibility for any shortcomings, errors of fact, and misstatements. Moreover, they alone are solely responsible for the interpretations contained here, which are intended more as analysis than a moral judgement on the Chinese government or the student movement.

We must thank the publisher, China Books & Periodicals Inc., for agreeing to see this volume into print, but would like to emphasize that the publisher should bear no blame for any errors that may appear in the text or for controversies arising from our interpretations.

San Francisco
November 1989

PART ONE ⬣

The students love the country; I love the students.

BING XIN
A famous Chinese writer

This storm was bound to happen sooner or later. As determined by the international and domestic climate, it was bound to happen and was independent of man's will.

DENG XIAOPING
China's senior leader

The Awakening of an Old Nation

People Revolt in Beijing

ROOTS OF THE UNREST

When Chinese people call for change, they begin by doing something symbolic. In 1976, the year Mao Zedong died and the "Gang of Four" was overthrown, people in Beijing called for the leadership of a man purged twice by Mao during the Cultural Revolution and still in disgrace when Mao died. Deng Xiaoping, an old revolutionary who was labeled a "capitalist roader" by Mao and his followers, was biding his time as people exhibited small bottles in the streets of the Chinese capital, hanging them in trees and placing them in windows—a sign of popular support for Deng, because in spoken Chinese, his given name, Xiaoping, could mean "small bottle."

Two years later, in 1978, Deng emerged from disgrace and became vice chairman of the Party Central Committee and vice premier of the State Council. Although he never took the position of chairman or general secretary of the Party Central Committee or prime minister after returning to power in 1978, by holding the title of chairman of the Central Military Commission from June 1981, Deng gradually emerged as China's paramount leader. It is generally believed that he became the chief power broker as soon as he made his comeback in 1978. In fact, on June 29, 1981, in his acceptance speech after being elected chair of the Party Central Committee, Hu Yaobang

3

said clearly that "originally, in accordance with the wishes of the majority of the Party as a whole, it is Comrade Deng Xiaoping who should take this title."

Shortly after his return to power, Deng began and masterminded what the Western media have called the "second revolution." With the support and confidence of the people, Deng began to reform China's economic and political structures left over from the Maoist period. In the countryside, China dismantled the largely ineffective communes, where hundreds or even thousands of people farmed on the same tract of land and were paid according to age and sex rather than the quantity or quality of their work. The "responsibility system," in which the land was allotted to households with responsibility for managing their own production and other economic affairs, was introduced to give the peasants more incentive to work harder for more personal economic gains.

In the urban areas, reforms have proven to be more difficult, but initial success was being achieved in separating the function of the Party from that of government administration, and a more effective system was set up in many factories to help increase productivity, although serious problems of potential worker dissatisfaction remained.

Deng's economic reforms have included the introduction of a market economy into the rigid state planned economy that had existed in China since the 1950s. However, due to different views within the communist leadership as to the proper role of a market economy in a socialist system, plus strong opposition from such senior statesmen as Chen Yun, Deng took a middle path by declaring that China would retain the planned economy while the market economy would be introduced as a "supplement." This policy, which was termed "socialist commodity economy," may have been necessitated by the need to compromise with the conservative forces led by Chen. However, it is doubtful if Deng himself had ever imagined that China would adopt a full-fledged market economy.

In any event, by introducing market economy features into the planned economy, Deng and other reformers aimed to correct serious problems caused by the planned economy, such as lack of flexibility in manufacturing and lack of incentives for workers. For example, the central planning bureaucrats, far removed from an industry, might set a quota for a factory to make a quantity of steel, but fail to insure that sufficient foundry equipment was provided to enable the steel to be molded into necessary products. A market-driven economy is expected to respond more directly and with greater flexibility to actual needs and conditions than the rather cumbersome system where information is first chaneled to central planners who then issue directives and quotas.

Incentive was reduced because there was little reason to innovate or work harder once a quota was met. In some cases, especially in agriculture, when peasants' income remained basically the same regardless of how much they worked, there was less motivation to produce a surplus beyond subsistence needs. In the rural areas, peasants are now allowed to sell commodities in the free markets, an activity branded and criticized as "capitalist tails" during the Cultural Revolution. In the cities, the private economy has reappeared and attracted a number of urban citizens to join the ranks of private business people, who have now become the richest individuals in China. The appearance of private business in both the rural and urban areas was a total departure from the orthodox Cultural Revolution experience, when all economic activities had to conform strictly to an abstract ideal of "socialism."

As the "chief architect" of the reform programs, Deng deserves immense credit for the past decade of economic reform which has greatly improved the living standard of the Chinese people as a whole. Modern devices such as television sets, refrigerators, and other electronic products, which few Chinese could afford ten years ago, are now standard equipment in most urban households and some rural families. In the countryside, where ten years ago the major concern of many farmers was sheer survival, the problems of basic subsistance have been solved, although there remains some grinding poverty, as can be seen in a few mountainous areas where family members still literally have to share clothes.

Deng's successful role in feeding China's 1.1 billion people resulted in his being hailed as a national hero until recently, when people began to see smashed small bottles in some universities of Beijing. This time, the students wanted Deng out. They wanted him to truly "retire." Indeed, they were hoping that Deng would live up to his own promise that personality cults like the one dedicated to Mao would disappear from China, and that no man would hold power until the end of his later years. In fact, it was Deng himself who initiated a policy in which collective leadership should replace absolute personal power and, while forcing many older officials into retirement or semiretirement, he vowed many times to retire and "give the younger comrades a free hand to work." At the 13th Party Congress in 1987, Deng retired from several posts, including the ruling Politburo, and retained only one official position— chair of the Central Military Commission.

However, events in May and June of 1989 revealed that Deng still had considerable influence in making decisions on all major issues, and he firmly believed that he and other senior statesmen had a duty to intervene in "such big events" (as he termed the student demonstrations), although he was truly "willing to retire."

It may be difficult for Westerners to understand how a Chinese leader can continue to wield immense power even after he no longer holds an important official position. In the West, when a premier or president retires, he may remain something of an elder statesman or a power broker, but he no longer has the legal right to direct state decisions. The person's authority vanishes when he loses the office. In China, however, the person can still command considerable authority by virtue of the fact that he *is* who he is. This is due partly to the legacy of China's feudal and patriarchal past, which has made the Chinese tend to be more willing than Westerners to respect the desires and decisions of patriarchal authority figures, even when these figures have no official positions. This explains why not only Deng, but other "retired" officials could emerge as such influential figures during the Tiananmen crisis.

But of course there is always an undercurrent of resentment of this individual power, and a grudging respect for authorities can turn into outright contempt if actual living conditions deteriorate. Thus, popular dissatisfaction with officials was rapidly increasing in 1988–1989, as political unrest grew and sharp inflation was eroding recent economic gains. Rumors that Deng's own son unduly profited from his business also contributed to the general dissatisfaction felt by the populace.

Interestingly, the Chinese people, who lack the proper channels available in a democracy to voice criticisms of their leaders, once again resorted to the use of folk rhymes to satirize social problems and express their resentment for corrupt officials. Such rhymes, which are never printed in any official publications, are usually passed on among the people in the form of folk songs. The rhymed verses make them easy to remember and recite. The verses of a once-popular song entitled "Socialism Is Good," for example, were changed by some people to satirize the contemporary situation. The original "The reactionaries have been overthrown; and the imperialists have escaped with their tails jammed between their legs" became "The reactionaries have not been overthrown; and the imperialists have come back with briefcases under their arms."

Folk rhymes like this abound in China today, a clear indication of popular dissatisfaction. And as was observed by a well-known film director, folk rhymes have sounded the death knell of many dynasties in Chinese history. Whether the current rhymes will signal the end of the current regime remains unknown. What is certain, however, is that they are more than enough to give voice to further unrest in Chinese society.

Ironically, this popular discontent stems directly from problems accompanying the economic reforms. In 1988, China decided to reform its price system by eliminating state price controls on major industrial and agricultural products and allowing them to be market driven. After ten years of successful reform, Deng wanted to achieve even more, and believed that state controls were a major obstacle to an improved market economy. This decontrol, however, opened the gates to higher prices, as manufacturers and distributors began charging what the market would bear. This rapid transition from control to decontrol, combined with an overheated economy, officials' profiteering, speculation, and other factors, eventually led to an inflation rate of 18.5 percent, according to government statistics. The economic gains people had enjoyed in the previous few years were quickly offset by price increases, and many began to suffer from deteriorating living conditions.

The inflation, which was by far the worst since the founding of the People's Republic in 1949, triggered bank runs and panic buying in many cities in the summer of 1988. Despite the government's effort to curb inflation by tightening economic controls and slowing down growth in the overheated economy, prices continued upward, and although the rate of inflation was lowered, prices remained distressingly high, given current income levels. The efforts to rein in inflation not only failed to solve the problem, but created confusion and frustration among reform-minded people, especially university students and intellectuals. Since people have benefited from and supported the decade-long economic reforms, many regarded the price reform as necessary, but believed that it could have been carried out with better timing and greater caution.

This new economic crisis aggravated longstanding grievances against widespread corruption among Party leaders and their families, neglect of education, the perceived decline of social morality, and a general sense of psychological dislocation that occurs in societies undergoing rapid change.

Corruption, which has been a predominant factor in the fall of ruling regimes throughout Chinese history, has once again become rampant in the last few years. The Communist government, which once drew the full support of the nation, has found itself increasingly alienated from the Chinese people due to its inability to stop corruption, especially among high-ranking officials and their children. Because of China's history, corruption is a far more serious issue in that land than Westerners can imagine. People still remember that forty years ago, the Nationalist government (Kuomintang or KMT) headed by Chiang Kai-shek was defeated by the Communist forces and fled to the island of Taiwan, due in large part to massive opposition to its overwhelming corruption. At that time, there was strong support for the Communist party, which was regarded as a "people's party," fighting for popular interests and basic needs. As a result, the Communists won the civil war and established the People's Republic in 1949, thus putting an end to a century-long foreign domination of China. As Mao Zedong proclaimed, "The Chinese people have stood up." The massive land reforms and other economic reforms that followed the founding of the People's Republic were hailed as highly successful experiments, which had given people high hopes for a bright future, liberating them from the feudalism and colonialism that had caused unspeakable suffering. Thus it is not surprising that for almost four decades, the vast majority of Chinese people have supported the Communist Party and government to a large degree, despite such disastrous events as the Anti-Rightist Campaign, the Great Leap Forward, and the Cultural Revolution.

But it is also not surprising that faith in the Party began to seriously erode in recent years as people recognized the extent of corruption among the Communist officials themselves. As a result, there developed the general feeling that the government had begun to lose not only the faith of many people, but also the "mandate of heaven."

Western commentators, however, impose their own biases when they attribute this loss of faith in the Party and the resulting "turmoil" to a supposed "failure" of Marxism or socialism. In their rush to attack Communism and revive the Cold War game of competing "systems," these observers fail to note that in many respects China has been relatively successful in comparison to many Third World nations in the capitalist sphere of influence. China has, in fact, made substantial progress in the forty-year period since the founding of the People's Republic, when it began the attempt to transform the nation from a woefully underdeveloped, war-ravaged, and feudalistic society.

Indeed, progress often creates the kind of rising expectations which trigger unrest. Only after an underdeveloped nation reaches a certain economic and intellectual level do expectations rise to the point where people feel sufficiently empowered to assert their demand for governmental accountability, democracy, press freedom, better education, and the other reforms called for by the demonstrators in Beijing and elsewhere. The new demands for further reform are themselves a result of partial successes in existing reforms. Dissent in China is a result of a complex mixture of successes and failures: success in tolerating increased criticism of the Party, but failure to allow critics to take it to its logical conclusion, which would be greater freedom of the press and of speech; success in raising the standard of living and success in initiating a market economy, but failure to maintain that standard and failure to check the abuses in the market economy, such as unbridled profiteering and speculation.

With these factors in mind, Western observers should be careful to avoid generalizations about Chinese affairs. After all, one reason that Western society was so taken by surprise by the crisis is precisely because some Western journalists and scholars had adopted a simplistic view—combined with wishful thinking—that China had "gone capitalist" or "Westernized"—and were happy about it.

One common problem that has raised the immediate concern of the people is what the Chinese have termed as *guandao*, or official profiteering, because it has affected the life of almost the entire population. For example, the officials who have control of rationing certain scarce commodities can make huge profits by issuing ration coupons. They give coupons to their relatives or friends, who in turn sell them to other friends. By the time the coupons reach the real consumers, they have passed through the hands of many people, each of whom has made certain profit on the illicit transactions. When consumers finally acquire a coupon to purchase a commodity, they may be forced to pay several times the original price. Products like color television sets, VCRs, steel, fertilizer and so on are usually purchased this way, except in cases where purchases are carried out under a state plan. The only winners are government officials and their children, while the losers could include the whole population.

Obviously, the higher the government official, the greater the public outrage. When Deng Xiaoping's own son, Deng Pufang, and Zhao Ziyang's son, Zhao Dajun, were widely rumored to be profiting unduly through *guandao*, it was a strong catalyst for discontent.

While such problems have certainly angered the people, who have demanded that the government do something to stop the corrupt practices, the Chinese were still far from prepared to challenge the legitimacy of the Communist government. People were hoping that the Party could change for the better by cleaning itself up. In fact, they have often expressed the desire to cooperate with the Party should it propose any substantive measures to end the unbridled corruption and to address other key social and economic problems. They would like to play a greater role in the political decision-making by being allowed a much broader access in meeting with and consulting with officials, who often make major decisions behind closed doors with minimal citizen participation.

The other reason that people still have hope in the Communist government is simply that no other political force has been developed to replace it. Even for some political activists among the intellectuals and students who had demanded a systematic change, there was no realistic hope of establishing an "opposition party" to compete with the Communist Party in the foreseeable future. However, there were indeed some people, such as Liu Binyan, a well-known journalist expelled from the Party in early 1987, who had advocated an opposition faction within the Communist Party. Given what was to happen after June 4, and the fact that the Chinese Communist Party has always placed strong emphasis on "unity," there is little hope for the Party to change internally or for the establishment of an opposition faction. Consequently, within the given political structure, people are actually demanding something that is more realistic and reasonable and less radical, or "reform within the system" *(tizhi nei gaige)*. They want more political reform toward a more effective and democratic system. They want more freedom of the press so that they can voice their concerns more freely. They want more support for education so that there will be sufficiently competent personnel to carry improvements in industry, agriculture, law, government administration, and other fields.

By "democracy," the Chinese do *not* necessarily mean what most Americans think of when they hear the word, namely, a US-style party "system" complete with elections and full-blown political campaigns. What the Chinese mean by democracy is a more broad-based decision-making process which takes into account a range of opinions. They believe that the current leaders at many levels make totally arbitrary decisions without adequate consultation either with citizens or sometimes even with experts in a given field. They also feel that this consultation must be conducted with much greater openness than currently exists, so that they may judge for themselves the fairness and rationality of decisions which directly affect their lives.

Regardless of the massive discontent then, it is unfair to say that the Chinese government was totally unresponsive to such popular concerns. In fact, political openness has greatly increased in the late eighties, especially since the summer of 1986, when the Chinese leadership itself publicly called for "democratization" and "scientification" in policy making. In doing this, the government was actually trying to take into account more and more public opinion, especially that of experts, when reaching major decisions, and the Chinese press has reported scores of examples of this. While this policy seemed to be putting China on the track toward a more democratic system, and had thus drawn widespread support in intellectual circles, many people still had serious doubts about its implementation. They were sceptical that the leaders were genuinely committed to surrendering their old privilege of making arbitrary decisions. And this doubt may have added to the dissatisfaction of the general public.

Part of the public discontent stems from the very fact that there *have* been recurring, government-sponsored crusades against corruption almost since the beginning of the People's Republic. In 1951, for example, there was the Movement Against the Three Evils (corruption, waste, and bureaucracy); the following year this was expanded to the Movement Against the Five Evils (bribery, tax evasion, theft of state property, cheating on government contracts and insiders' misuse of economic information). In 1983, the Central Discipline Inspection Commission reported on endemic corruption and outright crime. Late in 1984, the commission issued another report on the problem, and by 1986, there was extensive official reporting on corruption. In fact, various measures have been declared or are still in the making to curb such problems as corruption, profiteering by government officials, and insufficient investment in education. Party leaders have often reiterated their determination to solve such problems and present to the people a cleaner government.

The problem is that people have been largely disappointed because many of those clean-up measures so boldy announced remain on paper, or as the Chinese put it, "loud thunders bring little rainfall." Cynicism and discontent are bred because of the authorities' failure to match words with actions, especially when the problems involve higher officials.

In addition to this, despite government proclamations that it welcomes suggestions and criticisms from the people, the forums for speaking out assertively are still quite limited. And fear of reprisal still makes many Chinese extremely reticent to voice their opinions or become politically involved. As a result, an uneasy quietness prevailed in China in the last year or so, and people seemed to be waiting for the day when someone would break the silence and take the lead in voicing their concerns. And many knew that they would follow in large numbers.

DEATH OF HU YAOBANG

Opportunity finally came on April 15—perhaps prematurely in light of what occurred on June 3–4—when Hu Yaobang, the former general secretary of the Chinese Communist Party, died of a heart attack. Hu's sudden death sent a shock wave among Chinese college students and the intellectual community, which regarded the late leader as a symbol of political reform and a valued advocate of more tolerant policies toward critical intellectuals.

Only a few hours after Hu's death, *dazi bao*, or big-character posters (another popular traditional form of voicing protests and concerns in China) began to appear on the campus of Beijing University, followed by dozens of other universities. Many posters mourned the death of Hu, who had been a hero in the eyes of the students since he was forced out of office as the Party's general secretary two years earlier. On Beijing's campuses, the general sentiment was that "the wrong man died." Hu's relatively younger age—he died at the age of 73—and his decidedly more tolerant attitudes toward intellectuals made his death an especially emotional occasion. One poster at Beijing University read: "The one who shouldn't die died, while those who should die still live on."

In late 1986 and early 1987, a previous round of student agitation had occurred in some major cities such as Beijing, Shanghai, Hefei and Wuhan. The students were calling for "genuine democracy" and freedom, although few of them really knew what these words meant, and hundreds of thousands demonstrated in several cities.

The 1986–87 student movement occurred at a time when China was moving, however slowly, toward "socialist democracy" and political relaxation. As mentioned earlier, in the summer of 1986, the government openly called for "democratization" and "scientification" in policy making. As a result, 1986 became one of the "golden years" in the history of the People's Republic, one which was characterized by a remarkable degree of tolerance toward unorthodox views held by intellectuals. The then-Party Secretary Hu Yaobang and Propaganda Chief Zhu Houze, Hu's follower, initiated a new intellectual policy dubbed as *san kuan zhengce*, characterized by three words, *kuanrong* (tolerance), *kuansong* (relaxing control), and *kuanhou* (benevolent). This policy to a great extent gave the intellectuals a free hand to discuss the most serious political, cultural, and economic problems the nation was facing, and encouraged them to act according to their own consciences. If ever the Chinese intellectuals had really enjoyed the "fresh air of freedom," it was in 1986. And this new freedom was largely a result of this less rigid policy adopted by the top leadership itself.

However, for the students and some dissident intellectuals such as Fang Lizhi, an astrophysicist known for his dissident political views, "socialist democracy" as envisioned by Hu Yaobang was far from "genuine." Thus the predominant slogan during the 1986–87 student movement was *fight for genuine democracy*. Fang Lizhi reportedly argued face-to-face with a high-ranking Politburo member. In the argument, the Politburo member allegedly said that democracy was something bestowed from above, while Fang insisted that democracy could be achieved only through struggle from below. Fang's ideas were introduced to students through his speeches at dozens of universities in Hefei, Anhui Province, where he was serving as vice president of the China University of Science and Technology, and in Shanghai. His ideas were widely acclaimed by the students, who took to the streets to demand this "genuine democracy." The fact that the 1986–87 movement started from the China University of Science and Technology clearly indicates the key role of Fang Lizhi. He was subsequently expelled from the Communist Party together with Liu Binyan, a prominent investigative journalist from the *People's Daily*, and Wang Ruowang, a Shanghai writer. All three were accused of spreading "bourgeois liberalization."

Moreover, the aging leadership felt threatened, and attacked not only certain Western ideas as "bourgeois liberalization," but also the tolerant intellectual policies pursued by Hu and his followers. The policy of *san kuan* began to be openly criticized as "erroneous," and Zhu Houze was removed from the Party's propaganda department. However, Zhu was a much less important scapegoat than Hu Yaobang himself. On January 16, 1987, an enlarged Politburo meeting made the final decision to remove Hu Yaobang from the post of Party secretary, a position he had held since 1981, and accused him of being weak on opposing the above ideological trends.

Besides being a symbol of reform, Hu was also among the few Chinese leaders whose children were not believed to be involved in corruption or in unduly profiting from their business activities. He had gradually come to favor more openness and political reform during the years of China's general reform policy. It is apparent that his thinking had evolved since he became Party chief in 1981, as he had been influenced by extensive travel abroad. He came to feel that some kind of political reform or at least some sort of political input not necessarily restricted to the Communist Party itself was needed to revitalize its ideology and to give a creative impetus for new ideas relating to the political system.

Hu therefore took a completely new stand, which made him much more tolerant than most Communist leaders toward different opinions, especially those opinions critical of Party policy. On July 1, 1986, in commemorating the 65th anniversary of the Chinese Communist Party, he wrote in *People's Daily:*

> We should use totally different methods to solve the contradictions between different opinions that inevitably appear frequently in our work and in our thought. First of all, every major decision should be gone over carefully many times before coming to a final conclusion. Second, in Party meetings, Party members should be allowed to express their opinions freely and to criticize anyone, and they should be protected even if they are wrong. Third, the only important thing is that one should really try to think carefully, and then even if some kind of bias appears in someone's work, he should be allowed to change. Fourth, if someone disagrees with a main policy of the Central Committee, as long as he does not violate it and works to uphold it, he should be allowed to maintain his opinion.

Because of his thwarted demand for openness, tolerance, and fuller consultation (i.e., "democracy"), students felt that the loss of the strongest high-level advocate of political reform would leave a major gap at the top. Consequently, they decided to use the occasion of his death to continue to pressure the leadership for political reform. Otherwise, it was generally feared that the impetus for such reform would be buried in the bureaucratic morass of other priorities.

At the same time, the students also agreed that any serious political reform had to be accompanied by a widespread campaign against corruption. A cleaning out of some of the most flagrant examples of personal profiteering by high- and middle-level officials had to take place. If the most blatant cases of corruption were not rooted out, the students believed that the campaign for political reform would remain superficial and have no lasting impact on the economic and political system. In theory, this belief was not at all rebellious, but was closely linked to the Party's own recent policy statement that government administration should be separate from political status and that a professional civil service should have day-to-day responsibility for administrative affairs. The idea here was of course to have the Party set general goals on policy but not to interfere in those technical aspects of implementation which were not vitally linked to overall ideological and national policy. Instead of having incompetent administrators assigned to posts simply because of their Party affiliation, the government was planning to require civil service examinations.

It was not surprising that among the slogans and demands raised by the students one saw such big-character posters as "Down with corruption," "Root out government profiteering," and "Speed up democratic reforms." Another poster poignantly expressed in poetic form the grief, frustration and rage felt by the students:

The sincere man died,
The hypocrites live on,
The compassionate man died,
Buried by the cold-blooded.
Empty talk—TOEFL—bridge—Mah Jong
Despotism and reform,
Reform lies dead in the heart,
This world is a new enigma,
Let me ask you: Yaobang
Is China still hopeful?

The first four lines are a clear reference to the lack of credible leadership at the top. The next lines reflect the emptiness of the students' own lives filled with meaningless talk and card games. It asserts that the students' only hope is to study the Test of English as a Foreign Language (TOEFL), a prerequisite for study abroad, especially in the United States, where there are over 40,000 Chinese students today. Indeed, one point which drew a number of students to the movement was the fact that it suddenly gave them a strong sense of purpose and meaning which they had not felt before. Those who were cynical or indifferent or who had not been given a firm set of values became animated with a new, almost religious feeling of dedication to a cause. This "spiritual" dimension, through which the movement awakened these youth to a stirring sense of engagement in a larger cause, should not be underestimated.

In China, as in many other nations, students are often more prepared than any other sector of the population to advocate social changes whenever there is general discontent. The impatience of youth, the excitement of new ideas, the mere fact that students have more flexible hours, and that a campus is an ideal place for social ferment, obviously make universities potential centers of unrest. Chinese students and intellectuals have had a long tradition of serving as advocates of new and controversial ideas ever since the May Fourth Movement in 1919, when they became "the conscience of the nation." The uprising of students and intellectuals begun that day galvanized revolutionary and anti-colonial elements in China into organized resistance against Japan, and was partly responsible for the founding of the Chinese Communist Party itself. With such a past role as the "conscience of the nation" and having "a sense of loyalty to China," the students were not only mourning the death of a beloved leader, but also seizing an opportunity to agitate for more political change.

On April 16, several hundred students went to Tiananmen Square to place wreaths around the massive Monument to the People's Heroes, an action that should have alerted the authorities to possible unrest. On April 18, more than 6,000 students marched from Beijing University to Tiananmen Square early in the morning and launched a sit-in in front of the Great Hall of the People. And the next day, there were reports of conflicts between the students and security guards in front of Zhongnanhai, headquarters of the Communist Party and residential compound of many top leaders.

Meanwhile, the government, unprepared for and perhaps even frightened by the increasing number of students mourning the death of Hu, was apparently determined to put a quick stop to further unrest. Hoping to end the entire matter as quickly as possible, they declared an official memorial service for Hu Yaobang, to be held on April 22, one week after his death. The authorities apparently hoped that after staging the funeral, the student unrest would run out of momentum and quietly fade away. On April 20, fearing that the students would once again assemble in the square, the Beijing municipal government announced that the square would be closed off on April 22 during Hu's memorial service. However, the students outwitted the authorities simply by going to the square on the night of April 21. Consequently, by the next morning the number of students in the square exceeded 100,000, making it simply impossible for security forces to clear the square.

Hu's memorial was briefly held in the Great Hall of the People, where all the key players in Chinese politics appeared. Zhao Ziyang, then Party general secretary, delivered a speech in which he called Hu a "loyal Communist fighter and a great proletarian revolutionary and statesman." "As a Marxist," said Zhao, "Hu Yaobang led a glorious life." Zhao especially praised Hu for his work after 1978, saying, "Since the Third Plenary Session of the 11th Party Central Committee [in December 1978], our country has entered an important historic period of turning the wronged back to right and overall reform. At the 12th National Conference of the Chinese Communist Party [in 1982], on behalf of the Party Central Committee, Comrade Hu Yaobang delivered a report entitled 'To Open Up a New Era of Socialist Modernization Construction,' in which he further made clear the guiding principles for our Party in the new era. In the last eleven years, as one of the major leaders of our Party, he has devoted himself to the integration of the general principles of Marxism and the realities of our modernization construction. He has made significant contributions in upholding the lines of the Third Plenary Session of the 11th Party Central Committee, in adhering to the Four Cardinal Principles, in persisting in the policies of reform and opening to the outside world, and in building socialism with Chinese characteristics." [The Four Cardinal Principles are: 1) adherence to the socialist system; 2) the leadership of the Communist Party; 3) the people's democratic dictatorship, and 4) Marxist-Leninist and Mao Zedong thought.]

While Hu's memorial was held in the Great Hall of the People, the students assembled outside in Tiananmen Square listened to the live broadcast of the service. After the ceremony was finished, three student representatives were allowed to cross the police line to present a petition to the government asking for dialogue and discussion of problems. They knelt down on the steps to the hall, holding the petition above their heads, waiting for Premier Li Peng to accept it. At that time, word had spread among the students that Li Peng had agreed to come out to receive the petition. When he failed to appear, the students were angered, feeling that they had been duped. Subsequently, the government insisted that Li had *not* agreed to come out in the first place, which is quite possibly true. An article which appeared in *People's Daily* four months after the incident asserted that Wu'er Kaixi, a student leader from Beijing Normal University, "spread the rumor" that Li agreed to meet the students. Whatever the case, the students, facing their first humiliating failure, realized that further action would have to be taken.

Unfortunately the Communist government, like all Chinese governments throughout history, viewed public opposition to their official position only as permissible within certain boundaries. The students appeared willing to remain within these boundaries, while at the same time conscious of their role as "vanguard" of the whole population, not only in the strict Leninist sense, but in a genuinely populist fashion as well.

Therefore, the students could be seen as a pioneering force for the democratization of the political system in line with the Party's own well-publicized goals and economic reforms. The students were really telling the leadership that when Deng Xiaoping stated that he wanted to build China into a flourishing "socialist democracy" as well as to develop the country, it was incumbent on him and the Party leadership to take specific steps to realize such goals and not to repeat mere platitudes on this question. The issue here remained one of actually instituting political reform and not simply proposing it or discussing it. The students also knew that by pushing for political reform, they might give reform-minded individuals in the leadership the courage and support to press harder for reform themselves.

STUDENT DEMANDS

The students as a group reflected a host of basic problems in Chinese society that have been exacerbated by unanticipated or unintended consequences of the reform policies themselves.

Contrary to what the American media may suggest, despite the wonderful reputation for "pragmatism" the current Chinese leadership enjoyed until the recent events in Tiananmen Square, these officials have ignored certain crucial sectors of society. In contrast to certain segments of the rural population and people engaged in commerce who have enjoyed substantial increases in their incomes as a result of reforms during the past decade, teachers and urban workers saw their fixed salaries shrink drastically in purchasing power in 1988–89. Therefore, despite a sharp contrast between Mao's often misguided, anti-intellectual experiments in education during the Cultural Revolution and the new regime's return to a strict nationwide entrance examination system for universities, it should be noted that both Mao and Zhou Enlai placed far more emphasis on education personally than has the current leadership. It should also be noted that the opening to the West was in fact originated by both Mao and Zhou Enlai—although strongly opposed by the Gang of Four—and that the policy of the "four modernizations" is basically Zhou Enlai's policy, a policy which Deng Xiaoping may have carried out creatively, but which he certainly did not originate. Moreover, due to the incredible parochialism of the US media, few Americans realize that foreign students from Europe and Japan began studying in China by the fall of 1973, and in 1975 Canada started its exchange program with China, which meant that a new influx of ideas from the outside had begun over fifteen years ago. This, coupled with increasing numbers of Chinese studying abroad, also made inevitable the comparisons of Chinese education with that of the more modernized nations. It is only because the United States did not establish diplomatic relations until 1979 that no American students were present in the People's Republic until that time.

The point at issue here is that even during the past decade of reforms, the Chinese budget for education as a proportion of the entire state budget has been very low, despite the supposed break with the education policy of the Cultural Revolution years and despite the famous stereotype of the Chinese reverence for learning. This is true even when compared with many Third World countries and is especially striking for a self-proclaimed socialist state. Teachers' pay, particularly in elementary and secondary schools, remains very low and morale has not improved greatly since the late 1970s. During the ten years of economic reform, many sectors of society have largely benefited, but teachers' pay has only slightly increased, but definitely not enough to meet skyrocketing price increases. While people such as private businessmen make as much as 1,000 yuan (about US$270) or more a month, teachers have to live on fixed salaries averaging a meagre 80 yuan (about US$21) for elementary and secondary school teachers, and 150 yuan (about US$40) for college teachers. Thus the Chinese, when talking about the devaluation of knowledge, will make sardonic comparisons like "those who make missiles (*daodan* as pronounced in Chinese) are not worth as much as those who sell tea eggs (*chayedan*)."

A major reason for this is simply that the Chinese government has not been willing to invest more in education. Out of 149 nations surveyed by UNESCO in the late 1980s, China was 130th in the proportion of the Gross National Product allocated for education. In 1983, education absorbed 9.7 percent of national expenditures and was 9.6 percent in 1987 and 1988. Granted, a 15 percent increase in education spending was budgeted for 1989, but it is doubtful if this will keep up with inflation.

Facilities are another serious problem even at the university level. Student dormitories at universities in China have some of the worst conditions in the world, matched only perhaps by countries such as India, Indonesia, and Bangladesh. Even many of the struggling African nations provide better facilities for their college students than does the People's Republic. Study places are cramped and libraries are difficult to use. Ironically, despite the present government's heavy criticism of the Cultural Revolution and its extreme egalitarianism, to students and young faculty it seems that the policy has changed very little. They are still poorly treated in terms of material incentives and are often looked upon by the society with certain suspicions and an anti-intellectual bias. During the Cultural Revolution, the intellectuals were called the "stinking ninth category," and many people in and out of government still have problems with the image of the educated.

Other specific grievances of university students include the system of job assignment, whereby students are assigned jobs for life to a work unit chosen by the government. Too often, students are assigned to state companies or offices which are not suitable to their university preparation or for which they are overqualified or unsuited in some other way. Although the government has recently begun to relax the assignment policy to allow college graduates to look for jobs by themselves, most students still have to rely on their school to be assigned a job because school officials are involved in making assignments and recommendations. Only those who have *guanxi*, or connections, can get truly satisfactory jobs for themselves. Moreover, even if a suitable position is found, all too often in China promotion depends not completely on ability, but on relations with one's superiors to a degree unknown in Western nations. This reliance on connections and personal relations is but another aspect of the corruption which the students were protesting. The educational situation is so serious that the government itself has actually acknowledged it by recently upgrading the Ministry of Education to the status of a State Education Commission. New policies to deal with the problems outlined above are supposed to be elaborated, but given recent events it remains to be seen how much progress will be made in this direction.

Consequently, corruption is not merely a peripheral issue or an abstract moral question for the students, but something that very directly affects their everday existence and future careers.

Given this basic background for some of the specific frustrations felt by students and intellectuals in general, it would still seem that the initial demands made by the students were relatively moderate in character and only escalated in response to the reaction of the government. Before *People's Daily* printed a harsh editorial on April 26 which suggested that "a small number of people were manipulating the student movement to seize power," students had only demanded a "dialogue" with the government on the subject of recognizing independent student organizations and publications. Only after the publication of the editorial did the students add the demand that the government officially reverse its characterization of the movement as "unpatriotic."

A closer look at the student demands at different stages might give a more specific sense of how the students increased the scope and intensity of their protest during the course of the movement. The initial demands aimed mainly at solving some of the pressing social problems, including the punishment of corruption and government profiteering, in which party officials and their children made undue profits out of their business activities; freedom of the press, so that the opinions of the people could be properly voiced and that the student movement could be objectively reported; more money for education; and a dialogue with the government. In addition, the students cited the text of the Chinese Constitution which declares that citizens of the People's Republic should be allowed the freedom of speech, assembly, association, and so on.

After the first rather unsatisfying and inconclusive dialogue with government officials on April 29, the students demanded that representatives participating in the dialogue should not be picked from the official students union, which they thought was a puppet organization that could not represent their real interests, but rather from the newly established Autonomous Students Association of Beijing Universities. On May 3, the students handed in a petition to the National People's Congress and the Party Central Committee in regard to a new round of dialogue, in which they detailed their suggestions on conducting an equal and sincere exchange. The petition, which was published in official Chinese newspapers, included the following major requests:

1. Bilateral talks (between government and students) should be established on the basis of total equality. During the talks, opportunities for speaking and questioning should be divided equally.

2. Student representatives should be elected by the majority of the students. Since the official student unions in various schools do not provide real leadership to the current movement, students cannot accept representatives appointed by such unions. They also cannot accept the government hand-picked students as their representatives.

3. Chinese and foreign reporters must be allowed to cover the dialogue, which should be broadcast live on radio and TV.
   (See Appendix One for full text of this petition.)

However, the government rejected the student petition. Thus by May 13, when the students began their hunger strike, they had reduced their demands to only two, i.e., the retraction of the April 26 *People's Daily* editorial and a televised dialogue between student representatives and top leaders.

It was only with the declaration of martial law on May 20 that student demands dramatically escalated, with a call for the resignations of Premier Li Peng, Deng Xiaoping, and President Yang Shangkun. Even then, until the Tiananmen repression of June 3–4, the most often repeated demand was for the resignation of Li Peng and, in fact, demands for Deng's resignation were less noticeable in the last days leading up to June 4, when the crackdown took place.

At the same time the government was not accused of being a fascist regime, nor were any slogans voiced calling for the overthrow of the communist government itself until after the violent suppression in Tiananmen Square. Even then it was clear that the students were not demanding the end of the socialist system itself, but rather a drastic change in the particular kind of communist government that existed.

Basically, then, the students were calling for more accountability within the system itself and asking it to live up to its highest ideals rather than calling for its overthrow.

In terms of the philosophical and/or ideological background to the student demands, it is easier to examine the content by first suggesting what they were not. Thus if we take the two extreme interpretations—first the American one that they were calling for full-blown Western democracy and then the official Party position that they were calling for the overthrow of the Chinese Communist Party and the establishment of a "capitalist republic"—we can immediately sense that the real demands lay somewhere between the above two poles. Even students who were interviewed by American news reporters on television mostly suggested that their slogans of democracy were long-term goals and it would take many years to practically implement such institutions in Chinese society.

Finally, it was only after the bloody suppression of student and citizen protesters in Beijing's main streets that the first cry was heard for the overthrow of the Communist party. Even here one must be cautious in drawing conclusions. On the one hand, it could be argued that the increasing escalation of the crisis and apparent government overreaction may potentially result in bringing about the kind of revolution that the Communist party was hoping to avoid. As noted, however, it is not clear that any other organization exists to take its place nor that the students themselves were prepared to establish either an independent socialist party or a party dedicated to capitalism, despite the recent organization of the Chinese Democratic Front in Paris. With this in mind, it now remains to explore some of the more idealistic demands that the students have made.

It should be remembered that when asked what they meant by "democracy" by American reporters, many students were rather vague, and some of the more articulate among them even suggested that democracy for them was at the moment simply a slogan, and was in fact a goal they had no realistic hope of seeing established in the near future.

It is also quite likely that those people who have been presented by the American media as student leaders or those people who have agreed to be interviewed are by no means the leaders or the most serious individuals involved in the movement. It would be extremely naive to assume that the most serious organizers behind this kind of protest might have any interest in being "exposed" by any Western media, and thus face the possibility of arrest and retribution as well as having their movement branded as nothing more than an extension of some foreign organizations. If anything, the real purpose of certain people's appearing on television may have been to make it much more difficult for the government to engage in the kind of violent repression it conducted on the night of June 3–4. Key people in the student movement may well have avoided public exposure in the foreign media if they really intended to accomplish anything of lasting value internally—and the thousands of arrests which have occurred since early June confirms the wisdom of their reticence.

However, there are several things we do know. They include the fact that the students were singing the "Internationale" and that there were strong calls for democracy. But it is a mistake to confuse the students' idea of democracy with the American system or to give excessive credit to American influences. Rather than gullibly accepting pronouncements by some American journalists, who contend that only Chinese students who have been to Western countries can understand democracy, it should be realized that what the students primarily meant by the word was more accountability from and more input into the system by the mass of the population.

It is interesting to note that in one of the few substantive articles in the US press on the events, Lee Feighon, a visiting scholar from Colby College in Maine who spent several months at People's University, observed that some of the main theoretical impetus for the movement came from graduate students in the Party History Department at that school, none of whom have been interviewed or probably would even want to be interviewed by the American media (*New York Times*, May 25, 1989). His point was that these students were really attempting to help China begin in earnest its long march to a truly socialist democratic system. Therefore, it might be said that while it was not always clear what the students really wanted and while they themselves failed to spell out a detailed concrete program, they were certainly suggesting that the Communist Party could go considerably further than it had previously in opening up the political system and that their suggestions should be taken seriously as a starting point for discussion, though not necessarily for immediate implementation.

DIFFERENT APPROACHES TO RESOLVING THE CRISIS

Obviously there were many different approaches to resolving the crisis. To further complicate matters, the government was caught unprepared because the Gorbachev visit was the main priority at the time, deflecting attention from student unrest. Certainly, once the Gorbachev visit was completed, full attention could have been devoted to solving the crisis in a creative way. Of course the two extreme approaches were either full scale repression or full scale concessions, with a whole spectrum of possibilities in between. If, however, authorities had been more sensitive to the seriousness of the situation, they might have realized that after the bitter reaction to the April 26 editorial in *People's Daily*, the students would not easily be frightened into submission, and substantive talks might provide an easier solution. Such negotiations were the major demand and were the only opening for the discussion of other issues.

The government was not likely to launch a crackdown on May 4 as that would have put them in a very embarassing position, given the powerful patriotic appeal of the May Fourth Movement. It was obvious to the authorities that there would be huge demonstrations on May 4, and from a purely tactical point of view to attempt to disperse the demonstrators on that day would have been a potential disaster. Still, it seems clear that even after Hu Yaobang's death and before the April 26 editorial, the amount of prestige that the government would have lost in negotiating with the students was minimal. Certainly as was belatedly done, Yan Mingfu, member of the Secretariat of the Communist Party Central Committee and minister in charge of United Front work and Li Tieying, a Politburo member and head of the State Education Commission, could have been instructed to enter into substantive discussions with the representatives of the new, "illegal" independent students organizations instead of the officially vetted students union representatives. It seems clear that had that been done at the beginning, considerable tension would have been released, the students' demands would not have escalated, and the more moderate students could have made a very strong case that they were being taken seriously. Instead, the government treated the situation as a nuisance by refusing to deal positively with the student demands which had been long festering and which were symptomatic of a far wider social crisis throughout the nation—i.e., the unforeseen consequences of a very well-intended but not so well-implemented policy, namely the reforms themselves as a whole.

The problem of the student protest cannot be seen in isolation. As noted, the reforms necessitated tremendous economic, social, and political adjustments in Chinese society which it is dubious that the Party had really understood in all their multi-faceted implications. Thus one of the tragedies of the situation is that the student protest—partly inadvertently, partly inevitably, as is so often the case in China—became inextricably intertwined with policy differences over how to deal with the problems raised by the reforms. These differences eventually seem to have degenerated into a naked power struggle that toppled party chief Zhao Ziyang and several other reform-minded leaders.

The defeat of Zhao and his followers in the power struggle appeared to be inevitable soon after the student demonstrations began. Although he made a strong effort to gain the upper hand over the "hard-line conservatives," and he seemed to be succeeding in winning the power struggle during the first twenty days of May, Zhao was aware that his chances were limited. Contrary to speculation by the media that the student movement might provide an opportunity for Zhao to consolidate his power base, it was the conservatives who were taking the initiative and consolidating their power base, removing Zhao and his followers from the party leadership as they did to Hu Yaobang two years earlier. In fact, shortly after Hu Yaobang's funeral, Deng Xiaoping gave a speech at a Politburo meeting on April 25 in the absence of Zhao, who was on a state visit to Korea, and made two decisions: to publish a harsh editorial in *People's Daily*, which appeared the next day, and to crack down on student demonstrators by using whatever force necessary.

PATRIOTIC MOVEMENT OR A "TURMOIL"?

Prior to the April 26 editorial in *People's Daily*, there had been hints of government dissatisfaction with the protest and criticisms of those who had created some confusion on the occasion of Hu Yaobang's memorial service. The *People's Daily* had also called for the students not to disturb the stability of China and not to be fooled by a small number of instigators with ulterior motives. However, the April 26 editorial went much further than any previous government statements by declaring the student movement to be "riotous behavior" rather than a patriotic movement and went so far as to accuse the demonstrators of a naked grab for power on the order of the behavior of the Gang of Four during the Cultural Revolution.

Although it is true that the editorial still saw the majority of participants as patriotic, it directly accused certain university students, including the organizers of independent student groups, as intending to overthrow the socialist system and using the occasion of Hu Yaobang's funeral for their nefarious designs. The editorial stressed that it was impermissible to form illegal organizations, hold illegal demonstrations, or visit factories, the countryside or schools to instigate protest against the government. The editorial went on to attribute the massive disturbance to a small, conspiratorial group bent on destroying the system by poisoning the minds of innocent citizens:

> A handful of people with ulterior motives made use of the students' mourning of Comrade Hu Yaobang. They have spread all sorts of rumors to poison people's minds. They have resorted to big- and small-character posters to smear, scold, and attack our Party and government leaders. They have wantonly violated the Constitution to advocate opposition to the Communist Party's leadership and the socialist system. They have established illegal organizations in some universities to seize power from the official students' unions. Some have even taken control of the school's broadcasting system. They have also instigated class boycotts in some schools, preventing by force students from attending class. They have pirated the names of workers' organizations to spread counterrevolutionary leaflets. They have contacted many other places in an attempt to provoke bigger disturbances.

The editorial attempted to discredit them further by accusing them of undermining the very democracy they were agitating for:

> A handful of people were not really mourning Comrade Hu Yaobang, neither were they trying to push forward the process of the socialist democratic system, or simply expressing some grievances. They were in fact destroying democracy and the rule of law under such banners. Their purpose was to poison people's minds, put the whole country

under disorder, and sabotage the political situation of stability and unity. Thus it is a well-planned conspiracy and a turmoil. Its aim was to substantially negate the leadership of the Chinese Communist Party and the socialist system. *(See Appendix One for full text of the editorial).*

By branding the student movement a "turmoil," the government sent out a clear signal that the student protests should no longer be tolerated. The word "turmoil," or *dongluan* in Chinese, is in itself a heavily loaded term used by authorities to justify any crackdown on a popular movement. The word also has powerful resonance because it evokes memories of the nightmare of the Cultural Revolution, which is referred to as "ten years of turmoil." Therefore, the obvious intent in the use of the word is to identify dissent with a chaotic period of Chinese history, and by so doing galvanize popular support for government repression.

It has to be understood, however, that this reaction was not simply complete hypocrisy on the part of the government. Both for political and personal reasons, Deng Xiaoping and some other senior leaders may have had nightmares of another Cultural Revolution breaking out, this time completely out of control. While exaggerated, such fears were based on reality in Deng's case. During the Cultural Revolution, he was purged twice by Mao and was branded a "capitalist roader," for which he was sent to Jiangxi Province and spent some humiliating years as a common laborer there after being stripped of all his titles including General Secretary of the Communist Party Central Committee. However, this was not all. His son, Deng Pufang, who was a student at Beijing University when the Cultural Revolution began, was thrown out of the window of a dormitory building and lost the use of his legs. (The junior Deng now heads the China Welfare Foundation of the Disabled.) Moreover, there were also rumors of an attempted assassination of Deng Xiaoping shortly after his dismissal in April 1966.

A more fundamental problem than the personal history of Party leaders has to be understood to help explain the mentality of the editorial and the June crackdown. This mentality is usually characterized by a refusal to surrender power in any cultural or political area, an attitude described as "totalitarian." Regretably these attitudes toward power are more deep-rooted and systemic than merely personal, and seem to be deeply and sincerely held. Due to the way in which much of Marxist theory was transmitted to many present

Chinese leaders who studied in the Soviet Union in the 1920s, 1930s and 1950s through Leninist and most often Stalinist filters, much of China's leadership has a rigid, quasi-religious belief that their position is correct. The kind of socialism in which they were educated only reinforced the traditional Chinese view that the state must control all facets of society. To some extent, these leaders really do believe that independent student organizations and independent unions are not simply a threat to their power, but a crack in the foundation of socialism as they understand it. To fail to grasp this aspect of their consciousness by dismissing them as merely stubborn old men clinging to power would be to trivialize the seriousness of their refusal to make concessions. The real tragedy involved here is not that Deng Xiaoping and his allies were clinging to power, but that they ultimately believe that their views and their actions were fully justified. Only this intense belief in the righteousness of their views can fully explain their actions.

Although Li Peng is a full generation younger than Deng, he shares these beliefs to a considerable extent. It must be remembered that he studied engineering in the Soviet Union in the 1950s and that he was Zhou Enlai's adopted son. Therefore, he has been surrounded since childhood by the older revolutionaries, and influenced by elder Party leaders such as Chen Yun. While some in his generation might not share Li's strong convictions, others are willing to follow his lead for opportunistic reasons, in the same way that officials in any nation will support the status quo in order to advance their own careers.

TRIUMPHANT STUDENT DEMONSTRATORS

On April 27, the day after the hard-line editorial was published, the students found themselves much more defiant and courageous than two years earlier, when a reprimand in a *People's Daily* editorial could frighten even the boldest activists back into their dormitories. This time, the students responded by launching huge demonstrations the following day and for the first time in the history of the People's Republic triumphantly swept over police barricades and arrived at their strategic destination, Tiananmen Square.

Hundreds of thousands of students from dozens of Beijing universities began to march to Tiananmen Square early in the day. As the march began in the northwestern part of the city, students clashed with police briefly. Some students were kicked and pushed to the ground before the protesters changed direction and out-maneuvered police. Later in the march, a line of 300 policemen was forced to give way in what one observer likened to "watching an iron bar bend." As the students marched and shouted slogans, bystanders cheered and chanted "Don't hit them [the students]!" By the time the students arrived at Tiananmen Square, the number of protestors swelled to 500,000. They were triumphant and exuberant. As Wu'er Kaixi, a student leader from Beijing Normal University, proclaimed, "Finally we're victorious."

As usual, the students shouted slogans as they marched. What is interesting though was that on April 27, the protestors were not only shouting pro-democracy slogans such as "Long live democracy" and "Long live freedom," but also holding pro-Party banners saying "Support the correct leadership of the Communist Party." This was obviously a tactic used by the students for self-protection, to counter accusations in the previous day's editorial that they were trying to bring down the Communist government.

At the most superficial level, the huge student demonstration on April 27 suggested that the government had totally miscaculated the mood of the populace by issuing its harsh editorial of the previous day.

For the first time in Communist China's history, it appeared that society rather than the state was in a position to impose its will on the powers that be. Aside from the question of "face"—something never to be ignored in Chinese society—it is certain that this lesson was not lost on those elements in the government opposed to conciliation, among whom were some of the most prominent members of the Beijing city and Party leadership which have a long history of being among the most conservative elements at the municipal level in the entire nation. Whereas during the Cultural Revolution chaos could be blamed, if not on Mao himself, then at least on the Gang of Four, here the Party was confronting an entirely new situation in which society was escaping the control of the state. Put more bluntly, the people were asking to take control of their own lives—something anathema to old guard Leninist-Stalinist bureaucrats who believed they were the infallible guardians of the people's best interest.

The triumphant march on April 27 was also a clear indication of the extent of support the students had obtained, thus making this round of the student movement quite different from that of

1986–1987. Two years before, when the students took to the streets to demand democracy and freedom, they were largely isolated from the general population. Perhaps because of the less serious economic problems at that time, the students made no move to call on the masses to join in their ranks nor did the masses express a great deal of eagerness for solidarity with the students. Moreover, their demands included only some highly idealized and vague slogans such as "democracy" and "freedom," which few students really understood either theoretically or in terms of practical application to Chinese society. As previously mentioned, the general population in China —as anywhere—cares more about their daily lives than such abstract slogans, thus the ordinary workers and peasants might really think the students were doing nothing but "creating troubles." However, students did become conscious of this distance between themselves and the masses of common people, because in early 1987, shortly after the movement was put down, the students at Beijing University were arguing that if they really wanted to "create chaos," then they would have addressed such issues as price increases, which had already begun to incite popular dissatisfaction among urban people. They chose to ignore such problems of common concern while sticking to such obscure ideas as "democracy," because they said they did not want true social unrest. In other words, they did not, on the whole, solicit or even desire participation in the student movement by workers and ordinary citizens. This time, however, due to the drastically deteriorating economic and social situation, students openly called for the support of the general population, and their demands to eliminate corruption and official profiteering greatly appealed to the general sentiments of the people.

It was no accident that the Party began resurrecting once-discredited terms like "class struggle." The Party itself had, to some degree, abandoned this stereotyped sloganeering to counter the so-called remaining bad influence of the Gang of Four. Deng himself helped propagate such slogans as "to get rich is glorious" and declared that Marxism was too outdated to help solve some contemporary problems. His famous statement, "It doesn't matter whether a cat is black or white as long as it catches a mouse," was a relativistic comment that the end justified the means, implying to many individuals that if capitalist strategies brought them prosperity, such strategies should be used.

With officials slackening their own Marxist line, it is hardly surprising that the students took an interest in approaches to government now labelled "bourgeois democracy." The Communist Party has itself gone through some amazing ideological changes in order to justify sudden policy shifts. In 1956, for example, there was the Hundred Flowers Campaign, when intellectual and cultural openness was encouraged with the slogan "let a hundred schools of thought contend." The next year, however, this was reversed by the Anti-Rightist Campaign. Then came ten years of the Cultural Revolution. By the late seventies, recoiling from the rigidity of the Cultural Revolution's attempt to force communist society to emerge overnight, Party theoreticians began to search for a more pragmatic way to "build socialism with Chinese characteristics." The result of this ideological shift was the appearance of private enterprise, foreign investment, and an overall open policy.

While the standard of living did improve for a time, people also became disillusioned with capitalist-style profiteering followed by the explosion of inflation. In the wake of events in the spring of 1989, the Party shifted back to orthodoxy. In view of these sudden shifts in the Party line, it is not surprising that certain members of society would question the Party's right to rule and the legitimacy of its socialist credentials. (Indeed, if a political party or religious organization in the West had gone through similar reversals with such frequency its members would defect in droves.) It seems the government has only belatedly realized that by neglecting Marxist theory for the last ten years, it had let the "bourgeois" genie out of the bottle. At a far deeper level, the government stands as the emperor without clothes. In its panic to resurrect ideological orthodoxy to combat the real threat of mass discontent as implied above, the Party risks being so discredited by its own recent actions that even its claim to be socialist is now regarded by many to be nothing more than a figment of its own imagination. Ideological confusion and ideological bankruptcy stand revealed in the most profound sense as the "paper tiger."

ZHAO: MILD AND CONCILIATORY

In the wake of the student demonstrations, which had begun to spread to other parts of the country, Zhao Ziyang, general secretary of the Chinese Communist Party, took a much more moderate line toward the students than did the hard-liners within the Party leadership, who had originated the harsh April 26 editorial. Zhao, who became Party chief in early 1987 after then Party secretary Hu Yaobang fell from power as a result of an earlier round of student agitation, has been widely believed to be a reformer who was not only sympathetic to the students, but possibly intended to make use of the student movement in order to consolidate his own power base in his struggle against the hard-line conservatives. Unfortunately he suffered the same fate as his predecessor Hu Yaobang, whose death on April 15 set off the recent student demonstrations. On June 24, Zhao was to be formally stripped of power and accused of "having made very serious mistakes by supporting the counterrevolutionary rebellion and splitting the Party."

Zhao's fall from power is complex and cannot be fully discussed here. Of course it is obviously connected intimately with the disagreements not only over how to deal with the students, but more importantly, over how to deal with many of the problems raised by the reforms, which became not surprisingly linked up with the student movement. It is also connected to a power struggle between the so-called "liberals" and "conservatives" within the Party itself.

Despite the tense political situation and his own possibly precarious position, on April 24, Zhao left on a prearranged state visit to North Korea, two days after Hu Yaobang's funeral where he gave the memorial speech but noticeably before the April 26 editorial was published. According to a speech made by Yang Shangkun, China's president and vice-chairman of the Central Military Commission, Zhao was given a full text of the editorial in advance in a telegram, and he actually sent back a telegram from Korea in support of its publication. However, upon his return from Pyongyong, he immediately proposed that the editorial be retracted, possibly because of the bitter reaction it provoked. Due to his direct involvement in attempting to resolve the student crisis, *People's Daily* became more conciliatory toward the students, although its tone remained rather harsh from April 26 onward.

After Zhao returned from Korea, he called a Politburo meeting to discuss how to deal with the student movement. As a result of his personal influence, the Politburo reportedly agreed to major concessions to the student demands, including that officials above the minister level reveal their salaries and benefits, that the government take tough measures to fight corruption and official profiteering, and that top officials at the vice premier level and in the Politburo prepare for dialogue with the students. Zhao himself reportedly proposed to investigate one of his own sons accused of profiteering from selling color television sets.

Moreover, Zhao immediately suggested that Li Tieying, chairman of the State Education Commission, and Yan Mingfu, member of the Secretariat of the Party Central Committee, both of whom were believed to concur with Zhao's moderate line, take direct responsibility for extensive talks with the students. However, a problem that was not resolved at this point was that the leadership still refused to deal with independent student leaders and insisted that the majority component of the student delegation be composed of the officially elected student leaders.

It must also be noted in this context that Zhao himself had been accused indirectly of corruption, while he was in Korea. In a meeting between government officials and students, the officials suggested that they too were against corruption, especially where it concerned high officials who play golf, i.e. Zhao Ziyang himself (who alone among the top leaders enjoyed the game). Thus it seems clear that even by this point the student movement had already begun to be intimately linked with political rivalries at the highest Party level.

While not fully agreeing to all student demands, Zhao was certainly sincere in attempting to help defuse the crisis so that after May 4, a real dialogue with the students could begin and the daily situation would return to something more normal. He certainly took a far more conciliatory position toward them than did Li Peng, who, it is now clear, was already maneuvering not only to advance his own policies, but to completely defeat Zhao Ziyang as well.

MAY FOURTH:
PATRIOTIC STUDENT MOVEMENT REMEMBERED

The May Fourth Movement, as noted, has a long and honored tradition in modern Chinese history. It dramatically spread such Western ideas as "democracy" and "science" in China for the first time, in 1919, only eight years after the last feudal dynasty (the Qing) had been overthrown, while traditional feudal ideas still largely prevailed. The direct cause of the movement was China's failure at the Paris Peace Conference after World War I, where it was decided that Japan, as one of the Allies, like China, would take over the leased territory of the defeated Germans, in Shandong. Infuriated by the humiliating result, students at Beijing University took to the streets and called on other sectors of society to protest against the Chinese government's humiliating willingness to appease Japan's colonial ambitions. Students from other schools immediately joined in the protest and burned the houses of three top government officials in direct charge of China's foreign policy.

The significance of the May Fourth Movement, however, was that Chinese students for the first time initiated a mass movement not only to protest against government policies, but also to spread new ideas. Traditionally, intellectuals had served as apologists for and functionaries of China's 2,000-year-old feudal system rather than as harbingers of new ideas. Therefore, the May Fourth Movement opened a new era in Chinese history for intellectuals to play a far more active role in bringing about social change. After May 4, the intellectuals launched a widespread campaign to criticize the traditional culture represented by Confucianism and introduce modern thinking from the West, including Marxist theory, which laid the foundation of the Chinese Communist Party, which came into existence two years later in 1921.

In the following years of struggle for political power, the Chinese Communist Party, which itself developed partly as a result of the May Fourth Movement, made full use of student movements in fighting the Kuomintang before it finally established the People's Republic in 1949. Not long after, the party declared May 4 as National Youth Day.

Forty years later, when the students once again took to the streets to demand changes by making use of the occasion of May Fourth, the Chinese Communist Party leadership faced a great dilemma in how to deal with the student protestors. It is unlikely that even the most hard-line officials would have dared to launch a crackdown on such a patriotic holiday, particularly on the seventieth anniversary of this momentous event, which really marked the beginning of democratic mass politics of any kind in China's modern history.

According to some students interviewed by foreign reporters, there had been preparations for a large scale demonstration on May 4 long before Hu Yaobang's death, and it was only because of Hu's sudden death that they moved their schedule up by 20 days. This conclusion actually coincides with the official version of the events, which was delivered on June 30 to the National People's Congress by Chen Xitong, mayor of Beijing. In his report, Chen said that some dissident intellectuals such as Fang Lizhi, who together with his wife, Li Shuxian, took refuge at the American Embassy in Beijing after the June 4 crackdown, had been preparing for a march to Tiananmen for several months. Chen said:

> Collaboration between forces at home and abroad intensified toward the end of last year and early this year. Political assemblies, joint petitions, big- and small-character posters and other activities emerged, expressing fully erroneous or even reactionary points. For instance, a big seminar "Future China and the World" was sponsored by the Beijing University Future Studies Society on December 7 last year. Jin Guantao, deputy chief editor of the *Toward the Future* book series and advisor to the society, said in his speech, "attempts at socialism and their failure constitute one of the two major legacies of the twentieth century." Ge Yang, chief editor of the bi-weekly *New Observer,* immediately stood up to provide evidence in the name of the "eldest" among the participants and a party member of dozens of years' standing, saying "Jin's negation of socialism is not too harsh, but a bit too polite. . . . "
>
> [In early spring of this year,] a vast number of big-and small-character posters and assemblies came out on the campuses of some universities in Beijing, attacking the Communist Party and the socialist system. On March 1, for example, a big-character poster entitled "Denunciation of Deng Xiaoping—An Open Letter to the Nation" was put up at Qinghua University and Beijing University simultaneously. The poster uttered such nonsense as "the politics of the Communist Party consist of empty talk, power politics, autocratic rule, and arbitrary decision," and openly demanded "dismantling the Party and the Four Cardinal Principles." A small-character poster entitled "Deplore the Chinese" turned up in Beijing University on March 2, crying to overthrow "totalitarianism" and "autocracy. . . ." On April 13, the Beijing Institute of Post and Telecommunications and some other schools received a "Message to the Nation's College Students" signed by the Guangxi University Students Union, which called on students to "hold high the portrait of Hu Yaobang and the great banner of democracy, freedom, dignity, and rule by law in celebration of the May Fourth Youth Day." *(For the complete text of Chen's report on the demonstrations and the government's response see Appendix One.)*

Given the fact that the government was aware of what was going to happen on May 4, they might have handled the student crisis more effectively had the demonstrations been delayed until May 4, because then they could have at least been mentally better prepared for a crisis. However, with Hu's unexpected death and the quick response by the students, officials were obviously caught by surprise. Because of their inability to diffuse a sudden crisis, the situation had already gotten out of control by May 4, when the authorities could do nothing effective to prevent larger student demonstrations, since they were not willing to calm them by accepting student demands. On May 2, as mentioned, the students delivered a detailed twelve-point petition to the National People's Congress and the Party Central Committee, which was actually also an ultimatum, because in it the students demanded not only an equal dialogue with government officials, but also an answer before noon on May 3 from the government. Otherwise, they said, they would "reserve the right to continue our petitionary marches on May 4."

The government did not meet the student demands. On the contrary, it went further by accusing "blackhands" of manipulating the students. As a result, the expected demonstrations in Tiananmen Square took place on May 4, participated in by hundreds of thousands of students. Moreover, the demonstrations on May 4 gave the government more cause for concern, not only because of the enormous turnout of students, but also because the protest now attracted people from other sectors of society. More than 200 journalists joined the students calling for press reform, and workers and ordinary citizens came not only to celebrate May Fourth, but also to support the students. It can be certain that the officials were chagrined with what they could only see as student manipulation of the occasion of May Fourth to widen their support to almost every sphere of the general population in the urban areas. The implication clearly was that the general population regarded the student movement as a popular, patriotic expression of the people's will. Even more threatening to those at the top was the fear that other sections of the population might soon add their own demands to those of the students. Therefore, despite their apprehension about the further implications of not containing the broadening popular support for the student movement, the authorities wisely enough decided to take no further actions on this occasion.

STUDENTS RETURNED TO CAMPUS

Despite the government's extremely hostile editorial on April 26 and its refusal to meet all the student demands, the fact that Zhao Ziyang had even agreed to talk with them, combined with the overwhelming success of the massive demonstration on May 4, convinced the students that they could return to the campuses in preparation for the next round of negotiations with party and state officials.

Zhao's message to the students was reflected in two of his speeches. On May 3, he delivered a speech at an official meeting to commemorate the seventieth anniversary of the May Fourth Movement, in which he said little about the demonstrations directly. However, reiterating official policy, he did indicate that the students should help maintain order, by suggesting that democracy and reform could not materialize if China failed to maintain political stability. He also called on the students to guard against turmoil while demonstrating for political changes. Also in that speech, as was later revealed by Yang Shangkun, China's president, who is believed to have played a major role in the military crackdown in June, Zhao refused to stress "fighting bourgeois liberalization," although Li Peng and other hard-liners had requested him to do so.

On May 4, while the students were demonstrating in Tiananmen Square, Zhao made yet another speech during a meeting with delegations attending the twenty-second annual conference of the Asian Development Bank. In that speech, Zhao called for "soberness, reason, restraint, and order" and vowed to solve existing problems by a "democratic and legal means." Zhao expressed his understanding of the student demands and said he was confident that "there would not be serious turmoil in China." Talking about the student protest, Zhao said:

> I believe the majority of the students participating in the demonstrations are both satisfied and dissatisfied with the Communist Party and the government. This is their basic attitude. They are certainly not opposed to our fundamental (socialist) system, but rather are demanding that we eliminate the mistakes in our work. On the one hand, they are very satisfied with the progress and development in the last ten years of reform and construction. On the other hand, they are very dissatisfied with the mistakes in our work. Thus they want us to correct our mistakes and improve our work, which happens to be the goal of our party and government as well. *(See Appendix One for Zhao's speech.)*

Zhao's speech was actually an open challenge to the positions of the hard-line conservatives. It has now been officially branded a "turning point" for the "escalation of the turmoil." In Chen Xitong's report, the speech was accused of being "contradictory to the spirit of the [*People's Daily*] editorial." Chen also disclosed that the speech was drafted by Bao Tong, Zhao's important aide, who was later arrested on charges of leaking information to student leaders. According to Chen, Bao Tong also urged the *People's Daily* and other major news organizations to publish Zhao's speech in a prominent way. Chen said:

> On the afternoon of May 4, when meeting with representatives attending the annual meeting of the Asian Development Bank, Comrade Zhao Ziyang expressed a whole set of views diametrically opposed to the decision of the Politburo's Standing Committee, to Comrade Deng Xiaoping's speech and to the spirit of the editorial. First, as the turmoil had already come to the surface, he said "there will be no big turmoil in China"; secondly, when a host of facts had proved that the real nature of the turmoil was the negation of the leadership of the Communist Party and the socialist system, he still insisted that "they are by no means opposed to our fundamental system. Rather they are asking us to correct mistakes in our work"; thirdly, although facts had shown that a tiny handful of people was making use of the student unrest to instigate turmoil, he merely said that it was "hardly avoidable" for "some people to take advantage of this," thus totally negating the correct judgment of the Party Central Committee that a handful of people were creating turmoil.
>
> Comrade Zhao Ziyang's speech, publicized through the *People's Daily* and other newspapers, created serious ideological confusion among the cadres and the masses and inflated the arrogance of the organizers and plotters of the turmoil.

However, for the students, Zhao's speech was reasonable and convincing. That evening, the speech was broadcast again and again on many campuses in Beijing and was widely welcomed by the students, who at this point seemed to be ready to accept Zhao's assessment and return to classes the following day, thus ending the class boycott that had been in effect since April 23.

As a result, Zhao emerged with a more positive general image among the students than most of the rest of the leadership, partly because of his two speeches, partly because of his consistently more moderate lines toward students and intellectuals. It was felt that he had some sympathy for and some understanding of the student demands and would be willing to enter into substantive negotiations with them shortly. Obviously, the fact that Zhao Ziyang had adopted a relatively conciliatory attitude was not lost on Li Peng, who clearly wanted to use every advantage he could muster in what were already deep policy and personal differences in the party leaders' approach. He would certainly not hesitate to use Zhao's more conciliatory approach to turn Deng Xiaoping against Zhao, and he surely realized it would be relatively easy to manipulate Deng's extreme sensitivity to the student movement, given Deng's traumatic experiences during the Cultural Revolution. Again, the pity is that the student movement became inextricably involved with political rivalries at the highest level. However for the time being, things were quiet. Li Peng would have to bide his time, and it looked as if Zhao Ziyang's position might be relatively secure.

HUNGER STRIKE TOUCHES THE HEART OF BEIJING

The return to campus of the students and the peaceful end of the May Fourth demonstrations were a relief to both the leadership and to the general population at large. However, the students definitely had higher expectations in mind in terms of holding more serious dialogues with government officials, to address the issues they had raised during their demonstrations. Although the boycott of classes was officially called off by the Autonomous Students Association of Beijing Universities, the independent students union, many students did not return to class because they thought what the government had done was not enough to insure that their demands were met. On May 6, several hundred students demonstrated on the campus of Beijing University, calling on others to continue class boycotts until the government agreed to a dialogue with the "true representatives" of the students, namely representatives of the independent students union. However, the students did not come to any agreement among themselves over the question of whether or not to return to class. On the same day, student representatives issued another petition to the Party Central Committee calling for substantive dialogue with and demanding a satisfactory answer from the authorities. Otherwise, they said they would reserve the right to take further actions, which at this point were not specified and later turned out to be a hunger strike.

On the other hand, the government did not give any significant signals that it was prepared to hold serious talks with the students after May 4 and authorities were certainly unwilling to talk with representatives of the Autonomous Students Association, which they had declared to be an illegal organization.

Here it must be noted that the formation of such an independent students union was in itself an extraordinary event. It marked the first time in the history of the People's Republic that students openly demanded that the government accept the legality of an organization that was not formed at the behest of the authorities, but by the choice of the people. After the movement began in mid-April, many students felt that the official students unions in various schools could not really represent the majority of students or provide leadership to the student movement. Therefore they proposed that an independent students union be established to organize and coordinate actions in different schools. On April 19, the Preparatory Committee of Beijing University Solidarity Students Union was established at Beijing University, and the next day a formal organization, the Students Association of Beijing Universities, which later changed its name to the Autonomous Students Association of Beijing Universities, was formed, represented by students from dozens of universities in Beijing, with most of its major leaders from Beijing and Beijing Normal Universities.

While student leaders, such as Wu'er Kaixi and Wang Dan, had claimed that the independent union represented the majority of the students, it is not clear how and through what process such leaders were elected. It seems, however, that they naturally emerged as leaders because they had stood in the frontline of the movement and had played a major role in organizing the demonstrations. In other words, those who were willing to stand up became the natural leaders. Consequently, it is important to emphasize again that such leaders may not necessarily be the more sophisticated people who had chosen not to make public their role but who had provided substantial spiritual guidance to the movement. It is generally believed that some graduate students and younger faculty at various schools had played the most crucial role in organizing the movement and formulating and pressing their demands. Unlike those freshmen or sophomores on the front lines who might have had more emotion and courage than sophistication, these people were well-educated in and deeply influenced by both Chinese and Western cultural traditions. Although most of the latter may not have been to any Western countries at all, this of course did not prevent them from reacting to some of the most challenging ideas from Western culture.

Undoubtedly, Western influence played an important role in the "pro-democracy" movement. The tactics of the hunger strike and non-violent protest have even led some of the Western press to suggest that the students were particularly influenced by Gandhi and Martin Luther King. Although the histories of Gandhi and King were known to students, these men were by no means the primary influences. In fact, intellectual development in China in recent years has been a valuable source for encouraging Chinese students to be both idealistic and practical when calling for more democratic changes, which they know should be based on China's actual situation.

It is important to remember that the intellectual revolt in China did not begin only two years ago, as too many Western reports had suggested. Although it is known in the West that the "democracy movement" began in China as early as 1978, when some young people set up a "Democracy Wall" in Beijing, few Westerners have given attention to the student democracy movement of 1980 and 1985, both of which were of great importance in providing the students with the theoretical preparation for the recent "pro-democracy movement." Thus it is necessary to look back briefly to the recent history of the spreading of "democratic ideas" in Chinese universities.

In 1978–79, when Deng Xiaoping began economic reforms in China in an effort to realize the Four Modernizations, a group of young people in Beijing who had lived through the Cultural Revolution began to realize the defects of China's authoritarian political power structure. They rightfully blamed Mao Zedong for possessing absolute power, which they thought had at least partially caused the disastrous Cultural Revolution. Thus they felt that besides advanced technologies, a modern political culture characterized by democracy and political freedom should be introduced to China at the same time. As Wei Jingsheng, a prominent leader of the Democracy Wall movement, put it, China needs a "fifth modernization"—democracy.

The Democracy Wall movement marked the first time after 1949 that the Chinese turned to the West for concepts for establishing a modern political system. It was also the first time that some of the nation's best took "democracy," rather than "Communism," as the "objective of a struggle" (*fendou mubiao*). Although the Democracy Wall movement was quickly crushed by Deng Xiaoping, and Wei Jingsheng was jailed on charges of "leaking state secrets to foreigners," its impact on Chinese intellectuals was far-reaching. After that, the role of orthodox Marxism as the only "suitable means for China" came increasingly into doubt. It became inevitable that while China opened its door for Western technology—or "fresh air" as Deng Xiaoping referred to it, Western thinking—or "flies"—was bound to come in simultaneously.

Therefore, a year later, in 1980, a more extraordinary event that has never been fully explored by Western scholars, took place at China's most prestigious school, Beijing University, which had spearheaded most of the student movements since 1919. It began in the fall of that year, when a people's deputy had to be chosen from the students at the university to represent the Haidian District, where the university is located.

The election was the first of its kind conducted at Beijing University since a new election law had been passed in 1979 by the Second Session of the Fifth National People's Congress, China's parliament. The new legislation made it possible for the first time in the People's Republic to have a slate of more candidates than positions in the election of representatives to the nation's "highest power organ." It also stipulated that direct elections be held at the county level, a radical change from the 1953 law, which was based on a Soviet system of one candidate per location. The new law even allowed a fairly open process of nomination. Therefore, any organization or individual seconded by three or more voters can be nominated as a candidate for the first list. And, theoretically, campaigning for candidates is also permitted.

The new election law sounded quite democratic. However, actual practice proved to be a far different matter. Direct election at the county level was tested in some places in early 1980, but due to the fact that China's rural population is largely apolitical, the result was far from satisfactory. The same problems with participation also made it difficult for the new nomination process to function properly elsewhere, and campaigning for candidates had seldom been heard of except in some schools. Moreover, violation of the new election law was frequently reported, with local officials abusing power.

An extraordinary incident occurred at Mao Zedong's alma mater, Hunan Normal University, in Changsha, capital of Hunan Province, when the school authorities removed a candidate who was not a Party member from the list of candidates. As a result, 87 students launched a hunger strike, and 4,000 students took to the streets to support the hunger strikers. The students sent telegrams describing the affair to universities in Beijing and Shanghai, asking for support.

When the telegrams reached the campus of Beijing University, or *Beida*, as it is usually called, they touched off a wave of protest. Big- and small-character posters quickly covered the walls of the campus, especially in the area which the students have come to call the *sanjiaodi*, or "triangular area." At first, the students were expressing strong support for the students in Hunan, and gradually they began to advocate the new style of election, including campaigning for candidates and direct election of the "people's deputy." Given the new election law mentioned above, such demands were well within the law. Therefore, the school authorities accepted the student demands and for the first time in Chinese history a genuine democratic election was held at China's most prestigious school, Beijing University.

The election, which has come to be known as the "Campaign Movement" among Beijing University students, started as something like an American-style campaign. Five candidates were first nominated, among whom one was to be elected as the people's deputy. The candidates presented their viewpoints through big-character posters and by lecturing fellow students. For a time, wall posters were seen everywhere on the campus, and student rallies, big and small, were held in the classroom, in the hallways, or on the street. The candidates were also engaged in debates, where they were questioned directly by the voters. During the whole course of the campaign, which lasted about two months, the school authorities surprisingly accommodated the candidates by letting them use some school facilities and providing other services.

One most important issue during the campaign was the campaign itself. All the candidates expressed the same thought that "while it was not important to win, it *was* important to participate." In other words, they were hoping that by such a Western-style campaign, they could set up a model for the rest of the society and introduce to China some Western concepts which they thought could help China reform its own rigid, Leninist political structure. The campaign was mostly participated in and monitored by older students in their thirties who had entered the university in 1977 and 1978, right after China resumed the national entrance examination for colleges. All of the candidates had gone through the ten years of the Cultural Revolution and had considerable social experience, and most of them were very critical of the Maoist period and strongly advocated some new political thinking for China. Intellectually, they were influenced by writers and philosophers from the French Enlightenment, such as Jean-Jacques Rousseau, Voltaire, and Montesquieu, and the theory of *sanquan fenli,* or division of power among the three branches of the government, with complete checks and balances. Such an idea, which the West takes for granted, was strikingly novel to most of the Chinese students in the early 1980s. Soon after it was widely introduced to the campus of Beijing University, it almost instantly attracted the attention and interest of the students, who viewed Montesquieu's theory as a perfect lens through which they saw the defects of China's Leninist power structure and the way to change it, although they had no realistic hope of seeing it applied to all China in the near future.

Although the students were allowed to hold such a democratic election, Chinese leadership was by no means pleased. Soon after the Campaign Movement, Deng Xiaoping himself made an internal speech branding it as "bourgeois liberalism." In the speech, which was read to all Beijing University students shortly after the campaign, Deng insisted that such Western-style elections were not suitable for China's national conditions.

The experience of Hu Ping, the candidate who was actually elected, was somewhat more tragic. A graduate student in the Philosophy Department, Hu wrote an essay, "On Freedom of Speech," which helped win him the popular vote. Ironically, as a people's deputy, Hu could not find employment upon graduation, because he was deemed as "too dangerous," and he waited for almost three years before landing a job at the Beijing Academy of Social Sciences. In 1985 he came to the United States to do graduate work at Harvard and in 1987 he became chairman of the Chinese Alliance for Democracy, a New York-based organization believed to have received money from agencies related to Taiwan and therefore under suspicion in China. The organization has been declared "counter-revolutionary" by the Chinese government and Hu Ping himself was deprived of his Chinese passport after becoming one of the organization's top leaders.

However, the impact of the Campaign Movement was enormous. It educated the younger students, who entered Beijing University after 1979 and had grown up reciting Mao's quotations and knowing few foreign names other than Marx, Engels, Lenin, and Stalin. One immediate result of the movement was that almost all the students, regardless of their majors, began to read Rousseau, Voltaire and

Montesquieu, whether they could really understand them or not. Thus freshmen and sophomores at Beijing University in 1980 became the carriers of much "new thinking" in 1985 during an earlier period of student movement which was ignited by Japanese Prime Minister Nakasone's visit to the Yasukuni Shrine in Tokyo, where many Japanese war dead from World War II are still honored. However, as has often been the case, the thrust of the movement was quickly changed, with the demand for democracy supplanting the denunciations of Nakasone. The students planned a march to Tiananmen Square but they failed to carry it out or perhaps did not really intend to break through the locked gate, and the crisis was peacefully resolved after the authorities sent a state-run symphony orchestra to the campus to take part in a ceremony honoring the Chinese casualties of the Anti-Japanese War. Later, when meeting with a Japanese delegation, Zhao Ziyang, then the premier, praised the students for their patriotism instead of blaming them for making trouble.

The 1986–87 student movement that had cost Hu Yaobang his post and made Zhao Ziyang the Party secretary is well known in the West, and need not be fully discussed here. However, it should be emphasized that because of it, as well as the 1980 and 1985 movements, the students had gained a good deal of experience. Thus before the recent "pro-democracy" movement broke out in April 1989, students had become much more experienced in organizing demonstrations than before. They were also more deliberate in their tactics, although the strategies used, such as the hunger strike, might not have been as effective as they had anticipated.

After May 4, the students had to a certain extent made their point and it seemed that a peaceful and positive resolution was already in sight as they returned to class. However, for whatever reasons— neglect, bureaucratic inertia, incompetence, opposition by Li Peng and other officials, or because of the imminent arrival of Gorbachev —by May 12, the students realized that no substantive dialogue was about to begin before the arrival of the Soviet leader. They were left with the impression that either by omission or commission the government had broken faith with them. It was decided that dramatic action was necessary once again to put student demands at the top of the nation's political agenda.

A consensus was reached among the ad hoc leadership of the independent students union to return to the square in force, beginning

May 13. It was also decided to dramatize demands for serious dialogue and retraction of the April 26 editorial by using the tactic of a hunger strike. At the beginning, about 500 students decided to participate in this emotionally charged protest. At its height the number of hunger strikers reached 3,000, out of a total of 200,000 protesters.

However, it must be noted that the call for a hunger strike was at first met with limited enthusiasm. Many students felt that with Zhao Ziyang's conciliatory speech on May 4, they had already made their point. The majority thought it was more realistic to prepare for a long term struggle rather than to continue to pressure the authorities for an immediate resolution of their demands. In fact, many students interviewed by both the Chinese and Western media after May 4 declared they would not return to Tiananmen Square during the Gorbachev visit because they did not wish to jeopardize the Sino-Soviet summit. As a result, on May 12 when the student leaders began to enlist hunger strikers, only 150 students at Beijing University registered. However, the figure was soon doubled when students at Beida heard that 200 students had already signed up at Beijing Normal University. Beida, which had laid claim to leadership in student movements ever since the May Fourth Movement in 1919, of course did not want to be outdone by any other schools. According to a special report by ABC news, Chai Ling, the student leader who was originally an undergraduate student at Beida and was then enrolled by Beijing Normal University as a graduate student, actually felt "very sad" at the low turnout. Therefore she went to Beijing University to exhort more students to participate.

In any event, by launching a hunger strike during the Gorbachev visit, the students failed to consider fully its possible outcome. Of course they were expecting the best result, which at that point meant the retraction of the April 26 *People's Daily* editorial and a substantive dialogue with the government. However, they had misjudged the overall situation, or had at least seriously underestimated the potential reactions of government leaders, whom the students should have known would not easily relent. The students also underestimated the determination and convictions of those old revolutionaries, who would use any means they thought necessary, including a bloody military crackdown, to safeguard their position. Moreover, the students were misguided by a tragic lack of sophistication in other areas. For example, some even had the bizarre notion that according to an international convention any government was obliged to accept the demands of hunger strikers after a fast had entered its seventh day. On May 18, during a conversation between Li Peng and student leaders, Wang Zhixin, a student from China Political Science and Law University, declared to Li and other state leaders, "There is an international practice that any government should respond when a hunger strike has lasted for seven days. Even such a country as South Africa can comply."

Knowing that Zhao Ziyang was taking a different stand from other members of the Politburo, the students hoped that by putting more pressure on the government, they could even help Zhao win the majority over to his policy. Part of the problem, however, was that Zhao himself already faced serious difficulties surviving the political crisis, largely because leaders such as Deng Xiaoping and Yang Shangkun had firm control over the army, which still plays an important role in domestic politics.

Nevertheless, the students did hope that the tactic of a hunger strike would demonstrate both to the leadership and populace at large that their movement was patriotic and nonviolent. It was also hoped that the specter of students putting their lives at risk would pressure the entire leadership to begin negotiations of a serious nature.

In any event, before the hunger strike ended, more than 1,000 students who participated had to be taken to nearby hospitals for emergency treatment, and as long as the hunger strike continued, the government was, for public relations if nothing else, constrained from using force against the protesters.

Because of the emotionally powerful nature of a hunger strike, it succeeded to a great extent in winning the support of a large segment of the population. When more and more fasting students fainted and were taken to the hospitals, and the government failed to respond positively to the student demands, people in Beijing moved in to launch the largest demonstrations in the history of the People's Republic to express support for the students. On May 14, one day before Gorbachev arrived in Beijing, twelve well-known intellectuals, including Yan Jiaqi, Bao Zunxin, and Wen Yuankai went to the square. They first urged the students to end their hunger strike and leave the square to make way for the Gorbachev visit. However, they made it clear that they would not pressure the students to leave the square if they chose not to. On the contrary, they said they understood the students and that they would organize a support demonstration by intellectuals. Thus on May 15, several thousand intellectuals marched to Tiananmen Square and became the first non-student demonstrators after the hunger strike began.

Following the demonstrations by the intellectuals, more and more people demonstrated to support the students. Journalists, government empoyees, judges, workers and hundreds of thousands of ordinary Beijing citizens took to the streets, shouting slogans like "Save our kids!" (*jiu jiu haizi!*) Some more defiant protestors called for the retirement of Deng Xiaoping and the resignation of Premier Li Peng. Beijing's hospitals set up numerous emergency centers to treat the severely weakened hunger strikers, with many medical students volunteering to help. Ordinary citizens of Beijing donated money and other daily necessities because, as an old Chinese saying goes: "When one person is in danger, people from all over come to help."

It should also be noted that huge demonstrations occurred in many other cities as well, with some even continuing after the night of June 3–4. Thus demonstrations and riots were reported in Xian and Changsha before the climax of events in Beijing. Large demonstrations took place in Shanghai, where citizens and students blocked trains and took over the railroad station. In Wuhan, students blocked the main north-south railway bridge, and in Baoding, a city seventy miles south of Beijing, students from Hebei University and other schools blocked troops from proceeding and lay down in front of tanks. Demonstrations were also reported in Guangzhou, Shenyang, Nanjing, Hangzhou, Kunming and many other major cities, thus indicating the widespread involvement of China's urban population and widespread dissatisfaction with the government.

Some of the most serious demonstrations and riots took place in Chengdu, capital city of Sichuan, the home province of Deng Xiaoping himself, which may account for some of the harshness of the repression there after "rioting was reported" and some of the bloodiest suppression outside Beijing even after June 3–4.

Secondary and primary school students were also organized in other towns as in Beijing to participate in marches or help as messengers and support networks. This activity, and the help they doubtless received from sympathetic bureaucrats and others, may help explain why many student leaders have not yet been apprehended. It also may explain how some prominent student leaders and dissident intellectuals managed to flee the country after June 4.

GORBACHEV'S VISIT AND MEDIA COVERAGE

The official state visit of Soviet President and Party Secretary Mikhail Gorbachev to the People's Republic of China from May 15–18 was a historic occasion in many ways, and its importance in leading up to the events of June 3-4 cannot of course be underestimated.

Given its historic significance and the enormous press coverage it was bound to generate, Gorbachev's visit was an optimum time for the students to dramatize their cause. Moreover, given Gorbachev's dramatic policies of political reform, it provided them with an unparalleled opportunity to pressure their own leaders to follow the example of the Soviet reformers. It seems clear that one reason for the willingness to increase pressure on the government was specifically that shortly before Gorbachev's visit, when asked about China's own political reforms, Li Peng responded by suggesting that conditions in the People's Republic were quite different from the Soviet Union and that the People's Republic would follow its own timetable and policies in this regard.

For the Chinese leadership, the Sino-Soviet Summit represented a political victory, because the Soviet leader was coming to Beijing rather than the reverse. This was a powerful symbol of China's heightened status as a world power, a replay of the proud days of Nixon's historic visit to Beijing, putting China again at the center of the international stage. Gorbachev's appearance in Beijing indicated a dramatic change in the relationship between the two Communist giants. Stalin, for example, never paid a state visit to China during his years in power. Therefore, Gorbachev's presence meant that the People's Republic had risen to the Soviet Union's level in international status, a heady advance from its earlier role as a poor supplicant hobbling to Moscow to beg for aid. China had not only gained the respect of the Russians, but great respect for itself as well.

Although there were many unresolved major issues between the two countries, the Soviets had made major concessions on three key questions: Soviet withdrawal from Afghanistan had been completed in a humiliating admission of defeat for the USSR—at least in popular Chinese eyes—even though the Najibullah regime remained in power in Kabul. And pressure had been brought on Vietnam to agree to withdraw its troops from Cambodia. The Soviet Union had agreed to substantial reductions in the number of its troops stationed on the Sino-Soviet border and in Mongolia. In fact, on the occasion of his historic visit, Gorbachev made a dramatic gesture by proposing to reduce the number of Soviet troops in Mongolia by 50 percent, a move bound to improve the atmosphere at the summit.

Moreover, the summit could be seen as a personal triumph for Deng Xiaoping, capping his long career. It was announced shortly before the Gorbachev visit that Deng would step down from his last post as chairman of the Central Military Commission before the anniversary of the inauguration of the People's Liberation Army on August 1, meaning that Deng would relinquish his last official post even before the fortieth anniversary celebrations of the founding of the People's Republic on October 1, which would have been the ideal ceremonial occasion for presenting the succession leadership to the people. The fact that the 14th Party Congress was not scheduled to convene until the fall of 1992 added to its appeal as an occasion to present to the world the official lineup of the post-Deng succession leadership. The Gorbachev summit, then, could have been the last dramatic act of a heroic statesman, who presided over a major period of reform, had been in power since the establishment of full diplomatic relations with the United States, was the guiding spirit in negotiating the eventual return of both Hong Kong and Macao to the motherland, and had initiated a new policy of moderation toward Taiwan. To have stepped down immediately after the normalization of both state-to-state and party-to-party relations with the Soviet Union after a three decade period of varying hostilities between the two giant nations would have sealed Deng's place in history.

On another level, the Gorbachev visit provided the Chinese leadership an opportunity to go beyond their internal political concerns and offer the students a bold gesture of good faith. For Deng Xiaoping, it was at least as much a prime occasion as a crisis. There was a general feeling that Mao Zedong and Zhou Enlai would not have squandered the opportunity offered by the Gorbachev visit to handle the crisis in a more creative manner. It is thus no accident that both before and after the Sino-Soviet summit, many of the protesters carried photographs of both of China's preeminent former leaders.

Instead of reacting creatively and flexibly to the unprecedented situation with which the Chinese leadership was presented by the Gorbachev visit, the government reverted to the old patterns of orthodox political rhetoric. Nor could the traditionally conservative Beijing city leadership itself be counted on to attempt novel solutions, especially if conciliation were involved.

From the beginning of the Gorbachev visit, the path of least re-sistance was followed. The arrival ceremony was moved to the airport to avoid possible incidents in the square and Gorbachev was spirited to the Great Hall of the People by a rear entrance. It seems dubious that there was any serious physical danger to him at any point during his visit. Half of the square in between the Great Hall of the People and the Monument to the People's Heroes could have been cleared, and the arrival ceremony could have taken place in the usual location. It was clear that the students who already had the opportu-nity of attempting to break into the Great Hall of the People and Zhongnanhai itself made no serious attempt to do so, then or later. The only danger was that the students might have attempted to persuade Gorbachev to publicly endorse their demands and embar-rass the Chinese leadership. This in itself was probably the real motive behind the Chinese leadership's refusal to compromise with the demonstrators during the summit, but on a more sinister level it implied both that they did not take the student movement seri-ously and that they would eventually resort to force to suppress it.

The rest of Gorbachev's stay followed the same pattern. Instead of calling in the student leaders and asking them to withdraw from the front of the imperial palace so that Gorbachev's planned appear-ance there could take place, the visit was simply canceled and re-placed by other activities. Despite the enormous praise previously lavished on China's reform leadership by the West, the fact remains that the authorities were not able to respond in a reform-minded, flexible manner to the events during Gorbachev's visit. While the American media were right in suggesting that the summit was "up-staged" by the student protest, the leadership might have been able to upstage the students with its own dramatic gesture, had it been as innovative as the American press suggested before the student crisis erupted. Moreover, agreeing to change Gorbachev's schedule so that he could have, for example, spoken at Beijing University—a privilege granted to someone as far-removed from the communist spirit as Prime Minister Nakasone in 1984—might even have gone a long way in signaling that the government was serious about polit-ical reform and meeting student demands.

Instead, authorities were confronted with a far more embarassing situation by the statements Gorbachev made at his final press con-ference in Beijing which implied that the Chinese leadership had lost total control of the situation by letting their visiting dignitary criticize their ossified and unimaginative policies to foreign journalists in the middle of their own capital. At that press conference, which was held at the Diaoyutai State Guest House, Gorbachev suggested that he understood the students' desire for more openness. Whether intended or not, it seems most likely that certain people in the Chinese leadership might find Gorbachev's comment very embarrassing.

Not much more initiative was shown by the Shanghai authorities who were supposedly prevented by the masses in the center of the city from even allowing Gorbachev to visit the downtown area. Here again, effective use of a mass police presence, blocking certain access roads and bringing in Gorbachev by side streets, would have allowed him to have at least seen Shanghai's famous former commercial center.

Again, as evidenced by charges subsequently made against Zhao Ziyang, the Gorbachev visit became involved with the power struggle among China's top leadership. One complaint against Zhao was that he commented to Gorbachev that Deng Xiaoping was still the final authority on fundamental questions of policy. That was hardly a state secret to anyone and subsequent charges that Zhao betrayed confidentiality by making the remark only seem to indicate how highly charged was the internal political atmosphere at the highest levels of the Chinese Communist Party on the occasion of the Sino-Soviet summit.

We still do not know enough about the internal situation in the Chinese hierarchy at this time to make a definitive comment, but it certainly appears that the aging Communist leaders like Chen Yun, Li Xiannian, Bo Yibo, and Peng Zhen, who shortly afterwards began to appear out of their supposed "retirement" or "semi-retirement," would have been more than naive if they had not used the combined protests and Gorbachev visit to exercise their own influence against policies they did not particularly approve of, which were closely associated with Zhao and Deng himself. Thus the Gorbachev visit can be seen as a major impetus for making even more acute the policy struggle at the heart of the Chinese Communist Party that in a sense made the student protests irrelevant.

TOP-LEVEL DIALOGUE CALLED

After Gorbachev's departure there were expectations that the government would turn its attention to the students and begin seriously negotiating on the issues that had been raised. Encouraged by wide support from large sectors of the population, the students called for a dialogue with high-level leaders of the Party. They were hoping not simply for a meeting with some of the most important officials of the country but for the opening of a substantive dialogue as well. They were also encouraged by the fact that several top leaders, including Zhao Ziyang, Li Peng, Hu Qili, and Qiao Shi even went personally to some of the hospitals to visit students who had grown so weak from fasting that they had to be taken to medical facilities. It was hoped that once the leadership had agreed to a dialogue and substantive discussions began, the strike would dissipate even if the student demands were not immediately met. The government's willingness to negotiate would diffuse the increasing polarization between itself and the people.

By May 17, four days after the hunger strike began, the students got even stronger support not only from ordinary Beijing citizens, but also from members of the Party-controlled organizations and leaders of various democratic parties, who called on the top leadership—Zhao Ziyang and Li Peng in particular—to talk to the students directly.

The amount of pressure on the authorities was enormous. Even those who had been widely regarded as conservatives, such as Hu Sheng, former head of the Social Sciences Academy, and leaders of the democratic parties, who had always closely followed in the footsteps of the Party, called on the top leadership to enter into serious dialogue with the students "as soon as possible" so that the hunger strike could be concluded.

Beginning May 17, the *People's Daily* devoted much of its coverage to the appeals made by various sectors of the society to the leadership to engage in serious dialogue with the students. First, there was an open letter signed by ten university presidents in Beijing saying "Under the current situation, the only correct choice is dialogue. . . . In order to hold constructive dialogue, soberness, reason and a realistic attitude are needed. . . . We hope that the top Party and government leaders will hold direct meetings and dialogue with the students as soon as possible."

The next day, Fei Xiaotong, Sun Qimeng, Lei Jieqiong, and Zhou Peiyuan, chairmen of four respective democratic parties, signed an open letter to Zhao Ziyang, calling on him to meet with the students. The four chairmen wrote: "We believe that the student movement is patriotic. . . . And we suggest that the top leaders of the Party

Police stand, faced off by citizens on April 27.

Determined demonstrators link arms.

Faces and flags in the demonstration.

Trucks carry sympathetic police along Changan Avenue, towards Tiananmen Square.

Demonstrators in the afternoon, May 29.

Workers from factory who turned out to support students on May 17.

Criticism of the press in Poster Form

The poster offers pointed criticism of the media in China, saying:

People's Daily (Renmin Ribao) *"deceiving people"*
Beijing Daily *"recklessly concocts"*
Beijing Wanbao (Evening Paper) *"talking nonsense"*
Guangming Ribao (Brightness Paper) *"not bright, all darkness"*
Science and Technology Daily *"newspaper of truth—has been banned"*
The Central Radio Station "confuses right and wrong"
Broadcasting Station "false reporting"

Monument to the People's Heroes, focal point of the hunger strike.

The aftermath: tanks near southwest corner of Tiananmen Square the morning of June 4.

Students attempted to talk soldiers out of entering the back of the People's Congress the afternoon of June 3.

Tank at Tiananmen Square at about 5 a.m. on June 4.

Central Committee and the State Council meet with the students and hold dialogue as soon as possible."

Rong Yiren, president of China International Trust and Investment Corporation and vice chairman of the Standing Committee of the National People's Congress, made the same appeal in his letter to Zhao. Bing Xin, a prominent woman writer—aged 89—called on the "parents of the people" to "save my kids." She said, "I believe that if only one or two top Party and government leaders appear in Tiananmen Square and say to the thousands of people only one or two sentences to show their sympathy and understanding, the situation will develop in the direction of reason and order. If so, our children will not have to pay the unnecessary heavy price." The renowned writer also said, "The students love the country; and I love the students."

Similar appeals were made by many other prominent Chinese. Writers, artists, scientists, and journalists all came forth to show concern. Most prominently, the Central Committee of the Communist Youth League, the All-China Youth Federation, and the All-China Students Federation, which are all directly affiliated with the Communist Party, jointly issued a three-point emergency appeal stating: "1) We do not want to see the lives and health of the students threatened. Neither do we want to see a subversion of the process of reform and construction. We hope that the top Party and government leaders will meet with the students as soon as possible so as to fully understand the students' patriotic enthusiasm and reasonable demands and diffuse the situation. 2) We believe that the only correct choice is, under the leadership of the Party and through sincere dialogue, to resolve the question by democratic and legal means. 3) We sincerely hope that various sectors of society take a humanitarian stand, help and protect the students who are on the hunger strike, maintain order in the square, and insure the lives and health of the students."

Again, under this situation, the crisis could have been better handled if it were not for the political power struggle at the very top. As was evidenced later, Zhao Ziyang was ready to meet both of the student demands and proposed going to the square himself to talk to the students. He proposed retraction of the *People's Daily* editorial and taking personal responsibility for its publication.

However, he was strongly opposed by Li Peng and other conservatives and was thus accused of "splitting the party," a very serious charge. In the end, Zhao failed to convince the party leadership to take his conciliatory line, and it was up to Li Peng to meet with the student leaders and provoke further antagonism by his uncompromising stand on May 18, which was not softened by Wu'er Kaixi's own arrogance.

LI PENG: CONFRONTATION WITH STUDENT LEADERS

In the early afternoon on May 18, the same day Gorbachev ended his historic visit, Li Peng officially met for the first time about ten leading representatives of the student protest in the Great Hall of the People. Unfortunately, however, what might have been a breakthrough in the student-government conflict did not proceed in a very conciliatory direction.

To begin with, both sides may have had very different preconceived notions of the purpose of the meeting. The students may have been naive in their expectations, but they seem to have believed that such a meeting could be the beginning of a genuine dialogue to resolve the crisis and mark the beginning of real accountability on the part of China's leaders toward the demands of its people. The government officials may have been reluctant in agreeing to this meeting in the first place, because they may have regarded it as a loss of face. The mere acceptance of the students' call to meet was a major concession on their part.

Although accompanied by Li Tieying and Yan Mingfu, who could be seen as relatively sympathetic with student demands, Li Peng was also flanked by Beijing mayor Chen Xitong and Beijing party secretary Li Ximing, neither known for being particularly flexible individuals. In fact, his behavior at the session suggests that Li Peng's only purpose in meeting was to make a token appearance and possibly convince the strikers to return to the campuses, because at the time of the meeting the power struggle in the top leadership was almost over, and a hard-line policy had already taken shape. This conclusion is based on a highly confidential speech made by President Yang Shangkun on May 24, in which he disclosed that originally both Zhao Ziyang and Li Peng had arranged to meet the students that day. However, Zhao did not show up, possibly because he was unwilling to project the image of a hard-liner, which would have been his only option.

The meeting did not proceed well from the beginning. Premier

Li Peng entered and apologized for being slightly late and was immediately chastized by the fiery student leader Wu'er Kaixi from Beijing Normal University who suggested that Li was very, very late, sardonically implying that Li had missed the whole point of the student protest. In this rather strained atmosphere, when the formalities had been dispensed with, the premier immediately came to the point and made clear that as far as he was concerned, the purpose of the meeting that day was not to discuss major issues, but mainly to bring an end to the hunger strike. Dictating the bounds of the discussion, Li Peng said:

"Today we will talk only about one thing: how to get the fasting students out of their plight. The Party and the government are deeply concerned and worried about the matter and their health. Let's solve this problem first and other matters can be discussed later. We have no other motives; we are mainly concerned."

Having reduced the entire protest to an issue of public health, Li Peng continued stiffly and defensively:

"You are all young, no more than twenty-two or twenty-three years of age. My youngest son is older than you. I have three children. None of them engage in official profiteering. To us, you are like our own children."

Before Li Peng could continue, Wu'er Kaixi cut him short by saying "If we go on like this, there will never be enough time" and they would never be able to discuss substantive issues. Raising his voice, the student leader went on the attack, saying "Just now you said we would discuss only one thing, but in fact it was not you who invited us to be here, but it was many people in Tiananmen Square who asked you to come. So as to how many questions we should discuss, it is for us to decide. . . . Yesterday we all listened to and read Comrade Zhao Ziyang's speech. Why have no students left the square so far? We believe that it is not enough, far from enough. You know our conditions and the situation on the square."

The students then proceeded to demand retraction of the April 26 editorial and reiterated their demand for having their organizations officially recognized. But despite the lack of substantive dialogue and the intense shouting match between the two sides, the meeting ended on a fairly cordial note. The atmosphere was such that it was hoped that other meetings which might lead to a real dialogue could follow. *(See Appendix One for full text of Li Peng's conversation with the student leaders.)*

However, the students were obviously not satisfied with the meeting, for the hunger strike continued. But it may have given them false confidence as well. They thought it would be possible to pressure Li Peng by continual protest, with the hope of forcing future meetings that might signal progress in the dialogue and a more positive response to student concerns.

ZHAO'S TEARFUL FAREWELL

The most crucial event of the following day, May 19, was Zhao's last attempt to convince the students to leave the square and more specifically to conclude the hunger strike so that no fatalities would result. As it turned out, Zhao's visit did have a major effect, for that very night at 9 p.m. the students declared an end to the hunger strike and transformed it into a sit-in. The most poignant scene of the day was Zhao's tearful farewell in the square to the students. At the time, it was not clear that it was a farewell, but Zhao himself definitely knew that it would be his last public appearance. As noted, by the previous day the top-level power struggle was already finished and Zhao had apparently lost out. His last attempt to talk to the students seemed only to fulfill his earlier wish to hold a direct dialogue in Tiananmen Square, a proposal that was strongly opposed by the hard-liners and was voted down by the members of the Standing Committee of the Politburo 4 to 1. It is now known that Li Peng tried to persuade Zhao not to go to the square that day, undoubtedly because he feared it could further encourage the students. Then Li himself also went to check on the hunger strikers, probably not wanting to be upstaged by Zhao, who had already rejected Li's plea not to take a last look at the students.

The image of Zhao's tearful response to the students may have been partially responsible for their decision to end the hunger strike that night. For the students, Zhao's sudden appearance on a bus that sheltered some hunger strikers from rain in the early morning of May 19 was unexpected. Although Li Peng went almost at the same time, he left the square after briefly asking and repeating the same question: "Which school are you from?" although from the very beginning, the hunger strikers had identified themselves as students from the Mathematics Department of Beijing Normal University.

As a sharp contrast, Zhao not only stayed longer, but also talked to the hunger strikers for twenty minutes through a megaphone handed over by the students. With tears in his eyes, stopping occasionally to control his emotions, he first apologized for coming to the square too late. "I am here not to ask for your forgiveness," he said. "We have come too late. You can criticize us." Zhao urged the students to end their hunger strike and not to give up their lives like that. "It won't help," he said. "You are not like us. We are getting old and don't count much. But you are still young. You should live on, live to the day when China realizes its four modernizations."

The students were obviously moved by Zhao's speech. They applauded as he finished and handed in notebooks, shirts, and other objects asking him to autograph them. *(See Appendix One for Zhao's full speech.)*

Despite Deng Xiaoping's later endorsement and his apparent approval of a hard-line policy, it remains unclear how objective a picture he had of what was actually taking place in the square and how much was filtered to him through Li Peng and others. In any case, Deng felt threatened by the kind of political reform the students were suggesting, which he thought would eventually lead to the total negation of the "socialist system" and "Party leadership," and the establishment of a "capitalist republic." For a pragmatic economic reformer like Deng, the Four Cardinal Principles were essential to China's communist system. (See page 17 for a definition of the Four Principles.) Within this framework, Deng was willing to experiment with a variety of political and economic reforms, but he definitely would not tolerate any moves to cross these lines. Contrary to what the Western media has suggested, at no point during the past decade was Deng attempting to lead China away from socialism and toward "Westernization" or "capitalism." All the reforms he initiated had to be carried out within the limit of socialism, or "socialism with Chinese characteristics," a slogan that has the vaguest of meanings for most people, but perhaps not for Deng himself, who envisioned an economically prosperous China within the framework of the Four Principles. As a result, it was not surprising that as early as April 25, Deng had already decided to take action against the protesters, although at that time he might not have expected eventually to bring almost one tenth of China's military forces to the capital merely to suppress the peaceful student demonstrators.

Moreover, given his previously mentioned Cultural Revolution experience, Deng Xiaoping was perhaps most deeply concerned about order and stability, a fear shared by even some of the most "liberal" leaders like Zhao Ziyang himself. For Deng, student protest was a major threat because it could well lead to social turmoil. In dealing with the student movement, Deng actually took a middle road as the liberals and the conservatives fought their bitter struggle over policy differences. He was ready to give support to whomever could restore order and send the students back to campus. Consequently, despite the fact that Deng had already made the decision to crack down on the students on April 25 when Zhao was in Korea on a state visit, Zhao was still able to take a much more conciliatory line upon his return to Beijing, even though Zhao's policy was in direct contradiction to Deng's decision a few days earlier. Moreover, Zhao's conciliatory policy was largely effective before the students began the hunger strike, and this policy was established for almost three weeks before martial law was declared on May 20. According to a report in a monthly magazine *Ching Pao* in Hongkong, Zhao met with Deng after he returned to Beijing and suggested that a more moderate policy be adopted. Deng, possibly due to the huge demonstrations on April 27 which were incited by the strongly worded *People's Daily* editorial the previous day, realized the failure of the hard-line policy and agreed to Zhao's moderate line. Deng reportedly said to Zhao, "The most important thing you should do is to maintain order. If this could be done, do it your way and don't mind what I have already said." While the substance of this meeting cannot be confirmed, it definitely would explain how Zhao could still be in control of the situation in May, when even Li Peng had to talk about conciliation and dialogue with the students. Of course Deng's support for Zhao did not last long. After the students began the hunger strike, Deng realized that Zhao's policy was failing to get them back to class, and the situation grew increasingly out of control. At this point, Deng obviously concluded that the only way to restore the order he thought necessary was to declare martial law and send in troops to clear the protestors out of the square.

THE FALL OF ZHAO ZIYANG

As suggested, it seems that the student movement, whether intended or not, crystalized a power struggle between Li Peng and Zhao Ziyang that had been going on since the dismissal of Hu Yaobang as the Party Secretary. The conflict had both a personal as well as a policy basis, not to mention the highly charged question of leadership succession. Here however, it must be noted that Deng Xiaoping seems to have played a role all too similar to that of Mao in his late years, adopting a relatively laissez faire attitude toward his successors, giving only vague outlines on implementation of specific policy and then intervening only at the last moment in crises that threatened to get beyond all control. Both men seemed to be dissatisfied with their chosen successors and both seemed to have precipitated a situation that would make a smooth succession transition extremely difficult.

Clear differences between Zhao and Li Peng over the direction and pace of the economic reforms escalated into an acute political struggle fueled by the student demonstrations. It became a situation where Li Peng may have seen his opportunity to depose Zhao Ziyang regardless of the consequences, and the student protest was the ideal pretext for attacking the Party leader, given Deng Xiaoping's and Yang Shangkun's strong convictions that order was ultimately a far more important value than independent expression.

A close look at a highly confidential speech by Yang Shangkun on May 24 to an enlarged meeting of the Central Military Commission supports the above supposition. According to sources familiar with the full content of this speech, Deng himself initiated hard-line opposition to the students and this policy was fully endorsed by Li Xiannian, chairman of the Chinese People's Political Consultative Conference, along with Chen Yun, Peng Zhen, former chair of the National People's Congress and other aging leaders in "retirement." They supported the view of the April 26 editorial which claimed that the movement, while generally composed of students with patriotic intentions, was manipulated by a group of people with ulterior motives. This group, it alleged, was responsible for slogans like "topple the corrupt government" and for even demanding the toppling of Deng himself. Therefore it was possible to claim that the ulterior purpose of these people was to set up a "capitalist republic" and it was determined that no compromise with such a group was possible. According to Yang Shangkun's speech, Zhao Ziyang's refusal to accept the above judgement made Zhao's actions objectively counterrevolutionary. Such a judgment was sadly and frighteningly reminiscent of the Stalinist practice of vulgarizing Marxist categories of objectivity and subjectivity by rather subjectively declaring what is supposed to be "objectively revolutionary or counterrevolutionary" —usually in relationship to power struggles at the highest level. The rather complicated idea of objective-subjective dichotomy was lifted from German idealist philosophy by Friederich Engels, somewhat simplified and vulgarized by Lenin, and then brutally manipulated by Stalin. It essentially means that an action may be neutral in itself (e.g., eating an apple), but that it can become "objectively counter-revolutionary" if it sends a "wrong" message to the people (for a Communist to eat that apple when others are hungry would no longer be innocent, but objectively counterrevolutionary because it conveyed a negative image of the Party). Unfortunately, the actual judgments on such questions are sometimes based more on the immediate needs of the leaders in power rather than on any genuinely objective assessment of benefits or risks for the Party or nation.

According to Yang, Zhao's major "mistake" was to attempt to retract the April 26 editorial after he returned from Korea, although he had supported it earlier. Zhao felt that the tone of the editorial was too strong and insisted that the student movement was patriotic. However, when the crisis developed, Chen Yun, Li Xiannian, Peng Zhen, and Vice President Wang Zhen, men who had never fully supported Deng's reform policies, were called by Deng to discuss the situation. As general secretary of the Party, Zhao had to play by the rules of top Party leadership and submit to the principles set by the Party elders. Therefore, when it came to making final decisions on coping with the crisis, Zhao found himself isolated and helpless. Despite his intention to make good use of the student movement and despite the fact that he was the "general secretary," Zhao could do nothing more than to express his "personal opinion" and protest in the form of his resignation. At a meeting of the members of the Politburo's Standing Committee (the time of which was not disclosed by Yang, but probably around May 18), Zhao offered to resign as Party secretary. "I disagree with the majority of you," he was quoted by Yang Shangkun as having told the other four members of the Standing Committee: Li Peng, Qiao Shi, Hu Qili, and Yao Yilin. "So I cannot continue to function as the party secretary. Therefore, I will resign immediately."

However, Zhao's fall did not happen overnight. In fact, there had been reports that he was losing power since last fall, when skyrocketing inflation began to hit the country even harder. Party elders such as Chen Yun, Li Xiannian, and Peng Zhen had put enormous pressure on Deng to replace Zhao as general secretary. It was reported that Deng insisted that Zhao should be replaced only after the Gorbachev visit, because he wanted to maintain an image of unity. Zhao of course knew very well about what was going on among the aging leaders and was aware of his own fate even before the student movement, which actually gave him a possible last chance to survive and which he attempted to make the best use of by taking a much more conciliatory line. He was not able to turn the tide, so he tried another tactic by openly distancing himself from Deng, in the hope that this might enable him to secure stronger support from the people. As noted, during his meeting with Gorbachev, he told the Soviet leader that Deng was still the helmsman of China. Although he was merely stating an open secret, this action was extraordinary in Chinese politics, especially under the circumstances, because it implied that Deng, rather than Zhao himself, should take responsibility for the chaotic situation. Zhao also tried to send out a message that he was personally prepared to accept the student demands, but was prevented by Deng.

Zhao was alluding to the kind of conflict which is considered a question of "inner-party struggle," and resolvable internally, according to Maoist and even later Chinese Communist thinking. In this situation, two differing points of view are considered a "contradiction among the people," and amenable to a peaceful resolution. However, when this internal dispute among Party members becomes closely linked to a broader outside situation, it may come to be seen in terms of "class struggle,"with one point of view deemed "counterrevolutionary" and subject to attack as inimical to Party policy. In other words, people within the Party are categorized as outsiders who are now identified with the enemy in the class struggle.

The same problem exists with "democratic centralism," which is supposed to mean that once a decision is reached all agree to present a united front to the outside. Unfortunately, however, instead of inner party democracy, this approach often results in the tyranny of the majority, which accuses the minority of violating the tenet of democratic centralism when it merely disagrees with the majority. People in the minority can then be removed from a position or purged from the Party on grounds of "splitting unity." Again, the basic problem is that with no open and legally empowered deliberative body to decide whether policy or opinion is "counterrevolutionary" or "revisionist," determination can be made arbitrarily according to the needs of power configurations or a change in Party line or an immediate crisis. "Objectively," again, it seems that such procedures undermine rational decision-making to the point where they raise questions about the legitimacy of the Party. It is this arbitrariness and lack of an open, legal process for making such decisions about individual allegiance which has given rise to many serious questions about the justice of the governance structure in the Party and in Communist nations in general.

MARTIAL LAW: DECLARED BUT NOT ENFORCED

The seemingly bleak view presented above was unfortunately borne out by what happened the following day. At 12:30 a.m. on May 20, on the occasion of the convening of a nationally televised major meeting of top military and party leaders in the Great Hall of the People, Premier Li Peng gave a key speech in the presence of Wang Zhen and other top leaders. It was followed by a briefer statement by Yang Shangkun which justified the dispatch of troops to the outskirts of Beijing while warning that unless the square were cleared by a certain deadline, troops would be called in to "enforce order," but not "against the students." At this point, martial law was not yet declared, but came into force ten hours later.

The meeting was the clearest public indication that Zhao had lost the power struggle and that the good intentions of the students had once again cost the political life of yet another "liberal" party chief in a repetition of Hu Yaobang's fall from the same post after the round of student unrest two years earlier. After Hu was deposed, students at Beijing University jokingly said, "The students want to have an electric light, but they turn over the candle," meaning that the students wanted more democracy, but what they got instead was tighter political control and a swing back to political orthodoxy. It now appears that after the recent round of student movement, not only such ideas as "democracy" are again just distant dreams, but that the hard-line policy which has followed the crackdown will damage overall reforms in China—although the more optimistic observers continue to refer to the situation as "temporary."

The meeting was also a final showdown between Zhao Ziyang and other hard-line leaders. By refusing to appear at the meeting, let alone to deliver the speech together with Li Peng, Zhao gave himself no choice but to take an opposing line to Li Peng and Deng Xiaoping. According to Yang Shangkun's confidential speech, the conservatives did urge Zhao to deliver a speech condemning the student demonstrations, but he refused. He was then asked to preside over the meeting and again refused. "Then at least you should show up at the meeting," Zhao was told, and he rejected that request by asking for a three-day "sick leave." Given Zhao's uncompromising attitude, it fell to Li Peng to deliver a strongly worded speech.

It was an extremely harsh statement, recapitulating many of the points of the April 26 editorial, and accusing the students indirectly of crimes and breaches of the peace that had not even been committed. Scapegoating outside agitators, he accused the movement of being controlled by anti-Communist plotters and stated that the movement itself was riotous, although no incidents such as had occurred in Xian and Changsha had yet taken place in Beijing. Indeed, those few counterrevolutionaries who might have fantasized seizing power would have been highly flattered—if they existed—to learn that they were in a position to take control of the volatile student movement in Beijing.

Li Peng also accused the students of trying to overthrow the socialist system and of attempting to set up opposition political parties, something which was never mentioned among the students' demands. It is possible he was referring to marginal groups, such as certain elements connected with China Spring, which has been accused of receiving support from groups close to the Kuomintang, but such organizations had little or no control whatsoever of the mainstream of the student movement. He even accused some people, whom he did not identify, of taking the hunger strikers as "hostages" and declared those who had shown sympathy and support for the fasting students as "non-humanitarian." Moreover Li Peng himself in this speech suggested that the reason the government had shown restraint up to this point was to "distinguish the large masses of patriotic students from the political conspiracy of a handful of people." As evidenced later in June, this supposed handful of people referred to such dissident intellectuals as Fang Lizhi, Yan Jiaqi, who made his way to the West after the June crackdown, and dozens of others, who were backed by the party chief Zhao Ziyang himself. *(See Appendix One for full text of Li Peng's speech.)*

Yang Shangkun's speech, interestingly enough, was a bit more moderate than Li Peng's. He stressed that the student demonstration was causing daily hardship for the majority of the population because it was making it very difficult for the capital city to function normally. According to Yang, the main concern of the government was not the actual question of the student demands as such, but the problems the protests were causing for transportation and communication in the capital city.

Yang also stressed the fact that the protest had necessitated changes and delay in the agenda of the Gorbachev visit, a "historic event," as he described it. "We were unable to hold the welcoming ceremony in Tiananmen Square as scheduled," he said. "Several meetings were supposed to be held at the Great Hall of the People, but we were forced to move them to the Diaoyutai State Guest House. We had to cancel some programs, and Gorbachev was not able to present a wreath at the Monument to the People's Heroes." Yang noted problems with the city's transportation which he personally encountered, adding, "We had to leave an hour earlier than usual in order to get here on time." He said that if this situation continued, neither the State Council nor the Beijing municipal government would be able to function properly. Therefore, he said, "for the sake of restoring order and defending public security, some PLA troops had to move to the outskirts of Beijing to maintain order." Yang continued to say that troops had been sent in because "Beijing's police department was already powerless in the face of such a massive disturbance." However, Yang vowed that troops would be used "only to restore order to the capital and to protect the important departments and offices from being interrupted or attacked, not to suppress the students."

Li Peng's and Yang Shangkun's speeches failed to send the students back to campus and "restore order" in Tiananmen Square. On the contrary, they provoked not only the students, but the general population to higher levels of outrage and opposition. Shortly after Li's speech, which was broadcast through the loudspeakers in the square, the students, who had decided to end the hunger strike and transform it into a sit-in the previous night, vowed to resume fasting instantly, and it was announced that all 200,000 people in the square would join in the hunger strike. Although this planned hunger strike did not actually materialize, by declaring it the students had shown much more defiance than ever in face of a government using military forces. Moreover, intellectuals and Beijing citizens once again came to the support of the students. On May 21, about 30 members of the Standing Committee of the National People's Congress called for an emergency meeting of the committee to override martial law and to dismiss Li Peng as premier. On May 22, thousands of intellectuals took to the streets to protest the declaration of martial law and Li Peng's speech. On May 23, over a million Beijing citizens, including people from government offices, held huge demonstrations calling for the resignation of Li Peng and Deng Xiaoping. The dominant slogans during these demonstrations were such as "Down with Li Peng," "Down with Deng Xiaoping." The leadership had now clearly lost its "mandate of heaven."

Due to the defiance of the students and the fact that they enjoyed overwhelming support from the general population, the immediate enforcement of martial law proved to be impossible, apparently because authorities had underestimated the resources needed to effectively enforce their decision. At the same time it also seemed that they had not given serious consideration to the necessary tactics and were either unwilling or unable immediately to use the massive force deployed two weeks later.

PEOPLE POWER TRIUMPHS:
HUMAN FLESH VERSUS TANKS

The first serious attempt, inept though it was, to remove the protestors from the square was on May 20, the very first day of martial law. Thousands of troops with tanks advanced from all the major access routes to the square, intent on clearing out the protestors and "restoring order."

However, they were prevented from reaching the square by a massive show of support by almost one million people. Citizens in the streets took such actions as lying in front of armored personnel carriers and tanks and attempting to reason with the troops by pointing out the contradiction of using the "people's liberation army" to suppress the Chinese people themselves. There was apparent sympathy for the cause among the troops. It was reported, though not officially confirmed, that the 38th Army, which was stationed seventy miles south of Beijing in Baoding, once refused to enter the city to enforce martial law. This was a very unusual action on the part of the military commanders because, as Yang Shangkun later declared in his confidential speech, those who did not follow orders would be punished by military law, namely, court-martialed. Yang's speech in fact tended to confirm speculation that there were military commanders, possibly from the 38th Army, who refused to crack down on the unarmed students. Those military forces which did enter the city but were prevented from moving into the square by Beijing citizens, apparently had no idea what they were really supposed to do in the capital. Some soldiers openly admitted that they did not know why they were there. Some were told by their commanders that they were going to Beijing to "make a movie." Most importantly, the soldiers admitted that they had not been allowed to read newspapers, watch television or listen to radio broadcasts for two weeks, so they had no idea of what was occurring in the capital city. Thus while blocking the access routes to keep the army out, students and ordinary citizens launched their propaganda campaign by reading government newspapers like *People's Daily* to the soldiers to make them aware of what was really happening. Finally, the army had to bow to the will of the people and retreated. Some soldiers said that some day they would come back to Beijing—"as tourists."

The first confrontation with the military was won by the population —a historically remarkable example of unarmed people defeating armed troops. The government not only was defeated but looked inept and out of touch because it failed to take account of the massive support engendered by the protests. Certainly such resolute and enthusiastic backing indicated significant frustration with many of the problems that had arisen in connection with the reforms of the previous decade, especially in the urban areas.

Even at this stage however, many observers have asked why officials found it necessary to send in the military, especially before they had even developed a strategy to control or respond to the situation in other ways. The question that immediately comes to mind is why massive police forces equipped with shields, gas masks and clubs were not used, supported by water cannons and bulldozers, if necessary, to smash through any barricades erected by the protestors to prevent the forces of the authorities from breaking through to the square. There were also other methods of crowd control, such as the use of helicopters to drop tear gas on the protestors to clear the square and to similarly gas the surrounding areas as the protestors departed to dissipate the crowds in the immediate vicinity.

The crucial issue here is that a number of tactics could have been attempted before resorting to overwhelming military force. No reasonable justification can be imagined for the presence of tanks, given the tactics of the students up to this point. The appearance of heavy military machinery so early in the crisis seems to confirm, especially in light of what took place on June 3–4, that elements in the leadership were prepared relatively early to crush the protestors with force, regardless of the cost. Otherwise there could be no logical explanation for the fact that massive police force or even unarmed troops in riot gear were not brought in to suppress the demonstrators. The only other reasonable explanation is that the Chinese government, being unaccustomed to nonviolent protest, has simply never even conceived of any other methods of quelling such large-scale dissatisfaction except with outright military might.

Although the masses of Beijing probably exulted in their victory over the authorities on May 20, their success was not due to the triumph of people's power alone, but also to the government's ineptitude in carrying out quickly and competently its intentions. In addition, the reluctance among certain elements of the military itself to resort to violence, only offers further evidence of how tragically out of touch with its own people the Chinese government had become. In this sense perhaps one could claim that temporary though it was, "people power" really had won the day.

FRUSTRATION IN TIANANMEN

In the wake of the withdrawal of the troops, several triumphant demonstrations attracted one million participants, again with people from many government offices, including the Foreign Ministry, the *People's Daily* and New China News Agency, openly displaying the banners of their organizations in a public show of support for the students. Moreover, the refusal of the troops to enforce martial law —due partly to persuasion by the masses of the population blocking the access roads to Tiananmen Square—had also encouraged the population. In addition, they were inspired by reports of reluctance on the part of different military units and certain elements of the high command that the People's Liberation Army be used to resolve what was essentially a *political crisis*.

Due to the strong speculation about the real intention of the military and the possibility that Deng himself was maneuvering behind the scenes to get full support from the commanders of the seven military regions, the students decided to protect themselves by visiting the two surviving marshals of the armed forces, Nie Rongzhen and Xu Xiangqian, on May 21. Although retired, Nie and Xu were believed to still be able to exercise certain influence over the younger military officers, many of whom once worked under their command. The students succeeded in getting a favorable state-ment from the marshals saying they hoped the situation would return to order and that the students would cooperate with the People's Liberation Army. They still suggested that the only role of the army was to maintain order and that there was no desire at all to spill the blood of the students. It was after the meetings with the two marshals that there were also reports of a letter drafted by seven senior gen-erals and signed by another 100 high-ranking officers protesting the imposition of martial law. Also Wan Li, chairman of the Standing Committee of the National People's Congress, before his return to China, indicated in the presence of President George Bush on the occasion of a state visit to the US, cut short because of the crisis, that the protests would not be suppressed by violence.

It was later discovered in fact that Deng Xiaoping had been able to get all the People's Liberation Army top commanders to agree to martial law, although whether or not they agreed to the bloody sup-pression on June 3–4 remains an open question. At this time, *People's Daily* also printed a rather ambiguous letter from Zhou Enlai's widow, Deng Yingchao, which called the students patriotic but at the same time seemed to suggest that they should return to class and leave the square quietly. In the letter, she called on the citizens and stu-dents to "believe in the Party, believe in the people's government, and believe in the People's Liberation Army." She said, "as an old Party member, I have always had deep feeling toward the kids." At the same time, she insisted that "the PLA has been ordered to enter Beijing with the purpose of restoring social order in the capital. I hope that the students and citizens will lend their support for this." (This letter contradicts reports in local Chinese language newspapers in New York, which suggested that Zhou's widow had stated that if any one fired on the students, she would publicly leave the party).

In this context, Deng Xiaoping apparently was strengthening his hand for a possible showdown, but found himself searching for allies among the very people whom he had recently forced to retire and who were not particularly sympathetic to his reforms. Thus the Central Advisory Commission of the Chinese Communist Party under its chairman Chen Yun convened a highly irregular meeting which strongly endorsed the declaration of martial law. Also Li Xian-nian, who is the president of the largely powerless but symbolic united front body called "Chinese People's Political Consultative Conference," made a strong speech supporting martial law. Li called the student demands to eliminate official profiteering and corruption reasonable but at the same time accused "a tiny amount of people" of plotting behind the scenes for the purpose of "negating the leadership of the Communist Party and the socialist system." He said the speeches of Li Peng and Yang Shangkun were "completely correct, and we must support them." Such support for Deng seems to have been gathered in order to counter the pending move by the students to ask Wan Li, upon his return to the country, to convene an extraordinary session of the standing committee of the National People's Congress, with the purpose of declaring martial law illegal. In any event, Wan Li himself was not allowed to land in Beijing upon his return from the United States on May 24, and was forced to disembark in Shanghai, where he apparently was detained until May 31.

Although they had prevented the military from entering the square and clearing out the protestors, the students' frustration increased because the government had still not responded to their basic demands. With all their efforts stymied, the argument some factions made for a return to campus became more convincing. They contended that the demonstrations had accomplished all that could be expected, and that the next step had to be a massive long-term educational effort among wide sectors of the population. The apparent sidetracking of Wan Li by the authorities suggested that the effort to convene the National People's Congress Standing Committee was futile and that a tactical change was necessary. A growing number felt they had made their essential points and it would be counterproductive to remain in the square any longer. A vote taken by all the participants in the square was conducted on May 28. According to Li Lu, a student leader from Nanjing University who later made his way to the West, representatives in the square from all the 228 schools involved took part in the vote, with each school having one vote. The result was that 160 schools, mostly from outside Beijing, voted to stay. The rest, mostly from Beijing, voted to leave. Li said that one reason the students outside Beijing opted to stay was that they did not want to pay extra travel costs should they have to return to the capital. They decided to remain until June 20, when the standing committee of the National People's Congress was officially scheduled to convene for a regular session. With the majority of the students from Beijing having decided to return home or to their campuses, the number of students in the square now fell drastically to about 5,000, virtually the lowest since the protest had begun.

GODDESS OF DEMOCRACY: SYMBOL OF PROTEST

While the movement was losing momentum, some students were casting about for new ways to revitalize it. In the early morning of May 30, students of the Central Academy of Fine Arts pulled into the square—where the number of protestors had dwindled to only several thousand—a twenty-eight-foot-tall statue called the Goddess of Democracy. Despite the American media's implication and the Chinese government's accusation that it was merely the Statue of Liberty, it had distinctly Chinese features with two hands holding a torch. Nor was the style that of the neoclassical nineteenth century Lady Liberty, but more in the form of the monumental sculptures of Chinese revolutionary heroes which appear in the square. Not a mere copy of the US symbol, it was therefore an ironic and rather complex expression of the desire to bring Chinese democracy into the modern Chinese pantheon.

The statue was constructed by about thirty students working three days and nights nonstop. When it was finally completed, they were preparing to bring it to the square by truck. However, a phone call from the Public Security Bureau warned them that anyone who drove the truck would lose his or her license. In response to this, the students separated the statue into three parts and brought it to the square with the large tricycles used in China for hauling heavy objects. They reassembled the giant figure in the square and unveiled it on May 30. Despite the government warning to remove it, the statue stood in the middle of Tiananmen Square, facing the huge portrait of Mao which has been hanging on the Gate of Heavenly Peace for almost four decades. On the night of June 3–4, the Goddess of Democracy was torn down by government troops in the midst of the bloody suppression.

In any event, the appearance of this new symbol of the student movement began attracting more people to the square and inspiring renewed participation. Although officials had ordered immediate removal of the statue, claiming it was preventing the activities of Children's Day (June 1) from being held, many parents in fact took their children to the square for the very purpose of having them view the statue.

Unfortunately, the "Goddess'" appearance had quite the opposite effect on the Chinese leadership. While inspiring students and attracting the curious public, it only served to further provoke the authorities, and Beijing radio and television denounced it as invasion of foreign symbols into the Chinese cultural context. The *People's Daily* claimed that the erection of the statue was "totally against the law and against the will of the people." The goddess' appearance also strengthened the position of those in the ruling circles who were arguing that a crackdown was necessary because, at least symbolically, the statue proved that the situation was again threatening to get out of control.

WORLDWIDE SUPPORT AND SYMPATHY

By this time, the students had already won widespread sympathy and support partly due to the nature of their grievances and partly due to the massive media coverage, which they were able to exploit for their own purposes especially due to the extraordinary occasion presented by the Gorbachev visit.

Moreover, given the enormous changes occurring elsewhere in the communist world, it was felt that such dramatic events in such a key country as the People's Republic were worth covering in depth by the world media. What also piqued the interest of the media was the fact that China, widely held up for the last decade as a model of innovative economic reform in the communist world, was now faced with the apparently contradictory phenomena that large sections, if not the majority, of the most educated among its population were clamoring before the entire world for political reform as well, implying that political reform had been neglected in the last ten years while undue emphasis was placed on economic matters.

The statue, which aroused the antagonism of a part of the Chinese leadership, perhaps can be seen as a capsule dramatization of the student demands, for its symbolism was playing for all to see and could be captured in a moment on the screen. Therefore, in terms of capturing the essence of the student protest movement of the spring of 1989, the statue could be understood at a glance by all classes of people around the world without necessitating lengthy explanation. In this sense, the statue could be said to be the visual crystalization of the movement's ultimate aim.

Widespread sympathy was also shown through support demonstrations around the world both by overseas Chinese communities and by ordinary citizens of the nations where they took place. Large demonstrations took place in Western Europe, North America, and

Japan, and the biggest demonstration in its entire history was staged in normally apolitical Hong Kong. At the same time, Chinese students abroad tried to collect funds to help defray publication and medical expenses incurred by the student protestors and also as a reserve fund for emergencies. In North America, US and Canadian citizens donated money generously and spontaneously. It is probably not an exaggeration to say that never before had the overseas Chinese community around the world taken such an active interest in events in China on such a massive scale—with the possible exception of overseas Chinese support for Sun Yat-sen's 1911 revolution against the declining Manchu dynasty.

As the student protest garnered both unprecedented world-wide news coverage and unprecedented popular support, it also raised the suspicions of the conspiracy-minded Chinese leadership, encouraging them to brand the movement as a foreign plot. However, such a groundswell of widespread sympathy and support for a mass popular movement at home has historically never been caused by outside agents, in any nation, even when foreign agents have been involved, as undoubtedly there were and are in China. As we have seen, social forces far more powerful than foreign agents were at work.

Regardless of how the government attempts to discredit it, the only plausible explanation for the broad support of the protests was the credibility of the students' cause and their tenacity in advocating it. Regardless of the immediate outcome of this movement, in the long term it is doubtful if Chinese society will ever be quite the same again. The nation's leadership may have taken a dangerous gamble in completely crushing this movement. The memories of the violence are not likely to die soon, regardless of what arguments are used to justify it, and the strong and relatively broad-based attitude of defiance born from this movement will make it more difficult for the leadership to maintain control in the future.

PART TWO ✿

On a day in June that should have belonged to a season of fresh flowers, my people, my countrymen, my classmates and my beloved comrades-in-arms fell . . .

WU'ER KAIXI
student leader

The People's Liberation Army is an army led by the Chinese Communist Party and serves the people wholeheartedly. They are ruthless to the enemy, but kind to the people . . .

CHEN XITONG
mayor of Beijing

June 4

People's Army
Against the People

AFTER TWO WEEKS of stand-off between the defiant Beijing citizens and the People's Liberation Army forces, China's authorities finally decided to enforce martial law and clear out the students in Tiananmen Square by "all necessary means." In the early hours of June 4, some of the more than 200,000 PLA soldiers who had been surrounding the Chinese capital for several days were brought into the city along with tanks and machine guns to crush the student-led protest, which the government had now branded a "counterrevolutionary rebellion."

The events of June 3–4 in Beijing, which have become known as the "Beijing Massacre," have shocked the people of the world, as well as the citizens of Beijing, while most of the 1.1 billion Chinese still do not know what really happened in their own capital. This military suppression has given rise to a series of questions as to why the Chinese government chose to kill its own people to solve a domestic political crisis. The previous section discussed the socioeconomic background of the movement, and the power struggle that had been won by hard-line conservatives within the Communist leadership which is generally believed to be one of the main reasons for the crackdown. This section focuses on the violent events of June 4 and their aftermath. It is an attempt to provide an overall picture of the development of the events by piecing together information available from numerous eyewitness accounts and other sources.

10:45 p.m. June 2
A BIZARRE CAR ACCIDENT

As noted, the student occupation of Tiananmen Square and the erection of a statue called the Goddess of Democracy attracted more students and civilians back into the square, while deeply irritating the hard-line leadership, which accused the students of using a foreign symbol to "insult the Chinese nation." And on June 1, when the government accused the students of preventing the celebration of Children's Day in the square, many parents brought their children to the square just for a glimpse of the statue. Even *People's Daily* admitted in a short article on June 2 that many children were actually having a very good time in Tiananmen Square the previous day, and the atmosphere there was festive. Slogans hanging on the makeshift tents read: "Wish our little friends a happy holiday," and "We the elder brothers and elder sisters share the joy with you!" Students from the Central Academy of Fine Arts made sketches for the children on their clothes. Many students were asked to take pictures with children by their parents. And students from arts schools improvised some stage performances for the children.

Once again the government faced the troublesome holiday problem. With June 1 being a national holiday for children, it would have been awkward to launch a crackdown on young people, although the preparations for enforcing martial law were already underway.

On June 2, while many Beijing citizens were weary from days of blocking troops—perhaps knowing that they would eventually fail if the army did decide to enter by force, the government was speeding up steps toward a military crackdown. Large numbers of troops had been moved into Beijing below ground through the vast complex of tunnels dug below the city as a defense measure in the 1960s, when there was fear of nuclear war with the Soviet Union. Soldiers were stationed in the Great Hall of the People and other buildings around the square, and armed police with clubs and tear gas were also brought in.

At 10:45 p.m., a team of eight police jeeps were racing westward along Changan Avenue. When they arrived at Muxidi, a major intersection on Changan Avenue about four miles west of the square, the last of the eight jeeps suddenly veered off the thoroughfare toward the sidewalk. As more than 200 people watched, the jeep ran into a tricycle driver, two bike riders, and a woman pedestrian. The three riders, who were all workers from a Beijing construction company, died shortly after being rushed to the hospital while the pedestrian, later identified by reporters from *Wen Wei Po* newspaper as Liu Liwei, a 27-year-old English teacher at the Beijing Second Foreign Languages Institute, was seriously injured.

People who witnessed the accident reacted with shock and dismay. One man dragged the jeep driver out of the vehicle and slapped his face after the driver reportedly claimed that he had no responsibility for the incident. At this point, bystanders spontaneously organized themselves, surrounding the vehicle to keep the scene intact. A man jumped atop the jeep and called on the citizens of Beijing to carry the bodies of the dead and demonstrate the next day. Soon a team of bike riders marched eastward along Changan Avenue, spreading the news of the "accident" and shouting slogans such as "Oppose martial law!" "Blood must be paid by blood!" and "Down with Li Peng!" By the time the demonstrators reached Xinghuamen, more than 1,000 people had joined in. They marched around Tiananmen Square and informed the protesting students of what had happened.

Whatever the cause of the accident, the event deeply angered the citizens of Beijing, who had always been taught that the People's Liberation Army was the "people's army" and PLA soldiers were the "most lovable persons." Even during the days of confrontation since martial law was declared on May 20, people in Beijing had been using such familiar official slogans to try to persuade the soldiers not to resort to violence. Consequently, the death of the three workers caused by a police jeep served as a catalyst for further confrontations. At this point, the citizens of Beijing were spurred to take stronger actions against the military. Subsequent events clearly indicated the intensity of their anger, when they burned tanks and armored personnel carriers and beat some soldiers to death.

The Chinese government has stated that the accident at Muxidi had nothing to do with the army or the police, because the jeep involved in the accident had been rented by China Central Television for "several months" and the CCTV came out to claim responsibility the next day. However, the official explanation apparently did not sound convincing to many Beijing residents. They had become so sceptical by this point that they simply would not credit the alibi, even if the government's claim were true. What really took place may remain unexplained forever. While the government has accused "a handful of ruffians" of using the occasion of the accident to "step up their counterrevolutionary activities," it is not impossible that the military was using exactly the same strategy by taking the strong reactions from the people as an excuse to launch a brutal crackdown. For days, the nonviolent nature of the student-led protest failed to provide military commanders any solid reasons to use lethal force. Therefore, the strong reactions incited by such an accident could well serve as an excuse to justify the actions of the following night as "quelling a counterrevolutionary rebellion."

Morning June 3
PRELUDE TO THE CRACKDOWN

The incident at Muxidi the previous night was followed by large-scale military actions. In fact, as indicated, by the time the "accident" occurred, large numbers of troops had already been quietly brought into the city. By the dawn of June 3, many military vehicles had been seen at major intersections on Changan Avenue. At Liubukou and Xidan, both big intersections to the west of the square, students and Beijing citizens blocked three buses that carried weapons—machine guns, assault rifles and other equipment. The news that the troops had entered the city spread quickly, and people poured into Changan Avenue from many locations to see what was going on and, when needed, to offer help. At one point, some students climbed atop the buses carrying weapons and exhibited machine guns and other military equipment as testimony of the troops' presence in the city.

Early in the morning, a column of unarmed soldiers, which some Hongkong reporters described as "endless," were seen running toward the square from eastern Changan Avenue. Wearing green pants and white shirts, the soldiers had been running for two hours from the eastern suburbs of Beijing. Exhausted, the soldiers neared the square at dawn, only to find that they were unable to jog on any further because tens of thousands of people blocked their way near the Beijing Hotel, which was only a few hundred yards from the square. (Many foreign reporters stayed in this hotel during the military suppression.) The citizens apparently outnumbered the soldiers, who were too exhausted to break through lines of people blocking their way. Again, students and other citizens tried to turn the soldiers back, saying to them that "the People's Army loves the people and people love the People's Army." Some citizens offered food to the soldiers, and in some cases jammed food into their faces. Skirmishes, with injuries to both civilians and soldiers, were reported. In the end, the soldiers backed off and retreated in humiliation while the civilians applauded loudly.

Once again, people thought they had won the war. Late in the afternoon, about 100,000 of them went back to the square to celebrate their victory, as well as the scheduled opening of the "Democracy University," which the students had declared established in the square. The atmosphere became jubilant again.

In fact, while there was celebration in the square, the crackdown had already begun on western Changan Avenue. At about 2 p.m., loudspeakers near Liubukou broadcast orders from the martial law enforcement troops that people should disperse immediately, a signal that a crackdown was finally about to begin. Shortly after the announcement, over 1,000 soldiers and armed police rushed onto the streets, firing tear gas at the protestors and clubbing whoever stood in the way.

In the afternoon of June 3, reports of soldiers and armed police beating and clubbing protestors came from many parts of the city.

Evening June 3
KILLING ON THE AVENUE OF ETERNAL PEACE

On June 3 there were ominous signs that a military reaction was taking shape. Between 7 and 9 p.m., the government-controlled radio and television repeatedly broadcast an announcement by the "Martial Law Enforcement Troops," warning people not to go out on the streets or otherwise "they should bear responsibility for their own fates." However, the government warning did not keep the defiant citizens at home. Hundreds of thousands of them, flouting government orders, went out on Changan Avenue to block the troops as they had been doing since martial law was declared on May 20. After all, despite the government warning, most people still did not believe that the "People's Army" would really fire on the people.

As the warnings of the martial law enforcement troops were broadcast on television and troops began to move toward Tiananmen Square from all directions, people again resorted to setting up road blockades and lining up in front of the troops to prevent them from penetrating further into the city. Only this time, they met with an army that was not to bow to the will of the people. The soldiers were prepared to carry out the deadly orders of top military commanders.

Shortly after night fell, the 27th People's Liberation Army, along with several other armies, was brought in along Changan Avenue, or the Avenue of Eternal Peace, from the west of the city. Armed with tanks, assault rifles, and machine guns, troops arrived at Muxidi at around 10:30 p.m. Thousands of Beijing citizens gathered there and clashed with the soldiers when they approached. According to several eyewitnesses who came to the United States later, the clashes between the civilians and the soldiers had at first made it impossible for the latter to fire because the two sides were engaged in direct physical confrontation. It was the students who begged the civilians not to engage in such clashes. At this point, the students were still attempting to maintain a nonviolent protest. As a result, according to some eyewitnesses, people lined up and sat down on the ground, thinking that the army would not drive over them and that in this way they could effectively block the troops. But other reports noted scorn for the students' "naïveté" from people who ignored students' pleas and physically attacked the soldiers. In any event, however, all reports concur that the army, facing the clashes, began firing into the air and later at lower levels, for many people standing at a distance were killed or wounded as the bullets rained down on them. Then the troops began to fire directly into the crowd.

The live ammunition shocked the crowds with disbelief. At first they thought the army was using rubber bullets, but when they saw people dying before their eyes, their last illusion about the "Army of the People" was shattered. Terrified by the attack, many started to run away at full speed, leaving behind the dead and wounded. But there were also many people who risked their own lives, carrying the wounded or dead to hospitals, mostly using tricycles.

However, the army could not be appeased by the retreat. They clearly meant to take full control. As the civilians began to disperse, mostly in panic, soldiers ran after them, spraying bullets in their backs. Machine guns were used too. People fell, one after another. It didn't take long before the "Avenue of Eternal Peace" became what people in Beijing have called the "road of blood."

After Muxidi, the troops continued marching eastward toward their final destination: Tiananmen Square. As they passed the intersections of Xidan and Liubukou, the same thing happened, only by this time they fired not only at those on the streets, but also into buildings on both sides of the street. Curious people who were looking out of their windows were shot at, and some were killed in their own homes.

At the same time, troops entering the city from the east met with strong resistance before they began killing people near Dabeiyao and Huojialou on eastern Changan Avenue. Killings were also reported in other areas, but it is generally agreed that the heaviest gunfire was at Muxidi, Xidan, and Liubukou, all to the west of Tiananmen Square.

One point that must be noted is that the 27th Army, which was widely reported by the world press to be commanded by Yang Shangkun's nephew, did most of the killing during the whole course of the crackdown. While the 38th Army, stationed south of Beijing, was once rumored to have refused to enter the city to enforce martial law, the 27th Army was brought in to carry out the orders because it was loyal to Yang Shangkun and his family. In addition to serving as China's president, Yang is also the vice chairman of the Central Military Commission. As one of the conservatives who strongly supported the military crackdown, Yang played a major role in bringing in the troops in an effort not only to suppress the student movement, but possibly also to use the situation to encroach on the power of Deng Xiaoping himself. For Yang, the military suppression would not only wipe out political opponents within the top leadership such as Zhao Ziyang, but it could also clear the way for himself to become chairman of the Central Military Commission after Deng Xiaoping. In recent years, Yang had been actively establishing and consolidating his power base in the army. While he was vice chairman and general secretary of the Central Military Commission, he installed relatives in some of its most important posts. At least one of the three major departments under the Central Military Commission is controlled by his relative. His younger brother, Yang Baibing, is director of the General Political Department of the People's Liberation Army. And there have been unconfirmed reports that Chi Haotian, director of the General Staff Department, is his son-in-law.

12 a.m. to 6 a.m. June 4
WHAT HAPPENED AT TIANANMEN?

After the killings on eastern and western Changan Avenue, the army forced its way to Tiananmen Square after midnight. Troops emerged from all directions to surround the square and several thousand soldiers rushed out of the Great Hall of the People, ready to use all-out force.

According to several student eyewitness accounts, including that of student leader Chai Ling, the students began to be aware of the imminent danger of bloodshed in the afternoon of June 3. At about 4 p.m., an anonymous phone call from a military commander alerted the students that troops would forcefully clear out the square that night. Thus, the students were actually prepared for the worst possible situation.

At 9 p.m., all the students—there were still several thousand of them left in the square, approximately 30 percent from Beijing, the remainder from other cities—stood up in the square and took an oath: "I will defend Tiananmen Square with my young life. My head may be chopped off, my blood may be shed, but the people's square must not be abandoned. With our young lives, we are willing to fight until the last minute." At ten o'clock, the students clustered around the Monument to the People's Heroes in the center of the square, holding an opening ceremony for the "Democracy University." At midnight, Yan Jiaqi, a leading political scientist who had been a close advisor to the ousted party secretary Zhao Ziyang, delivered a half-hour speech amid gunshots on Changan Avenue, calling on the people to overthrow despotism and autocracy.

Meanwhile, troops were approaching. Shortly after midnight, two armored personnel carriers sped along the two sides of the square, running over any obstacles in their way. They then advanced in opposite directions along Changan Avenue back and forth. When one of them came close to the Gate of Heavenly Peace at around 1 a.m., the enraged civilians jammed its tracks with iron poles and stopped it. They then set fire to it, and the carrier was soon covered in flames.

At the same time, about 1,000 fully armed soldiers moved into the east side of Tiananmen Square. In the north of the square, troops accompanied by tanks and armored personnel carriers that had been advancing eastward along Changan Avenue arrived at the Great Hall of the People at around 1:30 a.m., while troops advancing westward came close to the Beijing Hotel at 2 a.m. Shortly afterwards, the two columns converged in front of the Gate of Heavenly Peace, under Mao's huge portrait. On the west side of the square, soldiers came out of the Great Hall of the People's main entrance fully armed. To the south of the square, troops occupied Qianmen Street. By 2 a.m., Tiananmen Square had been sealed off.

As the troops were surrounding the square, an "Emergency Notice" was broadcast through loudspeakers at 1:30 a.m. The notice said:

> "Tonight, a serious counterrevolutionary rebellion is occurring in the capital. Ruffians are savagely attacking PLA officers and soldiers, seizing guns and ammunition, burning military vehicles, setting up road blockades, and kidnapping military officers and soldiers. They are attempting to subvert the People's Republic of China and over-throw the socialist system. For many days, the People's Liberation Army has been highly restrained. Now they must resolutely counter-attack the counterrevolutionary rebellion. The citizens of the capital must observe the rules of martial law, cooperate with the PLA, reso-lutely defend the Constitution, and defend the safety of the great socialist nation and the capital. All the citizens and students in Tian-anmen Square must leave immediately so that the martial law enforce-ment troops can carry out their duties. For those who do not listen to this warning, their safety cannot be guaranteed, and they themselves must bear all responsibilities for whatever happens to them.

The notice was repeatedly broadcast for three hours. Many civilians began to leave the square, while several thousand students stayed, waiting for the army to clear them out. At this point, the students remained resolute and serious. They were ready to die if, as they wished, their deaths could serve as inspiration for the people to carry forward their struggle for democracy in China. Many even wrote their "wills," that is, final statements about their lives and their dedication to the cause.

Shortly after 2 a.m., the martial law forces which had secured the sidewalks in front of the Gate of Heavenly Peace in the north of the square slowly began moving toward the center of the square. Then two buses suddenly rushed dead ahead into the forces in front of Tiananmen. The drivers, which some reports say were students, while others disagree, were felled in succession by gunshots. One was shot in the back and the other through the stomach.

Facing increasing danger, the students began broadcasting through their megaphones to the troops: "Stop betraying the people and the country!" But the soldiers continued to press ahead. For those who were serious about sacrificing their lives to the cause in Tiananmen Square, the hour was approaching.

As noted by Hou Dejian, a pop singer who was on a hunger

strike with three other intellectuals, the square "was ruled by a strong atmosphere of death and sacrifice."

Hou, who defected to the People's Republic from Taiwan in 1983, was a popular figure in China. His song, "The Dragon's Descendants," had made him a household word. On the night of June 3–4, he was in the square with Liu Xiaobo, Zhou Duo, and Gao Xin, who were also on the hunger strike. When the danger of a massacre became imminent, the four fasting people decided to try to get the students out of the square safely. Hou went to talk with an army commander, Ji Xinguo, and urged the troops to give them time to leave.

After June 4, Hou went into hiding in the Australian Embassy and stayed there for seventy days before returning home on August 16. During his stay in the embassy, he wrote an account of the events of the night which was later published in overseas Chinese newspapers and also in part by the *People's Daily* and appears to be the most reliable and authoritative eyewitness account of what happened in Tiananmen Square on the night of June 3–4.

According to Hou, the decision to evacuate the square was made after 3 a.m. in the early morning of June 4, when "the atmosphere of terror reached its peak." Hou recounted that

> . . . almost no one in the square was still able to think about the situation calmly and rationally. Although no one was weeping because of fear, I could clearly feel that the calmness shown on many faces was forced. In fact, even the four of us hunger strikers in our thirties were not able to control ourselves, and our feelings were fluctuating with the changes of atmosphere in the square. Gao Xin and Zhou Duo could not bear seeing it any longer. They decided to get the students out of the square alive, and came to Xiaobo and me to ask for our opinions. Xiaobo was the only one who insisted on staying. But he had to, and he did give in, because the three of us all agreed to leave.
>
> As we were still struggling to make a final resolute decision, there came Chai Ling's excited yet weak voice, which showed an obvious lack of self-control. She was talking to the people in the square through the loudspeakers positioned near the command post. She told them that the final moment was coming, and those who wanted to leave could do so, while those who wanted to stay would live or die with the square. The four of us immediately realized the danger of such words. At this point, they could only serve to shake the already fearful yet unified will of the people in the square. If many people

Helping evacuate Tiananmen Square.

Demonstrators protecting a soldier who was pulled from a tank and beaten by people in the crowd around 10:30 p.m. June 3 on Changan Avenue. He was escorted to a first aid station.

This soldier's charred body was hung from a pedestrian overpass on June 4 by angry citizens who beat and killed him after he shot unprovoked into a crowd of civilians the night before, killing three people—including a child—according to Chinese and British witnesses.

Burned vehicles were put up by civilians to barricade army at Chongwenmen.

Armored personnel carriers and military trucks burned where soldiers had fired on the crowds on June 3.

Some of the fifteen dead civilians found in one section of a hospital near Muxidi.

Veteran professors from Beijing University join the demonstrations on May 15, a historic day when Mikhail Gorbachev came to China.

Staff members of the English language China Daily *on May 17, advocating a free press.*

Latest News about the Student Demonstration—May 8
Clippings from the New York Times, San Francisco Chronicle, *and the* Los Angeles Times *at Beijing University's "democracy corner" indicate to the demonstrators how widespread is the attention to their activities.*
The dazibao *(big character poster) says: "What is our purpose in boycotting classes. It aims to bring pressure to bear on the government, forcing them to accept our demands.*

While it is true that we won a victory in yesterday's demonstration, it is a small one. The government has only agreed to a dialogue with students. They still maintain that our demonstration is a riot. Obviously, to stop our demonstration and go back to classes would mean that all we achieved is tossed away."

did begin to leave, the square could easily fall into chaos. More dangerously, such chaos, if it happened, was bound to give the soldiers reasons to kill. The obvious result would be that not only those who wanted to stay would surely die, those who chose to leave might not be able to leave alive as well. It was within the second [that we heard Chai Ling's words] that we decided to persuade all the people in the square to withdraw peacefully.

The decision was made. Then the four summoned some student leaders to a nearby tent and revealed their plan. "Chai Ling did not make any comment," Hou recalled.

The student leaders raised two questions: first, if they left, they would not have lived up to the expectations of the students and citizens who had already died; and secondly, they were worried about the reprisal that was bound to follow. And we convinced them on both accounts. But Chai Ling came up with the rumor that Zhao Ziyang and Yan Mingfu had hoped that the students would hang on till daylight, because by then they would be able to bring the troops under control. The four of us immediately dismissed this idea. After all, we should not sacrifice so many young lives just for such a rumor.

As Hou and his fellow hunger strikers were trying to think of their next step, two doctors from the Red Cross came to their tent and suggested that they take an ambulance to go to negotiate with the troops. The doctors also offered to go along. "The suggestion was immediately accepted," Hou said. "And I volunteered to go, because I was the best choice. Since my face was familiar to them and everybody knew me, it would be safe if I went, and I could also be easily accepted by the troops. . . . In order to let the army feel that we had authority over the people in the square, we decided to ask Chai Ling to go with us. But Chai Ling declined. She said that as the chief commander, she could not leave the square. It was already 3:30 a.m. and we could not find any other proper choice, so we decided to go alone."

Hou and Zhou Duo and the two doctors rushed down the monument and stopped an ambulance.

We drove to the north of the square. When we arrived at the northeastern corner, we saw thousands of troops along Changan Avenue taking the assault position. The amublance came to an abrupt halt. We rushed down and ran toward the troops. There was nobody near the place where the ambulance parked, and we had no idea how long the troops had been waiting there. In any event, when they saw us running over, they all began to load their guns and shouted at us, ordering us to stop. We stopped and the doctors hurried to show their identity. They told the soldiers that I was Hou Dejian, and that I wanted to talk to their commander. The furious soldiers calmed down a bit and I could hear them snickering about my name. I didn't know what they were saying exactly, but I felt that they were not hostile.

A moment later, Ji Xinguo, a regimental political commissar, came over and met with Hou. Hou presented their plan to evacuate the square. Ji said he had to report it to the headquarters and went back in the direction of the Gate of Heavenly Peace. Five minutes later, at 4 a.m., all the lights in the square were suddenly extinguished. Hou remembers that they were "extremely frightened. The soldiers were getting furious again. They began to load their machine guns and shouted loudly. . . . The four of us were standing in the vast and empty northeast corner of the square and were very conspicuous. We dared not move in any direction. . . . About three minutes later, the commander showed up again and told us that the headquarters had agreed to our request and that the safest route of withdrawal was in the southeast corner of the square."

After the army promised them time to leave, Hou and the others rushed back to the monument where the students were clustered. He grabbed the megaphone and urged the students to leave. At this point, the students were divided as to whether to leave or not. A voice vote was taken, with the result that the students shouting "Yes" were obviously louder. However, before Hou could convince all of them to leave, he said

> . . . the gunfire became more intense and was getting closer. I saw large numbers of soldiers approaching us from south of the square. I began to worry that this would shake the students' confidence in the army's promise, so I immediately went with Zhou Duo and two doctors toward the northeastern corner of the square, urging the troops to show restraint and give us more time.
>
> At this point, the troops in the north were on the move too. We ran into Commissar Ji in the center of the square. Ji became more severe this time. He said that he had heard our broadcast, but time was up and that they had to finish their task before the given time. He said that if we couldn't take the students out, we had better leave

ourselves. But we told him that the four of us had to leave after all the others left, and that if we were afraid of death, we would have left the square long ago. Perhaps irritated by my words, a soldier standing beside Ji flushed and opened his eyes wide. He seemed to be utterly frustrated and shouted furiously at us. He couldn't wait to point his gun at us. Seeing this, we knew that we had nothing else to say, so we rushed back to the monument.

As we were running, we shouted to the students: "Leave quickly! Go to the southeast corner!" By then, many people had already begun to withdraw. When I reached the second tier of the monument I saw more than a dozen soldiers rushing to the third tier and firing furiously at the loudspeakers. Gunfire was everywhere.

It was 4:30 a.m. and the troops were continuing to press ahead toward the center of the square. Meanwhile, a notice was broadcast through the government-controlled loudspeakers declaring "The martial law enforcement troops are now entering the square. [The troops] agreed to the student request to leave the square. Everyone must leave immediately." This notice was followed by an order from the Beijing municipal government and the Martial Law Enforcement troops, saying:

Tiananmen Square is the heart of Beijing, capital of our great motherland. It is an important place for political assemblies and receiving foreign dignitaries. It is the symbol of New China. But now it has become a market for a handful of people to create turmoil and disseminate rumors. In order to restore order in Tiananmen Square as soon as possible, [the troops] have decided to carry out immediately the duties of clearing the square.

Soon after the notice was announced, at 4:40 a.m., a signal flare broke through the sky above Tiananmen Square, and all the lights were immediately turned on. The students found themselves being surrounded by fully armed soldiers on four sides of the monument. By this time, most of the students had already begun to retreat. With tears in their eyes, they sang "The Internationale," waved their school banners, and shouted to the soldiers that "The People's Army should not shoot at the people" as they left the square.

However, while most of the students began to leave, there were a number of students on the north side of the monument who remained seated and showed no sign of moving. Seeing this, Hou Dejian rushed to the north with Zhou Duo and "Dragged up everyone we saw and pushed them to the southeast. . . . When the last group of students stood up, a team of soldiers were closing in on us like a human wall. They were barely five yards from us. The students had all stood up. Perhaps it was because the soldiers had approached too quickly, we in the last group to leave looked like water in a fat bottle with a tight neck. It was so crowded that we could hardly move." When Hou finally squeezed his way out of the crowd with the help of two student pickets, he collapsed and was taken to a nearby Red Cross emergency center near the west gate of the History Museum.

Hou's account contradicts the numerous press and student reports that hundreds or thousands of people were killed in Tiananmen Square. There were other student eyewitness accounts that tell a very different story. There were reports that after the lights were turned on again, the troops were found to have come very close to the monument, which was surrounded by armored vehicles. Similiar reports also stated that machine guns were lined up at the north side of the monument, which has several steps on which the students were clustered. Soldiers were sent to force their way up to the top level and beat the students down to the bottom. According to these reports, as soon as the students came down, they were machine-gunned. Thus, the students were caught between troops who shot at them at the bottom of the monument and those who beat them up at the top.

The various and sometimes conflicting eyewitness accounts and other reports cannot be absolutely confirmed, and some important details of the situation may remain a mystery forever. However, if people were machine-gunned, Hou Dejian, who was among the last to leave the square, should have seen this. Hou actually went to the north side of the monument, where other eyewitnesses reported that machine guns were lined up, and pulled up the sitting students, literally one by one, and pushed them to the southeast. The assumption that the students were beaten and machine-gunned by troops around the monument also contradicts several other reports, not only that of the Chinese government, which insisted that no one was killed in the square, but also the eyewitness accounts we have received from photojournalists on the scene and US media reports, including the *New York Times*. On June 13, 1989, the *Times'* Beijing correspondent Nicholas Kristof questioned the major points of an eyewitness account which originally appeared in the Hong Kong newspaper *Wen Wei Po*. In the *Wen Wei Po* article, someone who claimed to be a "Qinghua University student" reported that soldiers beat and machine-gunned students clustered around the monument. This account has become the major source for many other similar reports. However, as Kristof pointed out, "several others say this did not happen." He went further to quote witnesses as saying "armored vehicles did not surround the monument—they stayed at the north end of the square—and that troops did not attack students clustered around the monument. Several other foreign journalists were near the monument that night as well and none are known to have reported that students were attacked around the monument." *(See Appendix Two for the* Wen Wei Po *article.)*

However, many witnesses heard gunshots in Tiananmen Square. And it is not clear if all the gunshots were fired into the air or if there were students being killed by such shots. Eyewitness accounts often differ and even contradict each other. Different reports put the death toll in the square at from zero to several thousand. However, it is generally believed that such a term as the "Tiananmen Square Massacre" is not only inaccurate, but an exaggeration of what occurred. If by "massacre" we mean large numbers of people being slaughtered, then the massacre took place along Changan Avenue, not in the square. It is possible that those students who chose to stay were killed, as reported by many witnesses, but the number would be relatively small. There were also reports of tanks crushing students who stayed in the tents, but as Chai Ling, the student leader, stated, many students had come out of the tents at around 9 p.m. the previous evening and had gathered around the monument. As a result, even if there were students who stayed in the tents, the number again would be very small.

Tanks did, however, begin rolling into the square at around 5:30 a.m. After the students left the square, the army moved to crush its next target, the statue called the Goddess of Democracy. At 5:30 a.m., under flames of a huge bonfire in the square, the martial law enforcement troops knocked down the statue, and Tiananmen Square, which had been the center of the student movement for seven weeks, fell completely into the hands of the People's Liberation Army. Shortly afterwards, the PLA in-house newspaper, the *People's Liberation Army Daily*, claimed in an editorial that the "martial law enforcement troops have achieved a great victory in quelling the counterrevolutionary rebellion," while Chen Xitong, mayor of Beijing, announced in a broadcast message that the PLA had achieved only an "initial victory."

June 4
A CITY OF DEFIANCE AND TERROR

It might have been premature for the People's Liberation Army to claim a "great victory," and Chen Xitong was more accurate in calling the troops' reclaiming of Tiananmen Square an "initial victory," for the fighting continued. As dawn began to break on Sunday, June 4, stunned Beijing residents faced violent attacks from the PLA troops with much defiance. Despite the initial horror of the situation and despite the fact that the troops numbered over 100,000 (some reports put the figure at more than 200,000), students and Beijing residents began to fight back. Armed with sticks, rocks and clubs, they counterattacked. The soldiers' violence was met with violence and, when possible, pleas for Chinese people to stop attacking Chinese people. Using the same guerilla tactics perfected by this same army forty years earlier, the citizens of Beijing attempted to wage a last-ditch people's war against their "People's Army."

As the army sealed off Tiananmen Square, workers and students vented their outrage by burning isolated military vehicles. Soldiers separated from major convoys were attacked and killed. One soldier was burned and hanged on a public bus after being lynched. Others were burned to death after their vehicles were set on fire. Chen Xitong's report to the National People's Congress on June 30, described the events in the early morning of June 4 this way:

> Just after dawn on June 4, more military vehicles were burned. Several hundred military vehicles on dozens of road crossings were attacked with Molotov cocktails. Some soldiers were burned to death, and some others were beaten to death. In some areas, several dozens of military vehicles were burning at the same time. At the Shuangjing crossroad, more than seventy armored personnel carriers were surrounded, and machine guns were ripped from twenty of them. From Jingyuan crossroad to Laoshan crematorium, more than thirty military vehicles were burning at the same time. Some rioters with iron bars and gasoline drums waited at the crossroads to burn passing motor vehicles. . .
>
> In the several days of the rebellion, more than 1,280 military vehicles, police cars, and public buses were wrecked, burned, or otherwise damaged. Of the vehicles, over 1,000 were military vehicles, more than sixty were armored personnel carriers and about thirty were police cars. More than 120 public buses were destroyed as well as more than seventy other kinds of motor vehicles.

It is of course obvious that Chen was trying to justify the army's suppression of the protestors by presenting such a graphic picture of "mobs" attacking soldiers. However, he failed to depict the more graphic—and incriminating—scene of PLA soldiers killing people who did not directly attack the soldiers or their vehicles.

A number of people did assault soldiers and military vehicles, using bricks, rocks, poles and whatever came to hand. In fact, the defiance of Beijing citizens on June 4 provoked counterattacks by PLA soldiers. Gunfire continued for the entire day. Eyewitnesses reported that after the troops took effective control of Beijing's main streets, the soldiers shot at people who showed any sign of hostility or negative attitudes toward the troops. As one military officer, whose father is a high-ranking military commander, commented, "For the first time in my life, I found the People's Liberation Army a strange one."

Chen Xitong also failed to explain why tanks were necessary to clear out the students in the square. In fact, he did not even use the word "tank" in his 30,000-word report. Instead, he used the phrase "military vehicles" on many occasions, although he did identify "armored personnel carriers," "jeeps," and so forth in some cases.

At 5:30 a.m., while troops were knocking down the Statue of the Goddess of Democracy in the square, at Jianguomen intersection five tanks and one armored personnel carrier pushed aside a bus used as a barricade, and headed toward Tiananmen Square. They were followed by another column of two dozen tanks. People were asking: "What? Do they need tanks to clear out the students?" Many were afraid that there might be a military coup d'etat.

At 6 a.m., at the intersection of Dong Daqiao and the main avenue leading from the Changan Avenue to Beijing Airport, ten tanks and twenty military trucks headed toward the center of the city. Suddenly dozens of tear gas capsules were thrown among the citizens in the vicinity and the crowds began to scatter.

At 6:30 a.m., thirty-eight tanks entered Changan Avenue from the road on the west side of the Beijing Hotel, and the sounds of gunshots and engines came from behind the Gate of Heavenly Peace toward the square. The crowds began running to escape, and some people set fire to a police car.

Violence occurred in other parts of the city as well. In the northwestern suburbs of Beijing, where some of China's best universities are located, there were rumors that the campuses had been surrounded by troops. Throughout the day, students mourned their dead comrades. Some were advocating revenge. Many fled the schools and returned home or sought refuge in friends' or relatives' homes. Despite the defiance of Beijing residents, the city was now largely ruled by horror and despair.

After June 4
A CITY RULED BY UNCERTAINTY

The bloody crackdown on June 4, 1989 marked what many now regard as the darkest day in the history of the People's Republic. However, horror did not stop as the day ended. Despite the fact that tanks had occupied Tiananmen Square and the army had claimed "victory" over the "counterrevolutionary thugs," violence continued. It seemed that the army intended not only to clear out the students from the square, but to wipe out all dissent in the city. Therefore, after June 4, as people in Beijing continued to show defiance, though on a much smaller scale, soldiers continued to fire, mostly into the air. Although gunshots could be heard for several days after June 4, the casualties were minimal compared to those on that deadly Sunday.

On June 5, a dramatic event crystalized the defiance of the students. Wang Weilin, a student, showed his outrage and courage by standing in front of a column of tanks trying to halt their progress. Wearing a white shirt, Wang walked into the street and stood there alone as the tanks approached. He raised his right hand and signaled the driver to stop. The first tank halted right in front of him, having no idea whether to press on or to retreat. After a moment of stalemate, the lead tank angled to its right, trying to drive by him. But Wang stepped to his left a bit and was firmly in front of it again. Then the tank inched to its left but Wang moved to his right, not allowing it to pass. When the tanks finally stopped, Wang Weilin climbed up and talked to the soldiers inside. He reportedly shouted to them: "Why do you come to my city? You have brought only misery. We do not need you. You go back!" After he climbed down, several people rushed to the scene and dragged him away.

Throughout the day of June 5, soldiers continued to fire on civilian protestors. As night fell, rumors began to spread that army units clashed in the northwestern suburbs of the city and near Nanyuan Airport in the south. Other rumors claimed Deng Xiaoping was dying or already dead, and that there was an assassination attempt against Premier Li Peng. For a time, it seemed as if no one were in charge, as there were no public appearances by any leading figures. Beijing was ruled by rumors, confusion, and fear of a possible civil war.

However, such rumors were officially denied the following day. On June 6, the CCTV evening news denounced reports of clashes between army units and Deng's death as "sheer fabrications intended to poison people's minds." Nevertheless, strange movements of troops, such as the tanks positioned on the Jianguomenwai Bridge in the east of the square near the foreign diplomatic compound, seemed to have little to do with "quelling the counterrevolutionary rebellion."

In any event, the maneuvers of the troops in and around the city added to the fears of the people. Foreigners scrambled to leave Beijing as tension increased. On June 7, the army fired into the diplomatic compound, reportedly in an attempt to stop a sniper, an event which provided more solid reasons for most foreign embassies to urge their foreign nationals to leave China immediately. As foreigners fled, two Chinese dissidents sought refuge at the US Embassy in Beijing. Fang Lizhi and his wife, Li Shuxian, both leading physicists who requested and were granted protection by the United States were labeled by the Chinese government as traitors.

In response to the terror and isolation being directed at the residents of Beijing, people throughout China began to demonstrate in the streets. In Shanghai, where the massacre in Beijing was quickly made known to the people, demonstrators effectively shut down all public transportation, commandeering city buses and using them to build barricades at over fifty thoroughfares. Train transport was also tied up for days. When a train smashed into the demonstrators on June 6, killing six and injuring six others, the train was set on fire and burned.

More bloody scenes were reported in Chengdu, capital of Sichuan Province, where troops fired at the protestors and dozens were killed. Chengdu was the only city outside Beijing where troops were sent in to "quell a counterrevolutionary rebellion," although demonstrations took place in many other cities.

Back in Beijing, the uncertainty about who was in charge ended on June 8 when Li Peng appeared on national television to congratulate troops on their actions. Li's reappearance was a clear indication that hard-liners had consolidated their power and had gained full support, at least on the surface, of the military. On June 9, Deng Xiaoping also made his first public appearance since May 16, at a pavilion in Zhongnanhai, on which occasion he met the chiefs of the military and the People's Armed Police responsible for suppressing the "counterrevolutionary rioters." He was accompanied by Li Peng, other members of the former Politburo such as Qiao Shi and Yao Yilin and such elder statesmen as Li Xiannian, Wang Zhen, Bo Yibo, and Peng Zhen, some of whom held no official positions. It was also announced that Chen Yun, who was too sick to attend, had sent a letter of support to the troops as well as condolences for those soldiers killed in the suppression. Such indeed gives a sense of the feeling of the leadership toward the situation. No expression of condolences for murdered civilians or students was forthcoming on that occasion.

With the hard-liners and the army tightening their grip, Beijing gradually returned to "normal." The crackdown was followed by widespread arrests. Student leaders and dissident intellectuals were put on a government wanted list. Executions took place in several cities. People were ordered to study the "important speech of comrade Deng Xiaoping," and in many respects China seemed to be returning to "normal" by the standard of certain elderly revolutionaries.

MYSTERY OVER THE CASUALTIES

In sifting through the often conflicting reports and eye-witness accounts, the most difficult question is the actual number of casualties —a question that has been asked again and again by people around the world. Thus far, the reports on this issue have been largely contradictory, and it is impossible to arrive at an exact figure. Notably, the Western press has taken a safe approach in presenting the figures by asserting that "hundreds, perhaps thousands of people were killed." However, other reports have stated it in more definite terms.

First there was the official government report which put the death toll at around 300. In Chen Xitong's report to the National People's Congress on June 30, he said:

"According to the information we have gathered so far, more than 3,000 civilians were wounded and over 200, including thirty-six students, died during the riot. . . . More than 6,000 martial law soldiers, armed police and public security officers were injured and the death toll reached several dozens."

Chen also insisted that no one was killed in Tiananmen Square.

The Chinese Red Cross reported a total of at least 2,600 confirmed dead, an estimate that the organization later retracted, possibly as a result of government pressure.

On June 4, shortly after the shooting began, the official Radio Beijing reported that "thousands of people" were murdered, "including our collegues at Radio Beijing." However, the announcer who broadcast the report was quickly removed from his anchor post and substituted by another individual who repeated the government's account.

Finally there were reports from students who claimed that at least 6,000 people were killed and 20,000 were wounded. Some put the death toll as high as 15,000, an obvious exaggeration. Some students also claimed that 1,000 to 2,000 students died in Tiananmen Square alone, but numerous eyewitnesses have denied that anything approaching this kind of slaughter occurred.

Since estimates and eyewitness accounts vary so tremendously, there is still no way to determine which is most accurate. While the official statement is obviously too low, it is doubtful that eyewitnesses, traumatized by the violence, could give a reliable estimate. The fact that the killings took place at separate locations obviously compounds the problem. The actual death toll may remain a mystery forever.

However, the number of casualties should not be the major issue here. The real issue is the way the Chinese government reacted to a domestic political crisis. By using live ammunition against the protestors, the government made a tremendous policy mistake. Even if only one person had been shot dead by live ammunition, it would not have changed the substance of a homicidal policy. Although the leadership had made clear its determination to squash the student movement, the actual decision and its final implementation was haphazard and unprofessional at best and, at worst, homicidal.

To begin with, by the time the decision was made, the students had already largely left the square and its occupants had dwindled to several thousand. Despite the decision made by the students to stay in the square until June 20, when the Standing Committee of the National People's Congress was scheduled to convene, it remained uncertain how many people would have actually remained in the square. It is perfectly possible that support would have dwindled and that by June 20, the numbers would have been negligible.

Even if such were not the case, postponement of the National People's Congress Standing Committee could have been announced due to unsettled conditions, and the worst that might have occurred would have been one large, final, defiant demonstration. With summer vacation approaching, it is even more dubious that any significant number of people would have remained in the square much after June 20.

Moreover, as indicated previously, the Beijing students had already voted to disperse and the authorities could have selectively made arrests and instituted measures behind the scenes subtly if they wanted to exercise more control in the fall. Besides, as the most articulate students themselves had indicated, democracy faces a long uphill struggle in China, and they realized that education and organizing in the long term would be more important than prolonged demonstrations. Finally, it remained to be seen how active student organizers would be once they left the university for regular employment, assuming of course they were not blacklisted from jobs by the authorities.

In any event, the bloodshed seemed to have been unnecessary, half-provoked, inconsistent, and based on the inexperience and incompetence of troops apparently not precisely informed of whom or what they were going to suppress. What is certain, however, is that it shattered China's image around the world, an image carefully constructed since the beginning of the reforms in the late 1970s. As a result, the government itself started an intensive damage control effort shortly after the crackdown. On June 9, in a speech to top military commanders, Deng Xiaoping declared that China would continue its reform and open door policy, although it is dubious that future developments will follow his wishes in this regard. Although the Chinese government has tried hard to lure back foreign investment and foreign tourists, some of the scars left will not be easily removed. Internally, an opposite type of damage control is taking place, namely, a campaign against "spiritual pollution" from the outside. It is doubtful, however, that the government will succeed in keeping the economic doors open if it completely closes the doors to new political and cultural concepts.

The damage created by the crackdown was perhaps worsened when the authorities tried to justify the use of force. Various official accounts of the events appear one-sided, in that they justify the army's actions as quelling "anti-government riots" without acknowledging that the the army's behavior itself might have provoked a violent crowd response or that the government's refusal to yield to at least some student demands escalated the level of protest. Nor do the reports suggest the possibility that some soldiers may have overreacted or that innocent civilians were killed.

On July 1, Li Peng made an astounding comment while meeting with Daniel Wong, the Chinese American former mayor of Cerritos, a suburb of Los Angeles, that the government had used live bullets because the troops did not have enough tear gas and no rubber bullets or water cannon. He insisted that the soldiers "did not want any bloodshed." "They wanted peace," he said. "They knew the students' intentions were good."

RETURN TO ORTHODOXY

It might have been easy enough for the current Chinese leadership to suppress a popular student-led movement by force. However, it is doubtful that they will either drag the country back to the Cultural Revolution era or restore the era of "reform and the open door" as has been practiced for the past decade. In fact, the government seems to be moving, to use a Maoist aphorism, on two legs, one of keeping the door open and the other of suppression. These two sides of the current policy sound so contradictory that it is difficult to imagine them realizing Deng Xiaoping's own program, i.e., development and stability.

In the months following the June crackdown, the government did take some steps to resolve the serious issue of corruption raised by the student protestors. The government was clearly responding to student demands in this area. Thus, on July 29, the *People's Daily* declared on its front page that "the Party Central Committee is determined to accomplish seven tasks of great concern to the people." The resolution adopted by the Politburo listed the seven areas in which the government will attempt to uproot corruption:

1. Further clean-up and rectification of companies, with emphasis on closing those with excessive commercial, foreign trade, or materials supply, and closing of certain financial firms. Abolishing two firms under the State Council, the Kanghua Development Corporation and the China Industry and Commercial Economic Development Corporation. Publishing of audits of these and several other government firms.

2. Prohibition on the children of senior officials from engaging in commercial activities. Children and spouses of members of the Political Bureau and Secretariat of the Communist Party Central Committee will not be allowed to engage in commercial business or assume posts in trading companies, and those who held such

posts were ordered to relinquish them before September 1, 1989. Leading officials are also forbidden from abusing their power to provide conveniences for their relatives and friends in commercial activities.

3. Cancellation of all supplies of special food to leading officials, who will be required to pay the same price as ordinary citizens to acquire specialty foods.

4. Tighter policy on alloting cars to officials and requiring high officers in the Party and government to use Chinese-made cars only. (The conspicuous use of expensive vehicles by officials when most of the public travels by bicycle or mass transit is an obvious sore spot).

5. No entertainment of guests or gift-giving with public funds and no accepting of gifts from subordinates.

6. Strict limitations on officials' visits to foreign countries.

7. Severe punishments for corruption, bribe-taking and profiteering, with emphasis on the principle that all are equal before the law.

How strictly and impartially this policy is enforced remains to be seen, but the Party's image will not improve if it confines the penalties to window-dressing or a few highly publicized cases because, as noted, public scepticism is considerable.

Although a response to protests has taken place with this strong pledge in the area of cleaning up the government, far less emphasis has been placed on the other significant areas of demands, such as opening up Party and state governance or increasing freedom of the press. Enforcing public morality is, after all, a qualitatively different task from surrendering political power to the degree that some of the Chinese intellectuals were demanding. While the public still shows some resentment for the government's conduct in the June crackdown, the Party has focused on attacking "bourgeois liberalization" for causing the social unrest and reemphasized the study of "Marxism, Leninist and Mao Zedong thought."

On June 16, Deng Xiaoping reportedly delivered a speech to the Politburo, appearing to lay out his "instructions" for the future and policy guidelines, while admitting grave errors in failing to emphasize political thinking and Marxist-Leninist theory since 1978 as being partly responsible for what occurred at Tiananmen. Deng reiterated that the only reason China had progressed at all since 1949 was because of "socialism," whose guiding base for China must be strict adherence to the Four Cardinal Principles, i.e., adherence to the socialist road, to the leadership of the Communist Party, to the people's democratic dictatorship and to Marxism-Leninism and Mao Zedong thought—which rescued China from going down the road of other Third World countries and becoming ever more integrated into the "international capitalist system."

Such is no accident, nor is it an accident that Deng Xiaoping and other leaders have deemphasized politics since 1978. It was in revulsion against the ultra-politicization of the Cultural Revolution that the reforms were in part launched, and to rekindle the political debate would have put the reforms at risk, at least in Deng's mind.

Deng himself has acknowledged, on more than one occasion before the unrest in the spring, that the lack of political and ideological emphasis was a serious problem. For example, in speaking with Ugandan President Yoweri Kaguta Museveni on March 23, 1989, Deng said:

> In the past ten years China has achieved satisfactory progress. Our biggest mistake is in the field of education; ideological and political work has weakened and education has not been developed enough. The most important point is that while the economy has scored heartening progress and the living standards have improved, we have failed to tell the people, including the Party members, that we should keep up the tradition of plain living and hard struggle. With this fine tradition, we can resist corruption and veteran cadres can help their children to behave themselves. After sobering consideration, we feel that the mistake in this respect is more serious than the problem of inflation.

In the end, Deng wanted reform without paying a sufficient political or spiritual price for it. It is no surprise that with emphasis on platitudes such as "to get rich is glorious," corruption had become rampant among a largely ill-educated party cadre mass and that an ideological and moral vacuum came to exist. A long-time lack of creative political thinking, a neglect of ideology, and a failure to inspire people with a sense of responsibility and ethics, encouraged a thoroughly cynical self-interest that contributed to the present social and economic dilemmas.

Only when that ideological and moral vacuum resulted in the

student protests for "democracy" was the Party forced to deal with its lack of political foresight. It must be admitted that neither Hu Yaobang nor Zhao Ziyang themselves had provided a real political alternative, but that may have been as much due to their being stymied by Deng's ambivalence and pressure from the older conservatives as to their own lack of imagination. In the wake of tragedy, the conservatives in fact criticized Zhao precisely for lacking a political direction. But their remedy for this lack of direction has been a return to rigid orthodoxy. Certainly, however, Bao Tong, Zhao's important aide, was on the way to suggesting a more positive and innovative path of political reform than the rather stale "new authoritarianism" theory floated by Zhao. In an article published in the first (1 July 1988) issue of *Qiu Shi*, (Seeking Truth), a biweekly theoretical magazine directly accountable to the Party Central Committee, Bao Tong suggested that political reform will be successful only if a more democratic system is established to encourage people at the grassroots level to exercise more effective supervision of Party and administrative leaders. He cited examples such as the election of Party leaders in some areas after open competition, and said that "democracy should be first of all fully developed within the Party." One thing he strongly endorsed was an increase in *toumingdu*, or "transparency," by publicizing work regulations and work results at various administrative levels. In this way he argued that the Party should actually be inviting supervision from the people. Bao suggested that by doing so, the Party could actually accomplish two tasks at once. "It will not only help establish a cleaner government," he said, "but also help increase the efficiency of work. Because of the openness [in policy making], the masses will have more confidence [in the Party] and government workers will be more careful in observing the law." Bao's idea was thus in sharp contrast to the theory of "New Authoritarianism," which basically posits that successful reform must be guided by iron-fisted yet reform-minded individuals at the top of the hierarchy. When stripped of rhetoric, however, it is at best merely another definition of a benevolent dictator, and at worst a new rationalization for puerile dependence on an emperor figure, a sorry legacy of feudalistic tradition China has not yet been able to shake off. It is also not clear whether Zhao really believed in this theory formulated in his think tank or whether he simply used it as a ploy to satisfy conservative opponents that he was not neglecting Marxist-Leninist theory and to legitimize his leadership. In any case, it neither mollified the conservatives nor provided the students with the concepts and guidelines for developing a true "democratic socialist" path for China.

At the same time, for Deng Xiaoping to admit that the party neglected political training and socialist morality for ten years reveals an incredible lack of creativity and an ideological bankruptcy, in that it took the Tiananmen crisis to jolt the leadership into recognizing the real moral, social and ideological crisis they faced. It only proves again that Deng's abilities were overestimated. Though a great innovator and administrator of a policy previously outlined, he is by no means a fundamentally creative thinker. The real tragedy of Tiananmen and the reforms is that they necessitated a far more dynamic and creative leadership than was available to take charge of the major challenges required by the policies the Chinese Communist Party was carrying out. China needed more people able to forge new political institutions and to provide outlets for much-needed criticism of policy. The leaders were good technocrats, but not truly far-sighted and creative individuals, let alone visionary leaders.

Jiang Zemin, the new Party chief, may survive, and the reform policy may continue, although the role of the military seems to have been seriously increased due to its major role in imposing martial law. Of course it is possible that there will be a major succession crisis immediately after Deng's death, and his self-appointed Politburo will not be able to muddle through. But even if they succeed in muddling through, it is unlikely that it will be the result of creative new policies and hardly seems to refute the conclusion that the reaction of the government as well as Deng Xiaoping's declining health seems to reveal the Party's basic political limitations at this point.

Moreover, the mixed signals of Chinese scorn for world opinion combined with hypersensitivity to outside criticism continue to manifest themselves, often in a style typical of a developing nation still bearing the scars of colonialism and ignorance, rather than that of a mature socialist or even developing socialist state.

Arrests are continuing, although less publicized than before, apparently to avoid adverse publicity. Agence-France Press has estimated that they passed the 7,000 mark (possibly an underestimate) and the overseas Chinese press speak of a new list of 3,000 prominent people in the intellectual, cultural, and scholarly fields who are to be interrogated if not arrested. Reinstitution of political study classes and informer networks on campuses have been emphasized, with what effect remains to be seen. The danger is that such a policy will lead to a further decline in attracting intellectuals to the Party and an increase in opportunist and mediocre elements applying for membership. The Party can ill afford enrolling even more members who are on an ethical and intellectual level as low as some of those who joined the organization out of similar opportunistic motives during and after the Cultural Revolution. The renewed role of political education is, on the surface, an attempt to fill the spiritual and ideological vacuum which has been criticized here. However, the problem is how to make that education more complex and challenging than mere indoctrination in orthodox principles. If the education only consists of old dogmas, with no encouragement of at least some of the rethinking of Marxism that is now taking place in other socialist nations, then the cynicism and selfishness which Deng and others have deplored will probably continue.

At the same time, Beijing showed its incredible clumsiness by announcing in the world press on July 14 further executions and a ten-year prison sentence for a forty-two-year-old factory official by the name of Xiao Bin for "rumor mongering." The particular individual in question had been interviewed on ABC news in Beijing and had spontaneously told the American television crew that solders had killed thousands in the June 4 crackdown, including students who had been run over by tanks. The footage of the interview was intercepted by the Chinese government from ABC's satellite feed of raw footage and was shown on Chinese televison. Hours later, Xiao Bin was recognized by two women in his hometown of Dalian and was turned in to the Public Security Bureau. He later appeared on television admitting that he was a "rumor monger" and deserved harsh punishment. Learning from this unfortunate experience, ABC declared it would avoid such interviews in the future, so that the individuals who agreed to speak frankly would be more difficult to identify and less subject to reprisals. Still, ABC's error pales in comparison with that of a government with a supposed 4,000-year-old political culture in making the announcement of such a harsh sentence for such a trivial offense—much less on the two hundredth anniversary of the French Revolution.

The purge of government officials continued, with Chen Xitong declaring that it had been insufficient and new waves of arrests seemed necessary to insure that the "counterrevolutionary elements" are "thoroughly uprooted."

What does the future hold for China and what advice should one give to Chinese youth? Perhaps one of the most balanced and intelligent evaluations is that given by Chen Ku-ying, a professor of philosophy from Taiwan, now living in the United States, who teaches half of each year in Beijing University's Philosophy Department and has just returned from Beijing. In a talk in Berkeley, California, on June 16, 1989, he apparently encouraged Chinese students and intellectuals abroad who did not face direct repression to return to China and become involved in pushing for further political and economic reforms within the system. Their willingness to participate in the reform programs is, in his opinion, perhaps one of the only possibilites for the reforms to have a serious chance of success.

Chen apparently went to the Tiananmen Square in late May and tried to persuade Wang Dan, the student leader from Beijing University, to leave, saying their point had been made and remaining longer was counterproductive. Wang Dan supposedly agreed, but then perhaps was overshadowed by events and his own inexperience. In retrospect, it seems Chen's advice and prediction were most sound.

Perhaps his real point is that if Chinese intellectuals really want to have a lasting impact, they must eventually reform and try to raise China's *political* culture to a new level of maturity, rather than merely criticizing from abroad. Although such work abroad may be valuable, Chen Ku-ying seems to argue that only by engaging in first-hand actions at home can Chinese intellectuals hope to introduce fundamental changes in the People's Republic. He is arguing that to help the country reach political maturity, instead of perpetually looking for a new domestic "hero-savior" or foreign help, this political engagement is China's best hope for a new society and new policies. *(See Appendix One for intellectuals' declarations of May 16 and May 17 on the need for this new level of political sophistication).*

Regardless of the above advice, Chinese nationals who have fled to the West have been actively involved in developing new political forces challenging the Communist Party. According to an announcement made in Paris on July 19, 1989, Yan Jiaqi, Wu'er Kaixi, Liu Binyan, Su Shaozhi, and Wan Runnan, the Chinese exiles in Paris have formed a new group, the "Democratic Chinese Front," which claims to be dedicated to the peaceful overthrow of the current Chinese government.

The Chinese government has strongly condemned this organization, and implied in an article in *People's Daily* that the group may have been connected to espionage and acts of violence and intimidation directed at Chinese citizens in France. Aside from the government's opposition (the founders are wanted on criminal charges), it remains to be seen how effective such organizations will be. When formed, the group announced it would be a broad coalition only dedicated to majority popular rule in China and the overthrow of the minority ruling clique. Liu Binyan, one of the front's founders in fact announced that the membership is open both to Marxists and non-Marxists, so long as they call for radical change in China's present political system. Subsequently, the organization issued a moderate and rather vague program of principles at the end of its first official meeting in Paris, at which it elected its leadership on September 24–25, 1989, still stating its belief in peaceful political change. However, the organization reiterated its basic position that single party rule by the Chinese Communist Party was the main obstacle to democracy, thereby saying that unless the Party reformed itself it would face continued moral and political challenges to its legitimacy.

These are the real seeds that have been sown by Beijing's actions at Tiananmen, and if the leadership wants to avoid further challenges to their authority they may have to develop more complex and pragmatic policies, rather than simply continuing a purge of "counterrevolutionaries," reciting shopworn slogans, and maintaining martial law.

PART THREE

The press must tell the truth.

STUDENT DEMONSTRATORS IN BEIJING

Comrade Zhao Ziyang did not do what he should have done when the situation quickly deteriorated, but instead stirred up the press with wrong guidance of public opinion.

CHEN XITONG
Mayor of Beijing

Telling the Truth

Press Freedom in China?

"MOUTHPIECE" OF THE PARTY

Countries under authoritarian rule always suffer from government control of the press. Freedom of the press, which citizens of Western nations now take largely for granted, was won after considerable struggle, is still not completely assured, and requires constant vigilance to maintain. (This is not to mention the more subtle forms of censorship that persist in the West, including control of the media by corporate monopolies, and advertising and marketing demands which run directly counter to the spirit of the laws protecting press freedom).

In China, freedom of the press in the legal sense is still only a dream for students and intellectuals calling for more radical political reforms. The Western concept of the press as a "fourth estate" which subjects the three branches of government to public scrutiny and criticism, is far from being accepted by the government. Chinese students, who have acquainted themselves more and more with Western-style democracy and are somewhat inspired by Gorbachev's "glasnost," knew very well that their call for political reforms had to be backed by freedom of the press, which they regard as the very first step toward genuine socialist democracy. At a more practical level, Chinese students in April and May of 1989 felt a particularly urgent need for a freer and more unbiased press—perhaps ultimately freer than even the European or American press—because they knew a free press was an important means of insuring that their motives and actions would not be distorted by any government point of view. Therefore, freedom of the press was a primary demand.

However, in demanding freedom of the press, the students were also not totally out of touch with reality. They understood very well that this was a highly sensitive issue for the Chinese leadership —perhaps even more sensitive than the question of democracy itself —and would require a fairly long-term struggle before it could be realized. In China, the role of the press, since the establishment of the People's Republic in 1949, had always been as the "mouthpiece" of the Communist Party. For the Party, the press is a tool to proclaim and reaffirm the legitimacy of its own power, which relies to a certain extent on controlling the press. Perhaps the closest analogy in the West today would be the "house organ"—a paper or magazine published by a business, labor, or religious organization to further the cause of that organization. The journalists who work for such publications are by no means free to speak their minds. They are expected to put on the best face possible for the organization, to handle controversial issues delicately, and downplay internal dissent. The content of such papers is subject to approval by the leadership of the organization and to some extent is dictated by the leadership. Such publications aim to achieve unanimity and loyalty within the organization so that it may accomplish its desired ends—and more than one editor of such publications has been fired for stirring up controversy, damaging the organization's public image, or generally failing to follow the "party line."

The Communist Party, being an organization with a serious mission, has therefore quite understandably used the press for the purpose of carrying out its mission. Indeed, at least in the midst of revolution, this may well be justifiable. (Western nations, during war, have also severely restricted freedom of the press for tactical and security reasons). However, once certain revolutionary goals are achieved, this power of the press is in grave danger of helping create a new form of tyranny, because it deprives the public of an effective mechanism to criticize, chastize, correct, enlighten, exhort, or expose errors made by those in leadership positions. And once basically immune from outside criticism or exposure, any leadership can reach a point where it is no longer accountable for its actions because the very nature of those actions remains obscure.

What China's leaders have failed to realize is that their work might be more successful if it were conducted more openly. For example, the corruption and inefficiency openly acknowledged by the Party as serious problems could continue to plague the nation if corrupt and incompetent people can operate without fear of public exposure.

Even before 1949, the Communist Party made effective use of the press—or "propaganda tool" as they preferred to call it—to attack the policies of the Kuomintang regime under Chiang Kai-shek and to win the support of the general population, mainly the peasants. As Mao Zedong explicitly put it, the Party had to have two "barrels" in its hands—namely the barrel of the gun and that of the pen—if it were to establish and consolidate its political powers. While the barrel of the gun did help Mao and his comrades establish a Communist government in China, the barrel of the pen has served the Communist government by providing people with "unified thinking" and, when viewed as tactically necessary, a distorted picture of events. In China, the traditional way of ruling has been to let people listen to and speak with one voice. Individualism, which Americans cherish (perhaps to excess) is simply out of the mainstream of Chinese life. Different views, or personal opinions expressed in public or privately, could be taken by the authorities as a disturbingly serious matter harmful to the ruling regime, and thus have to be suppressed. For more than 2,000 years, the Chinese have been accustomed to taking the words of their emperors or top leaders as the ultimate "correct line." They have always been ready to follow what they are told to do, and personal feelings have to be suppressed from within. For ruling regimes, this situation is of course the most ideal, because when people follow only one voice they are easily ruled. Since its founding in 1921, the Chinese Communist Party has adopted this traditional ruling style and has always laid supreme emphasis on "unity of thinking," and the press under Communist Party control has the most important role to play by "launching large scale revolutionary propaganda" and to make people "believe in the Party, love the Party and support the Party." However, before 1949, the Party had to combat another powerful propaganda machine under Chiang Kai-shek's Nationalist regime. It was only after the People's Republic was founded that the Party was able to take control of all the nation's press, a traditionally authoritarian ruling strategy.

In order to effectively control the press, the government has taken all the news organizations into China's huge state bureaucratic system. Newspapers, radio and TV stations are all funded by the government and thus follow the same editorial policy, i.e. to reflect Party and government lines. For instance, *People's Daily*, China's most important and authoritative newpaper, which is circulated nationwide, is directly controlled by the Central Committee of the Chinese Communist Party. In China's governmental structure, *People's Daily* is a ministry-level unit, and its editor enjoys the status and perquisites of a ministry-level bureaucrat who is often invited to important meetings of the ruling Politburo so that he will fully understand "the official line." For anyone wishing to know the official positions of the Party and government, *People's Daily* is definitely required reading, as it is "the paper of record," the voice of authority. Its editorials, like the one on April 26 that exacerbated the recent round of student demonstrations, always reflect the will of those in power and in fact are sometimes written by top officials themselves. Newspapers at the provincial and city levels are required to reprint the *People's Daily* editorials from time to time. Once these facts are understood, it should no longer be puzzling to outsiders that a "mere" newspaper editorial could trigger such a large and passionate response as that witnessed in Tiananmen Square.

The Party has its press office, called the Department of Propaganda, to control the press. Among all the departments under the Party Central Committee, the Department of Propaganda is one of the most important and most sensitive, because it has immediate charge of making propaganda directives and reflecting the "current Party line." From time to time, editors of major newspapers are called by the department to be briefed on new policies, or "propaganda lines" as they term it. It is in this department that decisions are made as to what people should or should not be told, and when. This makes it an important battleground for political power struggles, and anyone wanting to seriously affect the direction of the Party or defeat his political opponent has to exert control over this department. Therefore, the department head always bears certain political risks, for he can rise or fall as the result of top level power struggles. As observed half-jokingly by Wen Yuankai, a Chinese scientist well-known for his reformist thinking, who was reportedly stripped of his post as the deputy director of the Education Commission of Anhui Province for "counterrevolutionary" and "instigatory" speeches in Tiananmen Square, China's propaganda chief is among the four most risky positions in the world. The other three are, according to

Wen, the Soviet Union's agricultural minister, Egypt's defense minister, and the director of the United States' CIA.

To provide the "unified thinking" it believes necessary, the Party has to control not only the press, but the intellectual community as a whole. Besides journalists, who must always follow the Party line, writers and artists have to submit to the censorship of their superiors as well. All of them, without exception, are required to strictly obey the principles set by Mao Zedong that artistic works should serve the "masses of workers and peasants," of whom the Party claims to be the sole representative. Penalties for those who try to present their "personal ideas" could be severe. Indeed, many Chinese intellectuals now feel that they had been trapped by Mao Zedong in the mid-1950s when he proposed for writers and artists the so-called "Double Hundred Principle"—"Let one hundred flowers blossom; Let one hundred schools of thought contend." Mao urged the intellectuals to speak out their demands and complaints and to "help" the Communist government build a better country. The result was that many intellectuals became excited, took Mao seriously, and openly criticized the newborn government for what they considered its mistakes. However, it was not long before Mao launched the so-called "Anti-Rightist Movement" in 1957, and thousands of intellectuals who had criticized the Communist government in whatever ways, were labeled "Rightists" and many were sent to labor camps in remote areas. These people were in fact trapped by their own political naivete as well. It should also be remembered that the "Anti-Rightist" campaign was a policy strongly supported by Liu Shaoqi, Peng Zhen, and Deng Xiaoping, who were all purged by Mao during the Cultural Revolution. If the students had been less naive in 1989, they might also have had a forewarning of things to come, especially if they had remembered Deng's own Anti-Rightist attitudes in the mid-1950s.

However, after the downfall of the Gang of Four in 1976, Chinese intellectuals did begin to enjoy relatively greater freedom as a result of a somewhat relaxed political atmosphere and the government's "new intellectual policy," which once again emphasized the Double-Hundred Principle. Nonetheless, the intellectuals were still under strict scrutiny of the government and campaigns against them still took place occasionally, although control of writers and artists had been somewhat slackened in recent years. But the Communist authorities remain far from ready to completely relinquish control of the press. Even Hu Yaobang, who was generally believed to be the most liberal Party chief, took the stand that the Party could not let the press slip out of its hand. Four years ago, he declared that while writers and artists should have freedom of artistic activities, journalists should not be granted the freedom of reporting, especially on major domestic political issues, because the press is the "mouthpiece of the Party and so must serve the Party," he argued. In an article, "On the Party's Journalism," published on 14 April 1985, Hu asserted that "as far as its most fundamental characteristic is concerned, the Party's journalism is the Party's mouthpiece. This is not just a tenable position, it is an unshakeable one." Thus as more and more personal feelings and different views have been expressed by many Chinese writers in recent years—even sex and violence have been tolerated in Chinese literature and cinema—journalists have found it particularly difficult to report on certain events freely. As one former *People's Daily* commentator and former member of Zhao's "think tank," complained, "I could not say what I really wanted to say [at *People's Daily*], but fortunately I have said nothing I didn't want to say." So despite some progress in press reform in recent years, much remains to be done before the Chinese government really loosens control of the press and journalists acquire the freedom of reporting, or of saying "what I really want to say."

If even the most liberal officials like Hu had serious reservations about freedom of the press, it is not surprising that the current leadership still sees the media as the voice of the Party. Chinese leaders have become all too comfortable hiding the truth, or at least with presenting a well-laundered version of events. The leadership believes that the public should know only of the sunny side of contemporary society and assumes that too much negative reporting would lead people to challenge its power. The Party often publishes a distorted account of events in official newspapers while at the same time actually publishing the true story in the *neican*, or internal reference material, which is read only by officials above certain levels. It has been a common practice in the People's Republic for newspapers to carry primarily "good" news while omitting or downplaying any "bad" news, such as cases of official corruption. A few years ago, even natural disasters could not be openly reported. Corrupt practices of local bureaucrats and so on will, if reported, be kept from the public and put on the internal reference networks.

In recent years, however, the situation had slightly changed. Just as China's other reforms created increased expectations, the demand for greater press freedom resulted partly from the fact that there *had* been some relaxation of government restrictions of the press. Cases of corruption and abuse of power by officials at the ministry and provincial levels have been exposed by the press from time to time. However, compared to the depth and extent of official corruption, abuse of power, and other wrongdoings, such "negative" reporting is far from sufficient, especially when taking into consideration a decision made at the 13th Party Congress in 1987 that "crucial events should be made known to the people," a version of possible glasnost in China. Therefore, although admittedly a number of cases of corrupt officials at provincial and lower levels were reported in official newspapers in the late 1980s, corrupt officials at higher levels were not exposed in newspapers, not because reporters do not know of such cases: many of them are open secrets, such as Deng Xiaoping's own son Deng Pufang, and Zhao Ziyang's son Zhao Dajun both being involved in "official profiteering," but because it is not in the "Party line" to report such cases involving top leaders and their family members. It seems that too often the Party confuses a monopoly on information with a "correct line." It is more than safe to say that in dealing with propaganda work relating to recent events in the student movement and the Beijing final crackdown. Party leaders must be reading a story very different from the one they order the newspapers to carry about such events, one they are not especially anxious for the other 47 million ordinary Party cadres to hear.

So it came as no surprise that after the bloody suppression the Party has justified its action by glorifying the killed soldiers and attacking student leaders for trying to "overthrow the Communist leadership" and "negating the socialist system." They had also made full use of the "propaganda machine" to rewrite history. Therefore, while they knew very well how many innocent civilians were killed from confidential statistics carried in the internal reference for a few people at the very top—they have given out a rather unconvincing version of the events of June 3–4. Deng Xiaoping reportedly said in a speech after June 4 that the government must "create revolutionary public opinion on a grand scale and make the people understand what really happened." This statement itself is a telling example of the official attitude, which shows no qualms about manufacturing distorted history to suit the perceived needs of the Party.

"What really happened" was of course the killing of hundreds of unarmed civilians by the People's Liberation Army, but under the order of the Chinese leadership people were told that what actually took place was that "thugs" and "ruffians" wounded and killed "our beloved soldiers," who were only forced to fire in order to "defend themselves and the capital." People also had to be told that the fully armed soldiers suffered more casualties than the unarmed civilians. In fact, shortly after June 4, the government put out a six-segment documentary on the the day's events. The documentary, which was broadcast repeatedly on China Central Television, showed scenes of people burning military vehicles and several burned bodies of soldiers. But not one picture indicated that the soldiers ever opened fire on the civilians, an omission which was an obvious attempt to convince people outside the capital that the army never opened fire on anyone. The Chinese press also declared that the brutal show of force was another "glorious victory" for the PLA, an assertion which will do nothing but further damage China's reputation and convince the world that the "People's Republic" is anything but that.

STUDENTS CALL FOR PRESS FREEDOM

Based on earlier experiences, the student activists were more careful and better prepared in raising their demands in the recent round of demonstrations. One thing they came to understand was that in the past, Party progaganda against them effectively smothered their demands for political changes. They almost always found that the whole society would turn against them or was indifferent, and that they could hardly be understood by the masses of the population, including their teachers and parents, let alone ordinary workers and peasants, because the students themselves are a highly select elite in Chinese society. Consequently, it always required little effort on the part of authorities to present a distorted picture of the student movement and turn public opinion against it.

Another key problem is that the students made little attempt to bridge the gaps between themselves and the peasants and workers. It must be remembered that 75 to 80 percent of China's 1.1 billion people still live in the countryside. The interests of the students and of the rest of the population are often very different and it is a difficult task to bridge this gulf. For ordinary Chinese peasants and workers, adequate food and clothing, plus peace and stability, are sufficient for a tolerable society, and such words as democracy and political freedom, which the students want so much and for which they have been willing to die, sound somewhat strange. After all, peasants and workers do not read much Chinese, let alone Rousseau, Voltaire, and Montesquieu. Nor do they have international contacts. It would therefore require a sophisticated long-term campaign to bring the masses to an understanding of the students' concepts, let alone forge a political movement that joined these two segments of society.

However, in the most recent wave of protests, the students were also addressing far less abstract issues which touched intimately on the daily lives of the common people. The Party hierarchy obviously realizes that if people understood what the students really did and wanted, there could be a massive resurgence of the support which students enjoyed in May 1989. So instead of reporting on the student demands, the government-run official press concentrated on blaming the students for blocking transportation and incurring economic losses. Also, given the official assumption that the "majority of the people are good," students were always said to be "used by only a handful of instigators who have deep hatred for socialism." The authorities also encouraged some workers, peasants, and even intellectuals to express their objections against creating "turmoil."

Due to the monolithic nature of the Chinese media, government propaganda is largely effective and widely accepted by the masses of the population. In China, the *People's Daily* is regarded by many people, especially the less-educated, as the "documentation of the Party Central Committee," which of course must be true to the facts. This is especially the case in the countryside where people have little access to outside news from any source but the official press, and they have little scepticism toward the media. Although the monolithic nature of the Chinese press encourages the spread of rumors, and government propaganda after June 4 may have lost some credibility among the masses of the population, the general public usually views the official press as nothing but believable. Therefore, people may very well believe that the students were only a group of "trouble makers" if the *People's Daily* said this was the case. Consequently, the students have often found themselves helpless and isolated from society, and despite their good will, able to accomplish little significant change.

In addition, students face tremendous pressure from their families, which means so much to Chinese that before taking any actions an individual will usually consider the consequences for family members, with a caution and an anxiety that most Westerners can scarcely imagine. Parents would warn their children to stay away from "trouble" for fear of government retaliation, while the authorities would use their press to call on parents to prevent their children from "creating troubles" by suggesting that student activists would face certain punishment.

Because of this, a key strategic question for the students was how to win public support for their cause and prevent the authorities from distorting their movement. They turned to freedom of the press, a concept which they largely borrowed from the West and which was never heard of in China previously by the majority of the population, although Chinese journalists have been calling for press reform and even freedom of the press in recent years. The students felt that if the press could present the true face of their movement, or at least not distort it, other sectors of society would come to understand and support them. Of course it was an added advantage if the press called their movement "patriotic," as they considered it to be.

But a deeper issue than having the press help create a favorable public image, was the belief that freedom of the press is part of the overall political reforms which students had been pushing more strongly than other sectors of society. The students viewed freedom of the press as an indispensible means to solve many of the nation's current problems, such as corruption and popular discontent. They believed that putting public officials under the scrutiny of the press and the people would help check corruption. And by letting people freely express their views and complaints, the concerns of the general population could be properly voiced, creating a better understanding between the people and the ruling authorities. Moreover, democracy in itself should insure that different opinions could be expressed without reprisal. For the students, then, freedom of the press was both a fundamental demand and a strategic means to present a positive image of their movement.

STUDENTS PUBLISH INDEPENDENT NEWSPAPER

Given the fact that the Chinese press is under such tight government control, the students had little hope that their cause could be reported in a consistently fair and open manner by the official media, although that is exactly what they were agitating for. As a result, student activists in 1989 decided to launch their own propaganda campaign by sending out small detachments of people in an attempt to popularize their cause and gain support from the masses of the population. They also decided to publish their own newspaper to counter government propaganda.

At first student representatives were sent to the streets and factories to convince others that their cause was justified. They briefed people on what the student movement meant and solicited donations for the establishment of an independent student newspaper. They also mobilized even middle school and elementary school students in certain cases to expand their network of influence.

The students succeeded in winning broad support in Beijing when they discussed such problems as inflation and corruption, which appealed directly to the general dissatisfaction among the people. By addressing concrete economic and social problems rather than merely shouting pro-democracy slogans, they were speaking the language of the masses. Consequently, in sharp contrast to other student movements in the past ten years, when the general population showed indifference, if not antagonism, the citizens of Beijing now cheered and even supported the students with generous donations. As a result, substantial funds were collected from many different strata of society. This money, plus portions of the millions of dollars donated from the US, Hong Kong, and elsewhere, enabled them to purchase such basic materials as paper and mimeographs to start their own newspapers and a broadcasting station—by no means an easy task.

In late April, the Autonomous Students Association of Beijing Universities began to publish the *News Herald* to report on their own movement, despite the government warning that no state-run printer was allowed to print it and no official news organization was permitted to give any assistance to its publication. Given the government warnings, the students managed to mimeograph their papers, a practice which is not uncommon in China. The *Herald* was so popular that its first issue was immediately sold out as soon as it was available. (It is not known exactly how many thousands were printed). At Beijing University, the students took over the official broadcasting station and changed it into a "Democracy Broadcasting Station."

On May 22, two days after the declaration of martial law, a group of intellectuals and journalists published a four-page newspaper, the *News Bulletin*, in which it called for the repeal of martial law. Its editorial, entitled "Defend the Square, Defend the Capital, Defend the Republic," declared: "Since last April, the great patriotic democracy movement participated in by hundreds of thousands of Beijing university students has opened a most glorious page in Chinese history." The *Bulletin* made further appeals to the Standing Committee of the National People's Congress to convene an emergency meeting to lift martial law and dismiss Premier Li Peng.

During the days when the students occupied Tiananmen Square, the student newspaper and broadcasting system worked so effectively that they played an important role in coordinating the activities of the protestors in and outside the square. Student representatives were sent to all sections of the city to gather news and information so that the protestors, many of whom stayed in the square for over 20 days, could learn what was happening around them. The students were well informed when they printed and broadcast news about not only their own activities, but also top-level power struggles. Some information was being leaked to them from very high levels. Before martial law was declared, the students broadcast for the first time that a five-point proposal of Party chief Zhao Ziyang was rejected by the Party hard-liners. Zhao's proposal, which was indirectly confirmed by Yang Shangkun's confidential speech, included: 1) Retraction of the April 26 *People's Daily* editorial; 2) He personally would take full responsibility for the publication of the editorial; 3) Setting up a new organization under the National People's Congress to investigate the business activities of the children of top officials, including one of his own sons, and to investigate cases of profiteering by government officials and their children; 4) Publicizing the background and social relationships of officials above the vice-ministerial level; and 5) Publicizing the salary and benefits of top level officials, and abolishing certain privileges enjoyed by top level officials.

On the night of May 19–20, when Li Peng gave a harsh speech about the student movement and later declared martial law in parts of Beijing, the student broadcasting station reported that Zhao had resigned, which provoked further anger among the students, who decided to continue their protest in Tiananmen Square despite the declaration of martial law. The students were also able to obtain news about the activities of military officers. Among the reports printed and/or broadcast was the striking news that more than a hundred middle level military officers had written a letter in sympathy and support of the movement, and that a letter drafted by seven senior generals and signed by over 100 officers opposed the declaration of martial law and the use of military force to put down a peaceful and popular movement.

However, it must be pointed out that student newspapers were not following any strict professional standards of journalism, because their news included not only well-founded facts, but unfortunately also reports later proven to be false. On May 20, for example, after Li Peng declared martial law in Beijing, the student broadcasting station reported that the Chinese foreign ministry had declared that it ceased to recognize the Li Peng regime. Later the Hongkong-based Chinese language newspaper *Sing Tao Daily* reported this not only in Hongkong, but through its North American edition in New York and San Francisco.

The students also broadcast false reports that Li Peng had resigned in the wake of massive resistance against martial law. Moreover, the well-intended motives of the students in starting their private newspaper and broadcasting system were used by certain factions within the Communist leadership in their struggle for power. Allegedly Zhao Ziyang's people had deliberately leaked information about top-level power struggles. In his confidential speech, Yang Shangkun complained that results of Politburo meetings had often been leaked to the students, possibly by Zhao's followers, although Yang did not identify them specifically. But in his report on June 30 to the Standing Committee of the National People's Congress, Beijing's mayor Chen Xitong openly criticized Zhao's "think tank" for collaborating with the student leaders and leaking "top secrets" of party decisions. In the report, Chen disclosed that:

> Members of the Standing Committee of the Politburo of the Party Central Committee met to discuss the issue of declaring martial law in parts of Beijing on May 17. On the same day, a few people who had access to top Party and state secrets gave the information away out of their counterrevolutionary political consideration. A person who worked at the side of Comrade Zhao Ziyang said to the leaders of the illegal student organization: "troops are about to suppress you. All others have agreed. Zhao Ziyang was the only one who was against it. You must get prepared."

On the evening of May 17, Bao Tong [Zhao's former secretary] summoned some people from the Political Structural Reform Research Center of the Party Central Committee [Zhao's important think tank] for a meeting. After divulging the secret on declaring martial law, he made a "farewell speech" in which he warned the attendees not to reveal the schemes worked out at the meeting, saying that anyone who revealed them would be a "traitor," a "Judas." On May 19, Gao Shan, deputy bureau director of this Political Structural Reform Research Center, hurried to the Economic Structural Reform Institute to pass on to those who were holding a meeting the so-called instructions from "above." After that, the meeting, presided over by Chen Yizi, the institute director, [Chen is now on the government wanted list along with several other noted intellectuals and has escaped to Europe] drafted a "Six-Point Statement on the Current Situation" in the name of the Economic Structural Reform Research Institute, the Development Institute of the China Rural Development Center under the State Council, the Institute of International Studies of the China International Trust and Investment Corporation, and the Beijing Association of Young Economists. The statement, which was broadcast at Tiananmen Square and distributed widely, demanded "publicizing the inside story of the decision-making of the top leadership and the divergence of opinions" and "convening of a special session of the National People's Congress" and "a special congress of the Chinese Communist Party." It also urged the students on the square to "end their hunger strike as soon as possible," hinting that the government would use [military force]." Soon after that, some people, who identified themselves as employees of the State Commission for Restructuring the Economy, went to the square to deliver a speech in which they said: "With deep grief and extreme anger, we now disclose a piece of absolutely true news—General Secretary Zhao Ziyang has been dismissed from his post." The speakers called on the workers, students and shopkeepers to carry out nation-wide strikes and instigated the masses to "take immediate actions to fight a life-and-death struggle." The speech was soon printed in the form of a *People's Daily Extra* which was widely distributed. On the same evening, leaflets entitled "Several Suggestions on the Tactics of the Student Movement" were found at the Beijing Railway Station and other public places. It said that "at present, hunger strike and dialogues should no longer be our means and demands. We should hold peaceful sit-ins and raise clear-cut new political demands and slogans: 1) Comrade Zhao Ziyang mustn't be removed; 2) A special National Congress of the Chinese Communist Party be convened immediately; and 3) A special session of the National People's Congress be held immediately. . . . " At about four o'clock on the afternoon of May 19, someone, holding a piece of paper and identifying himself as a staff worker of a certain organization under the Party Central Committee, went to the "Tiananmen Square Headquarters" and revealed the news that martial law was about to be declared.

EDITOR FIRED

As mentioned above, Chinese students and intellectuals in general have long realized the defects of the kind of "China syndrome" caused by the fact that *1.1 billion people are being presented with only one viewpoint by their press.* They know that China's modernization would have to rely on a modern political cultural environment, in which the press should at least play the role of supervising the conduct of civil officials, particularly top-level officials, even if it were not completely free of government control. Such ideas were even supported by some high ranking reformers within the leadership, including Zhao Ziyang himself and even materialized three years ago in a small way when a Shanghai-based liberal news weekly, *World Economic Herald,* began challenging official Communist orthodoxy by advocating political as well as economic reforms in China in 1986. Since then, the *Herald* has been actively and explicitly calling for further political and economic changes, very often admittedly from a "liberal" rather than "radical" perspective, and has in a way become the "mouthpiece" of Party reformers. Founded in 1980 by a veteran communist journalist and a former editor on the *People's Daily* staff, Qin Benli, the *Herald* reportedly enjoyed the backing of Zhao himself, and also because of Zhao's opposition to shutting it down the paper survived the widespread campaign against "bourgeois liberalization" at the juncture of 1986–1987, when the student demonstrations brought down Party Secretary Hu Yaobang.

Hu's death was reported sympathetically by the *Herald*, which was also one of the few publications that presented the student movement in a positive manner before May 4 when Zhao made his conciliatory speech calling the students patriotic. One week after Hu died, the paper carried a six-page article commemorating Hu, in which a group of well-known intellectuals who knew Hu Yaobang personally reminisced on their experiences in dealing with the former Party chief. Most of them expressed anger at the decision to force him out two years earlier and suggested that Hu be rehabilitated. They also attacked Party hard-liners for manipulating his downfall.

Although the Communist government had praised Hu highly at a memorial service in the Great Hall of the People which was attended by almost all top party officials, and Chinese newspapers had carried lengthy reports on his death, the authorities, especially the hardliners, would not tolerate the suggestion by the *Herald* that the purge of Hu and the campaign against "bourgeois liberalization" in early

1987 were completely misguided. Such a rehabilitation, should it take place, would clearly indicate that Deng Xiaoping and other aging leaders such as Chen Yun and Peng Zhen themselves were wrong in sacking Hu. So the authorities simply banned the distribution of that issue of the *Herald*, their typical method of suppressing an opinion contrary to the official line.

On the day when *People's Daily* published its April 26 editorial, the Shanghai Municipal Party Committee took steps that created a further crisis by firing the *Herald's* editor, the 71-year-old Qin, and at the same time sending in a "work group" to reorganize the publication. The sacking of Qin drew strong reactions from various sections of the population. One demand of the students, for example, was that Qin be returned to his post. Qin's colleagues at the *Herald* even prepared a lawsuit against the Shanghai Party Committee, which the *Herald* claimed was not in a legal position to fire Qin, because the *Herald* was not directly accountable to the leadership of the Party Committee, but rather belonged to two Shanghai-based research institutes: the Shanghai Institute of International Economics and the Shanghai Academy of Social Sciences.

The pressure of the crisis focused on the Shanghai Party Committee and its head Jiang Zemin, a Politburo member who later in June was picked by Deng Xiaoping and other Party leaders to be the new General Secretary of the Party after they formally stripped Zhao Ziyang of his power. Jiang, who is believed to be a political conservative, although open-minded economically, has reportedly said in response to the *Herald's* lawsuit: "I am a Politburo member, can I not even fire an official at the bureau level?" (Qin as editor of the *Herald* is equal in official position to a bureau-level director.) He seemed to be prepared to take a hard line and ignore pressure from the outside in the hope that he could get support from the Politburo. In early May, he went to Beijing to attend a Politburo meeting where he tried to convince other Politburo members that the firing of Qin was well justified. However, he seemed to be unsuccessful because it was reported that Zhao Ziyang gave an ambiguous answer to his request by saying that the crisis should be resolved by the Shanghai Party Committee rather than the Politburo. Noting that Zhao was not in favor of firing Qin, Jiang seemed prepared to compromise and was about to agree to return Qin to his original post on condition that he make a public statement admitting his error in publishing the controversial article without editing it to the satisfaction of the authorities. However, Qin and his colleagues rejected this compromise, insisting that they had done nothing wrong and that it was the Shanghai Party committee which had acted illegally. Later the issue was put on hold when a more serious crisis emerged in Tiananmen Square.

The handling of the *Herald* crisis was later used by the conservatives to attack both the *Herald* and Zhao Ziyang as the Party chief. In Chen Xitong's report on June 30, he not only justified the decision to ban that issue of the *Herald* and fire the editor Qin Benli, but went further in accusing Zhao of opposing a "correct line." According to the report:

> On April 19, a forum was sponsored by the *World Economic Herald* and the *New Observer* magazine. The forum was chaired by Ge Yang [editor of *New Observer*] and its participants included Yan Jiaqi, Su Shaozhi, Chen Ziming [director of the Beijing Institute of Socioeconomic Science], and Liu Ruishao [Beijing bureau chief of Hongkong's *Wen Wei Po*]. It had two main topics: one was to "rehabilitate" Hu Yaobang; the other was to "reverse" the verdict on the fight against "bourgeois liberalization." They expressed unequivocal support for the student demonstrations, saying that they saw in them "China's future and hope." Later, when the Shanghai Municipal Party Committee made the correct decision on straightening things out in the *World Economic Herald*, Comrade Zhao Ziyang, who consistently winked at bourgeois liberalization, refrained from backing the decision. Instead, he criticized the Shanghai Municipal Party Committee for "making a mess of it" and "landing itself in a passive position."

The handling of the *Herald* crisis also revealed how different opinions in the top leadership on the role of the press make it embarrassingly contradictory for the Party to claim that the media is its own "mouthpiece." After all, with the constant power struggles between different Party factions, a question that often exists is who truly *does* represent the Party. It is also not uncommon that the Party finds itself playing into the hands of some individuals in power. Consequently, it may be more accurate to say that the press is the "mouthpiece" of those in power at the moment rather than of the 47 million citizens who are members of the Chinese Communist Party. Therefore it is not surprising that during the Cultural Revolution, the "Gang of Four" could use the same media to launch a massive campaign against Deng Xiaoping's "capitalist road," and ten years later Deng used the same tactic to send the Gang of Four to jail and justify doing so. So the *People's Daily*, for example, is in effect not the Party's "house organ," but has the even narrower function of representing those who happen to be in power.

Consequently, when Zhao Ziyang obviously took a stronger pro- "free press" position in the *World Economic Herald* crisis, he for a period of time was representing the party and a "correct line." With his fall and the fall of other reformers like Hu Qili and Rui Xinwen, the "correct line" has simply moved to the opposite side. Once that Jiang Zemin himself had become the new Party chief and the "true" representative of the party, the fate of the *Herald* was to be closed down.

STUDENT SLOGAN: "*PEOPLE'S DAILY* LIES TO THE PEOPLE"

The incident of the *World Economic Herald* brought home more forcefully than ever the necessity of a freer press. However, it must be reiterated that given the reality of China, the student demand for press freedom was at the beginning very low-key and tentative. They were not even demanding that the Party surrender control, but merely that major events be reported honestly, accurately, and openly.

At the beginning of the student movement and before the students brought out their own newspaper, they were not assured of success, for they knew that the officials would intervene and that the government would by no means allow independent newspapers to exist in the foreseeable future. Even if they could be so tolerant as to allow a student newspaper to continue, it would have very limited influence among the masses of the population. Obviously, a mimeographed student publication with limited distribution and operating capital was no match for the Party-run *People's Daily* in terms of influence. Therefore, while preparing for an independent campus newspaper, the students continued to demand that the government loosen control of the official press.

However, it seemed quite unlikely that the government-controlled press would carry unbiased reports on the student movement. As they have done many times before in controversial situations, the official press kept silent at the beginning of the demonstrations, acting as if nothing had really happened. It was only after the number of protestors swelled into hundreds of thousands and threatened to go out of control that the movement began to get some attention

—which was by no means positive—in the press. Therefore, although some daring editors at a few newspapers such as the *Herald* and the *Science and Technology Daily* began reporting on the student demonstrations right after Hu Yaobang's death, the *People's Daily* remained silent about the student activity until April 20, five days after he died. Then *People's Daily* published its first report on the student demonstrations in front of Xinhuamen, the ceremonial gate to Zhongnanhai, headquarters of the Communist Party and residential compound of many top Chinese leaders. In that report, the students were said to be used by a "handful of instigators" when they "tried to break into the gate and throw bottles and shoes at the security guards." The next day, *People's Daily* stepped up its accusations against the demonstrators, who were now reported to have incited troubles in their speeches and shouted counterrevolutionary slogans such as "Down With the Communist Party," a very serious charge in China. It also published a New China News Agency editorial referring to the students as "troublemakers" instigated by a very small group of anti-Communist agitators behind the scene.

Up to this point, *People's Daily* had failed, not surprisingly, to mention such student demands as "freedom of the press," "ending corruption," "cleaning up the government," "more funds for education," and the rehabilitation of Hu Yaobang. The call for a dialogue with government officials was also ignored by the press until April 29, when Party leaders finally agreed to talk with the students, largely because of their inability to quell the huge demonstration two days earlier, a demonstration partly provoked by the April 26 *People's Daily* editorial accusing the students of creating chaos.

On April 29, the first formal dialogue between the students and government officials was held in Beijing. Yuan Mu, the spokesman of the State Council, and several other officials from the State Education Commission talked with forty-five student representatives from sixteen Beijing universities. Among the topics they discussed was China's press system. One student from the Beijing Foreign Languages Institute called for the removal of press censorship and pointed out that it was the strongest demand of the students that the press should "tell the truth." Yuan Mu, however, responded by saying that China does not have such a thing as press censorship, which the students knew was not true. Yuan continued to say, in classic double talk, that "according to the Constitution, the press enjoys freedom, but at the same time, it has to be constrained by the Constitution and law. Since the press bears certain social respon-sibilities, it has to be responsible to its readers and cannot report on whatever happens. This is true in all countries."

The students, apparently dissatisfied with this rationalization, saw little hope of a sincere dialogue with the government on the issue of press reform. On May 10, about 10,000 students held a demon-stration on bicycles in protest against press control by the govern-ment. They proceeded to some important news organizations such as the *People's Daily, Guangming Daily,* Xinhua News Agency, and the Central Broadcasting Station. While they marched, the students shouted such slogans as "People's Daily lies to the people," "Guangming (brightness) Daily has no light." They even accused the Xinhua (New China) News Agency of being a "rumor-monger."

JOURNALISTS SPEAK OUT: 1,013 SIGN PETITION

In the wake of the students' call for press reform, Chinese journalists, who have long been regarded by many other intellectuals as self-serving, dishonest, or even "rumor mongers," felt the need to speak out for themselves as well as for a freer press in China. In fact, journalists, especially those younger ones who were recent college graduates, shared many common views with the students. As a well-educated group in China, most of them were even more eager than the students to demand freedom of reporting. However, given their position, they have to submit to the control of the government and serve, no matter how reluctantly, as the "mouthpiece" of the Party.

Many of China's senior journalists, however—especially those who began their careers during the period in the 1930s and 1940s, when the Communist Party was considered an outlaw force operating under extremely difficult conditions in the remote village of Yanan in Shaanxi Province or in the early 1950s shortly after the founding of the People's Republic—do not share the same concerns as younger reporters. Given the Party's persistent emphasis on propaganda work, they believe that journalists are supposed to be trained as Party loyalists, who would consciously "propagandize Party lines and carry out Party principles." For many, it is by no means hypocritical or narrow-minded to believe that the Party is always "absolutely right," for as they shape public opinion—or "reeducate" as the Party prefers to say—they must allow their own thinking to be bent along the party line. Although most of them have retired or are about to retire, their influence on younger generations should not be totally disregarded and the effectiveness of Communist propaganda should never be underestimated either.

Although there does exist a generation gap in demanding press freedom, it should not be overly exaggerated, because it is obvious that different opinions exist among people in the older generation. In fact, some senior journalists have been just as active as younger reporters in calling for an "open," if not free, press, by which they mean that the press should not only report on the sunny side—as the Chinese press has long been doing—but also the "dark side" of society. In other words, while recounting and analyzing the "important achievements of socialist construction," cases of corruption and other wrongdoings by public officials should also be exposed by newspapers. Although the Party has *theoretically* declared that such reports *should* be allowed, they are usually limited to exposing the crimes of lower-level officials and are always highly selective: in other words, an "excess" of such reports is not permitted.

This explains why the investigative reports by Liu Binyan, a senior journalist for *People's Daily*, were regarded as excessive in discussing the problems of society and were cited as examples of "bourgeois liberalization," for which he was expelled from the Party in early 1987. Liu had been one of the most outstanding journalists calling for a more open press in China. He once said that his function as an investigative journalist was to "expose the dark side of the Communist Party," and after the Cultural Revolution, he published a series of reports in the *People's Daily* criticizing some Party officials and discussing their illegal activities. As a result, when student demonstrations broke out in many cities in 1986–87, Deng Xiaoping personally gave the orders to strip Liu of his Party membership, along with two other prominent intellectuals, Fang Lizhi and Wang Ruowang.

However, Liu Binyan still has many followers and admirers both within and outside press circles. Shortly after the campaign against "bourgeois liberalization" in early 1987, Party reformers gained the upper hand over the conservatives in the 13th Party Congress in October 1987. As a result, a much more moderate policy toward dissident intellectuals was adopted, and Liu Binyan was even allowed to come to the United States as a visiting scholar in 1988, where he remained until after the military crackdown in June 1989. While in the United States, Liu continued to advocate a freer press in China, and there have been reports that he was planning to publish his own newspaper in America.

Back in China, when Party reformers began to face serious difficulties after the summer of 1988, controls on dissident intellectuals were resumed. Fang Lizhi, the astrophysicist who sought asylum in the American Embassy in Beijing after June 4 had been recently barred from going abroad to attend international conferences. More restraints were put on journalists as well, who warned that China seemed to be going back to the bad old days when the Party controlled everything. Also social morale was at its lowest point since 1949, and reforms in general suffered severe setbacks. Journalists felt that they had the responsibility to call attention to socioeconomic and cultural problems and to suggest solutions. However, due to Party control, they could not speak out freely. Like the general public, these journalists were also waiting for the opportunity to demand a freer press in China.

On May 9, a petition carrying 1,013 signatures was handed over to the All-China Journalists Association, calling for talks with the Party and government about China's press system. The signers of the petition came from over thirty news organizations in Beijing, including *People's Daily,* the Xinhua News Agency, *China Youth News, Guangming Daily, Beijing Daily,* and the *Beijing Evening News.*

The petition marked the first time in the history of the People's Republic that journalists attached to official news organizations massively called for reform while closely linking themselves with a student protest. The petition, which was read to foreign and Chinese journalists, requested a "sincere and equal" dialogue on press reform with leading Party propaganda officials. It also criticized the sacking of Qin Benli and refuted the statements made by Yuan Mu that "China has no press censorship," saying that this simply did not conform to the facts. The petition expressed special dissatisfaction with the press coverage of the student movement and demonstrations in the Chinese capital, saying the reports on the event had been "far from enough, not objective, and neither fair-minded nor comprehensive." The All-China Journalists Association pledged to see that the petition reached the appropriate authorities.

As the petition was being delivered, about 1,000 students from five Beijing universities gathered outside the All-China Journalists Association building to express their support for the journalists. They shouted such slogans as "It is crucial to speak for the people," and "Newspapers must tell the truth."

The petition was virtually unprecedented in demanding some freedom of the press from state control. It was all the more impressive in that the journalists had far more to lose potentially than the students because they were risking immediate loss of employment and possible ruin of their careers, whereas the students were mostly not yet installed in career positions. It was also a rare event for any communist country that such a large percentage of employees of the state controlled press called for freedom from total control by the Communist Party. The student movement had clearly provided the powerful catalyst the journalists needed to make such a bold move.

HU QILI: DIALOGUE WITH REPORTERS

Due to the unprecedented nature of the petition and the extraordinary situation in which the leadership found itself because of the student protest, on May 10, Hu Qili, member of the Standing Committee of the Politburo in charge of propaganda, who has now lost power as a result of the student movement, visited the offices of *China Youth News*. Because this paper is the organ of the Youth League of the Communist Party, the visit suggested that the government was willing to engage in a substantive dialogue.

On the following three days, May 11–13, Hu Qili and some other high ranking propaganda officials, including Wang Renzhi, head of the CCP Central Committee Propaganda Department, and both Rui Xinwen and Yan Mingfu, members of the Secretariat of the Party Central Committee later fired from their positions, visited Xinhua (New China) News Agency, *People's Daily*, Guangming Daily, and the *China Youth News*, to conduct further discussions with journalists. In those meetings, the journalists expressed strong dissatisfaction with the way they were ordered to report on the student movement and the editing of their articles, and they made a series of suggestions on the reform of the press system. The journalists asked for the right to criticize publicly leading members of the Party and argued that only if the press was democratically reformed so it could make independent criticism could a democratic system based on the "rule of law" really begin to develop. Thus the journalists were insisting that press reform should be a vital part of the reforms in general.

(As previously noted, the replacement of rule by men with rule by law is one of the most crucial issues in modern China. Even if a structure of rule by law is fully installed, it threatens to remain as arbitrary as the old system if decisions continue to be made in secret and there is no effective means of honest and open reporting on the activities of the courts.)

Hu Qili, on the occasion of his visits, seemed to have been in firm agreement with the outline and thrust of the opinions expressed by the journalists. He said "we have reached a stage where the press system has to be changed." He also called press reform an important part of the general reforms. However, at this point, no concrete steps could be taken except by the National People's Congress to implement press reform immediately. Despite Hu's assurances, no specific or tentative timetable or plan was worked out in detail. His comment may be evaluated more as a question of policy intent than as a detailed plan for actual implementation. It was also quite likely that no concrete policy changes could have been made at that moment anyway because of the party power struggle. It is also possible that the journalists' demands may have been such that the leadership as a whole, despite Hu's sympathy, was unwilling to meet the demands at that point or in the foreseeable future. Recognizing press independence would have implied a diminution of Party power and it seems that the Party was unwilling to give ground on that issue either then or in the near future.

JOURNALISTS MARCHED FOR PRESS FREEDOM

Despite the opening of the dialogue with Hu Qili, or perhaps because of the very fact that there seemed to be few immediate prospects for a letup in press regulation, the journalists felt that they were at least obliged to push for the right to report on what was literally occurring in Tiananmen Square, i.e. the details of the hunger strike and the general demands of the student protests.

In order to push for this right, they marched publicly in several large demonstrations. Marchers included staff from various newspapers and news agencies, most prominently from *People's Daily* and the New China News Agency. On May 18, the *People's Daily* itself reported that more than 1,000 journalists from *People's Daily* alone took part in the march. Among the marchers were not only young journalists, but also a large number of "famous editors and reporters in their sixties or older." The newspaper also published a huge picture of its own members on the march.

What was most compelling about this action was the fact that groups from these units publicly marched under banners of the organizations for which they were employed. Even during the Cultural Revolution, there was no such intergroup solidarity or unified opposition, which suggests the extent of the crisis faced by the present regime. The fact that journalists were publicly involved is also highly revealing of the extent to which support had been generated for the students in almost every sphere of society. Considering how tightly the official press is controlled in China, the journalists' display of support for the students indicated not only personal courage, but the enormous contradictions generated by the past decade of reforms crying out for resolution. Their involvement was another expression of frustration with the contradiction of the failure to match the opening of China to economic and technological change with a similar degree of opening in the political sphere.

Altogether several thousand journalists took part in the marches supporting the student protests. They were of course warmly welcomed by the students, not only because press freedom was itself a major student demand, but because of the obvious fact that an alliance with journalists would increase the opportunities for a sympathetic hearing in the press. The importance of these mutual interests cannot be overestimated, given the power of the government-controlled media in shaping public opinion. For the first time, the students felt the hope of enjoying the benefit of having their demands published and rationally discussed in the official media.

Due to the sympathy of journalists and a virtual power vacuum at the top level of the regime for almost a week—roughly from May 15–20, compounded by the Gorbachev visit—there was a respite from the usual control of the media. Moreover, it was hoped that Zhao Ziyang might be getting the upper hand and that a broader reporting of the purpose of the demonstrations might be helpful to his cause and enhance press freedom as well. In fact, in Chen Xitong's report, Zhao was specifically accused of encouraging the press to report on student demonstrations. Chen said:

> It needs to be pointed out in particular that Comrade Zhao Ziyang did not do what he should have done when the situation quickly deteriorated, but instead stirred up the press with wrong guidance for public opinion, making the deteriorated situation more difficult to handle.
>
> In his May 6 meeting with Comrades Hu Qili and Rui Xinwen, both then in charge of propaganda and ideological work in the Central Committee, Comrade Zhao Ziyang said, the press "has opened up a

bit and there have been reports about the demonstrations. There is no big risk to open up a bit by reporting the demonstrations and increase the openness of news." He even said: "Confronted with the will of the people at home and the progressive trend worldwide, we could only guide our actions according to circumstances.

His instructions were passed on to major press units in the capital the same day and many arrangements were made afterwards.

As a result, the *People's Daily* and many other national newspapers and periodicals adopted an attitude of full acknowledgement and active support of the demonstrations, sit-ins, and hunger strikes, devoting lengthy coverage with no less exaggeration. Even some Hong Kong newspapers expressed their surprise over this unique phenomenon.

Many of the journalists felt emboldened by this unique constellation of circumstances to write fairly frankly on events taking place in Tiananmen Square. They listed the student demands without condemning them and gave major emphasis to the fact that many students were expressing the strength of their commitment by means of the hunger strike. Given that the regime was about to declare martial law and brand the student movement as a gang of hooligans intent on fostering counterrevolutionary behavior, it is highly significant that some of the news people were willing at that point to report the real content and nature of the student demands. It was one of the freest periods of official press reporting since the Chinese Communist Party came to power in 1949. One intellectual who arrived in the United States shortly after June 4 summed it up by observing, "For a few days, the Chinese press became really free. We could know almost everything about the student demonstrations from the Chinese media, and this made the Voice of America virtually useless."

He was referring to the ironic fact that many Chinese students and intellectuals get their news about domestic events through the Voice of America, British Broadcasting Company, etc., because they are usually not reported in the Chinese press. He noted that for a few days, the program of the China Central Television, which has 300 million or more viewers, was packed with reports from Tiananmen Square and hospitals where many hunger strikers were treated. On May 18, the overseas edition of *People's Daily* devoted most of its two news pages to reports on the student hunger strike, actually crowding out the Gorbachev visit. Apart from a news report on the hunger strike and the one-million-strong demonstrations, it published letters from various organizations, mostly official state organizations, and well-known writers, artists, and businessmen calling for Zhao Ziyang and Li Peng to meet the students so as to peacefully resolve the hunger strike itself. Huge photos of hunger strikers and demonstrators, including some from the newspaper itself, marked the first time that such events were reported in a positive way. Most prominently, the paper published a long feature article entitled "History Will Remember This Day," which was written in a very emotional style, and showed solid support and understanding of the student movement.

Beijing Review, a government-controlled foreign languages newsweekly, devoted most of its May 29–June 4 issue to reporting on the student movement. It took a clearly sympathetic view of the students and indirectly criticized the leadership for their ignorance of popular demands. One article even went so far as to refer to China's paramount leader Deng Xiaoping as "doddery," an almost blasphemous adjective in a nation where reverence for age and fear of offending authority are so strong. It also expressed support for Zhao Ziyang's moderate policy and in one article even stated the fact that "Li Peng was attacked and asked to step down from his post by the demonstrators." More significantly, this issue of the magazine was published after martial law was declared and Zhao Ziyang by then was already losing power.

In those few days, Chinese journalists reported on the student demands in a sympathetic light and fairly extensive detail, noting the fact that some had to be taken to hospitals in conditions near death. Their reporting was extremely sympathetic to the students, and went as close as possible to outright support, within the restraints imposed by the Communist system. This relative freedom of the press was in dramatic contrast to what followed shortly after. For example, Wei Hua, the anchorwoman for the English language foreign news broadcasting for China Central Television, stated in several interviews with foreign reporters that one had to keep on fighting and she was not immediately worried by what might happen to her later. However, during the news clampdown shortly after, she was warned that further interviews would cost her job.

Although short-lived, China's press for a few days in May 1989 enjoyed an unparalleled freedom and reported fully on events and voiced controversial opinions without fear, an impossibility under normal circumstances.

PARTY RESUMED CONTROL OF THE PRESS

In conjunction with the announcement of the martial law decree on May 20, the propaganda department of the Party attempted to reinstitute strict control of the press. For the first few days, it was not overwhelmingly successful, partially because Zhao Ziyang's fall did not seem to be confirmed by authoritative sources until May 24. Until then, the press was making an obvious effort to tone down the government line in favor of the students.

By May 24, Li Peng had reorganized and purged the propaganda department at higher levels, and at the same time both Zhao Ziyang and Hu Qili had lost out in the power struggle. This was clearly reflected in less sympathetic press coverage of the student protests. In fact, Li Peng was so furious at the bold press coverage of the student movement in mid-May that as soon as the hard-liners gained control, Li himself began to take personal charge of propaganda by heading a new propaganda team, which was composed of five other officials, including Wang Renzhi, head of the Propaganda Department, Zen Jianhui, deputy director of the department, Yuan Mu, spokesman of the State Council, He Dongchang, vice-chairman of the State Education Commission, and Li Zhijian, propaganda chief of the Beijing Municipal Party Committee. The new propaganda team quickly resumed control of the press, which was once again made the "mouthpiece" for those in power.

As a result, sympathetic coverage of the hunger strikers became more muted and the press made increasing reference to the protesters as "hooligans" and "rioters." Reports of disorder and disruption of traffic increased while coverage of the demands of the protestors subsided.

The overall tone of reporting changed from one of suggesting that the government listen to the protesters to one of exhorting people to avoid the demonstrations and insisting that the primary problem that needed immediate attention was social order, whereas the demands of the protestors could be left for later resolution.

Even a brief relaxation of controls revealed the depth of the frustrations with the restrictions imposed by the authorities, especially in this case where the disparities between official reporting and reality were so widely known to the reporters themselves.

This can be most clearly seen by the restrictions which became even more stringent by the time of the June 3–4 violence and afterwards, where attempts to deviate from the official line were even more strongly dealt with. After June 4, the Chinese press fully resumed its orginal function as the propaganda machine used by the Communist Party to rewrite history—and manipulate the future.

After the crackdown, the government took further steps to control the press and purge those who had not fully obeyed Party rules. On June 23, *People's Daily* reported that its own director and editor had both been changed for "health reasons." Given the importance of the newspaper, such changes represented a clear sign of political transformation in the top leadership. Its new director, Gao Di, a Central Committee member who used to be the Party secretary of Jilin Province, was believed to have close personal relations with Li Peng, who worked for many years as chief engineer at a local hydropower station in Jilin Province. The new editor, Shao Huaze, was the director of propaganda in the army's General Political Department, which is headed by Yang Baibing, brother of president Yang Shangkun. Therefore, the new editor is assumed to have close relations with the Yang family. The ousted director and editor, Qian Liren and Tan Wenrui, both political moderates, were obviously fired because of the bold reports on the student movement in May and the demonstrations by more than 1,000 members of the *People's Daily* staff itself.

One more interesting fact to be mentioned is that after the shakeup in the Communist leadership, Li Ruihuan, mayor of Tianjin who is now a member of the Standing Committee of the Politburo, has taken charge of the Party's propaganda system. Li, a carpenter who has worked his way up to the top leadership, is believed to be an economic reformer but a political conservative, and is said to be largely unfamiliar with ideological work. He has replaced Hu Qili, a well-educated Party ideologue who has been expelled from the five-member Standing Committee of the Politburo along with Zhao Ziyang.

NEWS BLACKOUT

The reinstitution of strict control of the press was quickly followed by attempts at an international news blackout. On May 20, when martial law was declared, Chen Xitong, mayor of Beijing, issued three orders, including one regarding news reporting, which imposed tight restrictions on the activities of journalists, especially foreign

reporters. It said: "Chinese and foreign reporters are strictly forbidden to conduct instigating reports," and foreign reporters were
not allowed to go to the streets, official organizations, schools and
factories to interview people or take pictures. However, in the first
few days after martial law, such restrictions, like martial law itself,
were simply unenforceable. American journalists had reported that
it was in fact very easy to obtain information despite the restrictions,
because some students were eager to assist them.

The news blackout was especially targeted at direct satellite transmission. On the evening of May 20, satellite transmission for all
foreign news agencies out of the country was abruptly cut. American
audiences actually witnessed how Chinese officials stopped the
transmission by CNN and CBS. Three days later however, satellite
transmission was resumed only to be cut again one day afterwards.

It was widely suspected on each occasion that satellite transmission
was cut off, that a crackdown was imminent and that the reason for
cutting transmission was to avoid any negative publicity and embar-
rassment to the Chinese government should bloodshed occur. For a
moment, hopes were raised that confrontation might be avoided
when satellite transmission was resumed on May 23 for one day, for
many people interpreted this as an indication that Zhao Ziyang might
be making a comeback.

It is of course possible that Zhao Ziyang was temporarily victorious
in the power struggle which could have briefly affected the attitude
toward coverage by the foreign media. This remains speculation, for
it remains unclear exactly what did trigger the change in policy,
although bureaucratic infighting within different agencies or an error
in the chain of command might well have been responsible.

In any event, the blackout continued and foreign reporters were
warned to stay off the streets, especially not to talk with the Chinese.
Still, some of them remained in rooms of the top floors of the Beijing
Hotel until after June 4, close enough to the square to offer a fairly
good vantage at the height of the crisis.

There were, however, foreign reporters who remained in the
square during the military suppression, and although two CBS people were later arrested by troops and then released, it seemed that
the ban against the foreign press was rather sloppily enforced either
by design of those sympathetic to the students or due to incompetence combined with the confused situation.

Nevertheless, it is amazing that throughout the crisis, foreign
reporters were able to transmit live by telephone their evaluation of

events. On the other hand, it is true that the news blackout was effective in preventing live coverage in detail of some of the most violent suppression of the protests on the night of June 3–4.

DOUBLE-ENTENDRE IN THE CHINESE PRESS

Despite the news blackout and the reimposition of strict control of the media, Chinese journalists in some cases were so outraged by the the events of June 3–4 that they took some extraordinary steps to refute the official version of events.

The most dramatic example of resistance to the official line was the behavior of a reporter at Radio Beijing. Instead of announcing that patriotic troops had crushed "rioting hooligans" in Tiananmen Square, the outraged announcer reported that thousands of unarmed citizens, including his colleagues at Radio Beijing, had been shot by government troops and that he wanted the whole world to be aware of this outrageous behavior.

Shortly afterwards, however, he was replaced by another announcer who gave the official line, a condemnation of the "hooligans" for having caused the death of several hundred PLA soldiers who were only engaged in carrying out their "lawful duties." Still, the fact that the first announcer was even able to make his protest indicates there was probably strong support for the views he expressed among the staff at Radio Beijing. The *People's Daily*, too, showed its support for the students and attacked the use of military troops by the government to squash the protest.

Although it became virtually impossible for the press to continue to openly challenge the official line after martial law was declared on May 20, the journalists still used an oblique and often ironic strategy to send their message out to the public, most prominently through reports and comments on foreign affairs which were analogous to events in China. On May 22, for example, *People's Daily* reported on its front page that Hungarian Prime Minister Miklos Nemeth said troops should not be used to solve political crisis and that Hungary would definitely not do so. It quoted Nemeth as saying that "no political force should be allowed to use military troops to solve domestic political problems. One of the most hateful characteristics of Stalinism was that armed forces were willfully and recklessly used to suppress its own people. We should most resolutely break with such behavior."

On June 7, three days after the crackdown, the overseas edition of the *People's Daily* prominently reported on an appeal made by South Korean opposition leader Kim Dae-jung to punish those who initiated the bloody suppression of the 1980 Kwangju uprising. Although the article was a very short one, its title was printed in the boldest and largest type, which said: "Punish by law the arch-criminals who have suppressed the people's uprising, and launch a struggle to end the rule of the current regime." Clearly, the audience was expected to read between the lines and apply similar sentiments to the Chinese situation.

Aside from reporting foreign attitudes that contradict the official line, Chinese journalists have long practiced the technique of "double-entendre" to get around official restrictions on reporting. Slight differences in tone or nuances of expression will convey a message to the informed reader that the writer means the very opposite of what is printed. Unstated facts that everyone is aware of, or understated statistics and many other subtle hints will suggest to the reader that things are not at all what the surface of the text seems to proclaim. Or an article might repeat over and over, to the point of parody, the need for suppression of "hooligans" and the necessity of turning in "counterrevolutionaries." Such exaggerated repetition of the party line may suggest to the informed public not how fully in control the government is, but the very opposite, that it is facing a major crisis.

When the Chinese government itself makes abundant use of doubletalk to defend its own positions, it should come as no surprise that Chinese journalists have become as adept at using their own two-edged technique, mouthing official propaganda in a style which in fact turns it on its head.

Moreover, very little research has been done on mass communications in China and real attitudes of more sophisticated readers toward government propaganda. It is therefore difficult to gauge how much value should be put on interviews granted to Western reporters, especially after June 4, when people were under strong constraints not to express anti-regime opinions, particularly to foreigners.

We know from research in certain East European countries as well as the Soviet Union that large sections of the population have become so cynical about government propaganda that anything printed in the official press is likely to be taken as completely unreliable. Rather, the population is often inclined to suspect that the exact opposite is true.

Given China's lower level of literacy and development, the same may not be as true in the People's Republic. However, observers ought to be sceptical of what the American press might have gleaned from ordinary citizens in live interviews. The "man in the street" is not necessarily the most informed individual. Moreover, large numbers of the bureaucracy have access to various levels of uncensored daily translations from the foreign press about important events, so it is not clear exactly for whose consumption the official version of the incidents of June 3–4 has been concocted. It is apparently directed at the general masses of the population outside the big cities, large numbers of whom are seldom aware of what goes on at the top echelons of government in Beijing at any time. The official version may also be intended for large numbers of ordinary Party cadres and some gullible foreigners: for few others in the world will accept an account which is so thoroughly discredited by a mass of reliable evidence.

Another reason for rewriting history may be that at least some of the Chinese leaders are trying to justify to themselves what they may feel was an overreaction. This speculation seems borne out by a statement reportedly made by Li Peng on June 19, when he was quoted as saying that his government had shown enormous patience for almost 50 days before having moved troops into the square. He concluded by suggesting that not a single one of the many nations which criticized China's action would have exhibited the same self control, so that therefore none were in a position to criticize China's actions. This reaction in justifying the attacks on civilians could be regarded as a classic case of psychological projection, of shifting the burden of moral failure onto others in order to exculpate oneself.

But what truly gives the lie to Li Peng's rationalizations are the circumstances surrounding the demonstrations. As previously mentioned, from the domestic point of view, crushing a student movement on historic May 4, a day that symbolizes student activism and national rebirth, might have been dangerously counterproductive. Internationally, with the entire world watching and reading about Gorbachev's visit, drastic action would have been disastrous because this visit was a key event in Chinese history, a display to the world that China had achieved parity with the other great Communist power. To have carried out a bloody purge while being visited by Russia's angel of glasnost would have disgraced the leadership and destroyed China's new reputation as a modern, confident society. A third reason for the "restraint" lies even closer to home: the government's own inability to mobilize forces to crush the demonstrations as quickly as they wished.

The reality behind the delay also explains the frantic, and contradictory behavior of Chinese officials, who attempt to sell the crackdown to the Chinese by using the media to tell people that violence was necessary to quell "turmoil" and that a return to orthodoxy is necessary. At the same time, they are attempting to convince the rest of the world that they acted reasonably, and that China has returned to normal.

But such contradictory versions of reality cannot be credible, neither within an awakened China nor in a world that will continue to watch China closely. Indeed, the more loudly the regime proclaims its innocence and its legitimacy, the less it will retain. The more it boasts of its moral superiority to other nations, the lower will be their regard for its morality. The more it labels its own dissidents as "bourgeois liberals," the more it will undermine its own proclaimed goal of socialist development.

This image of a "normal" China is also contradicted by the extreme defensiveness of Chinese officials who claim that criticism from other nations is an attempt to meddle in China's internal affairs. Informed criticism from other countries is certainly different from the colonialist interference which China has suffered from so profoundly in the past century and a half.

There can no longer be two separate Chinas: the real world of corruption, repression and government control—and the censored and sanitized image that the government attempts to present to its people and the outside world. Modern governments that have succeeded in repressing the truth and squelching dissent and criticism have frequently led their people to disaster. Information control by any power elite, whether capitalist or communist, is a form of social control as powerful as any other cultural force. This is perhaps because journalism presents itself as "truth" or "fact," thereby taking on a character of scientific "accuracy" that no culture or belief system can lay claim to.

Journalism as an instrument of propaganda has proven to be such a potent weapon in this century because it helps shape a view of the world so distorted that unspeakable violence and repression are either completely concealed or promoted as positive values. Insofar as Chinese journalists realize this, they understand that the battle for the media in China is not merely a battle for some nebulous kind of "freedom," but an important part of a struggle for the soul and body of a great nation. It is a struggle that is even larger than China herself, for China's success or failure in building a more democratic socialist system will greatly influence the course of socialism throughout the world.

Epilogue

ON NOVEMBER 9, 1989, as this book was going to press, it was announced that Deng Xiaoping had formally resigned his final official position as chairman of the Central Military Commission, and was replaced by present Party Secretary Jiang Zemin. At the same time, however, Yang Shangkun's position as first vice chairman of the Central Military Commission was also confirmed.

This has occurred in an international atmosphere where the greatest changes in Eastern Europe and the Soviet Union since Stalin's days have been taking place. On the same day that Deng's resignation was announced, the German Democratic Republic made its own astonishing declaration that East Germans would be allowed to pass through any crossing into West Germany or West Berlin, including through the Berlin Wall. Thus East Germany has seen in less than a week a complete change in its government, its cabinet and its Politburo, and the opening, at least temporarily, of all its borders, with the possibility of dismantling the Berlin Wall itself.

If the events at Tiananmen had not taken place, Deng's announcement might have far more credibility than it does at the moment. While this retirement clearly signals an attempt to achieve a peaceful succession before Deng's death, Jiang's ability to survive politically after Deng's demise remains in doubt. Yang Shangkun's appointment and the promotion of his brother, Yang Baibing, to general secretary of the commission and to the Secretariat of the Party Central Committee may suggest an attempt to maintain stability but hardly demonstrates great originality or flexibility in dealing with China's political problems. Deng's resignation is a positive step, but if it had been taken after a more creative response to what happened in May and June in Tiananmen, its effect might have been far more beneficial and stabilizing than otherwise. This is precisely why we stated that Gorbachev's visit was both a crisis and an opportunity for Deng to initiate more creative policies to resolve the student protest in a peaceful and productive manner.

The appointment of Jiang Zemin as the new chairman was a clear attempt on Deng's part to stabilize the situation in order to dampen the threat of a fierce struggle for military power to be won by the conservative forces represented by Yang Shangkun. It is particularly doubtful if Deng really will relinquish all his power now that he has given up all his official positions. It may even be fair to say that his resignation was more of a symbolic action than an event of real substance. For the last ten years Deng has possessed the highest power without ever taking the highest positions, such as general secretary of the Party. It can be expected that he will continue to be consulted on major issues and exercise personal influence on national policy. This may be the very reason that he decided to resign, because in this way Deng would be able to see his chosen successor, Jiang Zemin, consolidate his power while Deng is still alive and is able to patronize the new leader. At this point, it seems that Jiang's base in the army is extremely weak and even his support in the Party remains in doubt. A great deal depends on how strongly Deng supports him and the kind of political consensus that can be worked out both within the Party and the armed forces. If Jiang Zemin proves as weak as Hua Guofeng, Mao's chosen successor who was outmaneuvered by Deng two years after Mao's death, there will be no Deng Xiaoping to replace him—and the possibility of return to power by Zhao Ziyang seems fraught with difficulties. Thus even if Deng Xiaoping had effected Zhao's dismissal without the crisis that pushed him to make such a move, its potential repercussions might not be as serious as they are now.

To be certain, Deng has promoted Jiang to the highest position both in the Party and in the army, but not without some compromise with Yang Shangkun. Although Yang did not get the job he most wanted, i.e., chairman of the Central Military Commission, he did become first vice chairman. Given Jiang's weak base in the army, Yang's power has been significantly strengthened rather than weakened after Jiang's appointment. The fact that Defense Minister Qin Jiwei, a long time loyalist to Deng and a rival to Yang, did not get promoted in the Military Commission says even more about Deng's compromise.

However, the historical significance of Deng's resignation should not be underestimated either. By resigning from all official posts, Deng may help China break away from its tradition of top leaders in modern governments continuing to rule like ancient emperors.

Although China's last feudal dynasty, the Qing, was overthrown in 1911, the traditional ruling style has not changed much since then, as Chinese intellectuals have often ruefully noted. Mao Zedong died in 1976 while Party chairman, as did Zhou Enlai, who died the same year while still premier. In Taiwan, the long time rival of Mao, Chiang Kai-shek, remained the paramount leader of the Nationalist government until his death and was succeeded by his own son, Chiang Ching-kuo, who held onto power in exactly the same way as his father. Therefore, seen in the Chinese historical context, Deng's resignation could be viewed as a very positive step, though far less inspiring than it might have been if the crackdown had been averted.

The resignation may also be viewed as a move to win back the confidence of the people, especially those in the capital and other big cities who are well aware of what actually took place in Beijing. However, given the rather predictable economic remedies announced in a communique issued by the Central Committee meeting, it is doubtful that Deng's resignation will arouse much enthusiasm among those who were calling for further political and economic reforms in the streets of Beijing. In the communique, it was said that the policy of economic rectification and retrenchment will continue along with an austerity program that will last for "three years or more." During the rectification, according to the communique, the government will lay emphasis in four areas: first, reducing overall consumption and tightening credit and finance; second, readjusting industrial structures and paying more attention to agriculture; third, cleaning up and rectifying all kinds of companies, especially those engaged in speculation rather than production; and fourth, improving business management and raising technological standards. Although the communique did mention several times "deepening the reforms," no concrete measures were announced to carry it out.

The result of the Central Committee meeting in many ways indicated that the leadership is trying to hold back the kind of political and economic reforms practiced in the last decade, especially after the convening of the 13th Party Congress in 1987. Given the fact that China was once a leading member among socialist countries in terms of reform, plus the dramatic changes in Eastern Europe in the past few months, the result of that Central Committee Meeting has to be analyzed in the international context. Professor Michael Oksenberg suggested in a McNeil/Lehrer report on November 9, 1989 that the events in East Germany may make the Chinese

Communist Party more cautious and by implication even more threatened by potential political change. The authors of this work, however, feel that the situation is more complicated. On the one hand, it is very possible that events in Eastern Europe will make the more conservative members of the Chinese leadership more fearful of making any concessions. It is also possible, however, that it may increase a push for change among more moderate members of the leadership. In other words, it seems that the Chinese leadership's handling of the crisis in June—particularly in light of the liberalization and opening up of Eastern Europe—suggests a potential for another major crisis even if they succeed in maintaining strict control in the next few years. Or it may make political stability even harder to achieve in the short run as it could further divide opinion in the Party and armed forces—both of which are far from unanimous in their approval of how events were handled in the spring of 1989.

Undoubtedly, all policies declared after June 4 bear the imprint of those tragic events. It is particularly significant that Deng chose to resign only after people like Jiang Zemin were in place to carry out his own policies of economic reform and opening to the outside world while at the same time they tighten political control. It seems that Deng has again managed to reach a new balance among different factions within the top leadership, as he has been doing for more than a decade. The promotion of Jiang, former Party secretary of Shanghai, and Li Ruihuan, former mayor and Party secretary of Tianjin, hardly suggest a strengthening of the hard-liners, and after Deng's death, it is possible that influence of the hard-liners will be weakened even further. Moreover, it is striking that no one from the Beijing city government and Party committee was promoted to the standing committee of the Politburo, which suggests some dissatisfaction on Deng's part with the city government's response to the situation and the interesting possibility that Deng is trying to balance his political repression with a reemphasis on his open door policy by promoting technocrats rather than ideologues into the ruling Politburo.

Again, as emphasized in this text, it seems that if Deng had really been in touch with events, he would have taken a "leaf from Gorbachev's book," and ridden the tide of the protests in Tiananmen as Gorbachev did in Eastern Europe and the Soviet Union by trying to anticipate events rather than merely reacting to them afterward. Clearly, the events alluded to in East Germany could not have taken place without the approval and the stimulus of the Soviet Union and of Mikhail Gorbachev in particular. It may even be that to some extent Gorbachev was influenced by what happened in China and was attempting to reduce the possibility of similar mass protests in Eastern Europe. Of course, the opening of the East German border and the possible dismantling of Berlin Wall does not imply instant German reunification or the instant disappearance of the Soviet bloc. But it does suggest a reasonably intelligent and innovative policy to outmaneuver the United States and to relieve certain unnecessary tensions between the East and West. It also promotes an international atmosphere which frees the Soviet Union to devote greater attention to its domestic problems rather than being preoccupied with crises in its bloc or with Cold War strategies. It was precisely this kind of constructive response to events that the Chinese leadership failed to provide.

Comparisons with the situation during the Cultural Revolution, which portray a leadership with no choice but to battle against total chaos, are therefore exaggerated and greatly misleading. China's international situation in 1989 was not that of the 1950s or even of the mid–1970s. She was not isolated as she was in the 1950s; she had diplomatic relations with almost every major nation on the globe; she had just repaired relations with the Soviet Union; and the return of Hong Kong was amicably settled; the general theoretical line of the Party was one of de-emphasizing class struggle and stressing a united front toward all classes in the country and especially toward the overseas Chinese for the purposes of helping achieve the Four Modernizations. Thus there was no logical reason for the government to react as it did during the seven most intense weeks of the student movement, with confusion capped off by a final act of desperation. The crackdown made no sense unless the demonstrators were burning shops, attacking armories, or seizing government buildings. In terms of law enforcement strategy alone, what happened on June 3–4 was a gross overreaction.

Again, we are struck by the fact the crisis was symptomatic of a social crisis engendered by the Chinese Communist Party's own policies in the last decade—a total de-emphasis on ideology and pure stress on economics. Especially given the vague guidelines of the anti-spiritual pollution campaign in 1983 and the anti-bourgeois liberalization campaign in 1987, there seemed to be a clear moral and philosophical vacuum within the highest levels of the government.

Consequently, the measures adopted after the June crackdown, such as sending first-year students to military bases for a year of training and reemphasis of ideological indoctrination ring hollow in light of events at Tiananmen. If the government had been serious about such questions, it might have adopted such policies at the same time it began reform instead of waiting until it was faced with a full blown crisis. It might have done more to teach the history and the meaning behind Deng's exhortation—after the crackdown—that "Hard working is our tradition. Promoting plain living must be a major objective of education." It might have insisted that officials live up to these values, rather than indulging in the conspicuous consumption and easy living that sparked such an outpouring of resentment from the people. It might have engaged more vigorously in the kind of stimulating exchanges Marxists in many other nations are having with other ideologies.

Although the government finally announced a winding down of martial law, critics argue that had more to do with creating a favorable impression on foreigners and preparations for the Asian Games to be held in 1990 in Beijing rather than with any serious self-reflection on fundamental changes in policy. Basically it became a question of crisis management and of "too little too late." While it is true that despite the military suppression and subsequent executions, the current purge appears to be rather limited in scope, and there is a deliberate attempt to neutralize some of the potentially damaging effects on China's international relations. China would have been far better served by a more sophisticated policy. Foreign tourists and international corporations may be lured back with China's new face of reasonableness by winding down martial law, but it is doubtful if the government's actions will mollify a large portion of its own population, especially people in the capital and other big cities who are fully aware of what happened on June 3–4. After all, it was the first time that martial law had ever been declared in Beijing since the founding of the People's Republic, much less that unarmed citizens had been fired upon by their own armed forces. The government still has much to answer for, and many citizens remain unconvinced by the official explanations of actions, even if they do not publicly express their doubts and their anger.

It is still too early to judge both the short and long term effects of the events of last spring. But it certainly seems plausible to suggest here that the halfhearted attempt at the recent Fifth Plenum

of the 13th Party Central Committee to continue to try to strengthen
the forces of compromise—first evidenced by the appointment of
Jiang Zemin as the Party Secretary last June—cannot begin to sal-
vage the loss of confidence engendered by the government's reactions to the student movement.

Appendix One

What Do They Have to Say?

Take a Clear-Cut Stand Against Turmoil

(People's Daily *editorial, April 26*)

This editorial which appeared in the April 26 edition of People's Daily *is the one which provoked such a strong reaction among the students that they demanded a retraction.*

In memorial activities following the death of Comrade Hu Yaobang, the broad masses of the Communist Party members, workers, peasants, intellectuals, cadres, officers and soldiers of the People's Liberation Army and young students expressed their grief in various ways, saying that they would turn it into strength and devote their efforts to achieving the four modernizations and the revitalization of China.

During the mourning period for former Party General Secretary Hu Yaobang, who died on April 15, an abnormality appeared. A handful of individuals took this opportunity to fabricate rumors against Party and state leaders, incited people to attempt to force entry through the Xinhuamen [gate] of Zhongnanhai [building complex] where the Central Committee of the Communist Party and the State Council are located, and even shouted reactionary slogans like "Down with the Communist Party." In Xian and Changsha, serious incidents of beating up people and smashing, looting and setting fire to public property by some lawbreakers occurred.

Considering the feelings of grief of the broad masses of the people, the Party and the government have exercised tolerance and restraint in dealing with inflammatory speeches by students. At the memorial meeting for Hu Yaobang on April 22, some students who arrived at Tiananmen Square beforehand were not turned away as would have

155

been done normally, but were asked to observe discipline and jointly mourn Comrade Hu Yaobang. With these joint efforts the memorial meeting was assured of proceeding in a solemn and quiet atmosphere.

However, in the wake of the mourning service a handful of people with ulterior motives have continued to use the grief of students to fabricate various rumors and incite the people, using big-character and small-character posters to defame, hurl invective at and attack Party and state leaders. They wantonly violated the country's constitution by advocating opposition to the Communist Party's leadership and the socialist system. In some colleges and universities they have formed illegal organizations to "seize power" from student unions, and some of them have forcibly occupied broadcasting rooms. Some incited students and teachers to stage strikes, even preventing students from going to classes. They have resorted to the unauthorized use of the names of workers' organizations to distribute reactionary leaflets, and continued to resort to demagoguery in an attempt to stir up more serious trouble.

But the facts show that these people are not engaged in memorial activities for Comrade Hu Yaobang. Nor are they advocating the advancement of socialist democracy or making mere complaints of dissatisfaction. Under the banner of democracy, they are trampling on both democracy and law. Their purpose is to poison people's minds, create national turmoil and sabotage the nation's political stability and unity. This is a planned conspiracy, a turmoil which, in essence, aims at negating the leadership of the Communist Party of China and the socialist system. This is a grave political struggle facing the whole Party and the people of all nationalities.

If unrest is given free rein, China will be thrown into confusion. The reform and opening up to the outside world, improving the economic environment and rectifying the economy, construction and development, price control, improvement of living standards, opposing corruption, and the building of democracy and legality which all Chinese people including young students desire will come to nothing and even the great achievements of the 10-year reform will all be lost. The nation's great desire to create a prosperous China will become impossible. A promising China will become a turbulent and hopeless one.

The whole Party and all the people must realize the seriousness of this struggle, unite and take a clear-cut stand against the turmoil and firmly safeguard the political situation of stability and unity which has not been easily attained, the constitution, and socialist democracy and legality. No illegal organizations will be allowed to be set up and any action under whatever pretext that encroaches upon the rights and interests of the legal student organizations is absolutely forbidden. Those who fabricate rumors and defame will be held responsible for their crimes according to law. Illegal demonstrations and parades are forbidden, as is the establishment of contacts in factories, villages and schools. Those who are engaged in beating, smashing, looting and burning will be punished according to law. The students' right to study must be protected.

The students' sincere demands for the elimination of corruption and the promotion of democracy are also the demands of the Party and the government. But only under the leadership of the Party can these demands be satisfied through improving the economic environment and rectifying the economic order, actively promoting reform and improving socialist democracy and legality.

The whole Party and the whole nation must clearly recognize that if the disturbances are not prevented, the country will have no peace. This struggle concerns the success or failure of the reform and opening to the outside world and the drive for the four modernizations and the future of the state and nation. Party organizations at all levels, Party members, members of the Communist Youth League, all democratic parties, patriots and all the people should make a clear distinction between right and wrong, actively go into action and struggle for the quick and resolute quelling of the turmoil.

Students' Petition for an Equal Dialogue

On May 2, student representatives from several Beijing universities handed in a 12-point petition to the National People's Congress, the State Council, and the Party Central Committee. In the petition, the students detailed their conditions for a dialogue with Party and government leaders. Following is a translation of the full text of the petition.

After the demonstrations on April 27, the government has expressed through the media its willingness to conduct a dialogue with the students. We wholeheartedly welcome this. In order to facilitate a substantial dialogue as soon as possible, we, as the chosen representatives of university students in Beijing, hereby present the government and Party Central Committee with the following demands concerning a dialogue:

1. Two-sided talks should be established on the basis of total equality for the sincere resolution of problems. During the dialogue, the opportunities for speaking and questioning should be divided equally.

2. Student representatives should be elected by the majority of the Beijing university students, especially those who have participated in the patriotic democracy movement in April. At the same time, we will by no means accept representatives appointed by the official students' unions or graduate students' unions in various institutions of higher learning, because we believe that these official students' organizations did not provide any correct leadership or play a positive role in organizing the student movement. Neither will we accept representatives hand-picked by the authorities without the approval of the majority of the students.

3. We propose the following procedures for composing the student delegation: In view of the fact that the spontaneously organized Autonomous Students Association of Beijing Universities has continuously provided leadership to and directly organized the student movement, and has received the approval of the vast majority of the students, the Autonomous Students Association could act as a liason organization, while the students in various schools choose their own representatives in proportion to the total number of students. Once the students' delegation is formed, the delegation will, after complete deliberation, select a certain number of student representatives to act as head speakers. The remaining members of the delegation will attend the dialogue as observers and have the right to give supplementary suggestions to the student spokespersons and question the government spokespersons.

4. Government officials attending the dialogue should be of a status equal to or greater than a member of the Standing Committee of the Politburo, vice chairmen of the Standing Committee of the National People's Congress, or a vice premier of the State Council.

They should have an understanding of important state affairs and have policy making authority.

5. Both sides must be allowed to invite any individuals or groups to observe the dialogue. Neither side may refuse or obstruct any such invited individuals. The invited observers do not have the right to speak during the dialogue, but have the right to express their opinions about the dialogue afterward.

6. Spokespersons from both sides must have equal opportunity to speak. Each time a spokesperson from either side speaks, there will be a time limit. Questioning should be subject to a three-minute time limit, while answers will be subject to a limit of 10 to 15 minutes. Spokespersons will be permitted to ask questions more than once.

7. Chinese and foreign reporters must be permitted to make on the scene reports of the dialogue. Meanwhile, the Central China Television and the Central People's Broadcasting Station should broadcast live the whole process of the dialogue. Both sides will have the right to photograph, record, and report on the dialogue. No group or individual may interfere with or obstruct such activities for any reason.

8. The location of the dialogue should be assigned alternatively by the government and student representatives.

9. In the course of the dialogue, government officials should, to the best of their knowledge, answer the questions [raised by the students]. And after the dialogue, they should, to the best of their ability, resolve these questions. If a particular question cannot be answered at once, the next meeting should be planned within a certain time limit agreed upon through mutual consultation. Neither party may refuse such meetings without solid reasons.

10. In order to protect the legal integrity of the results of the dialogue, the two sides should put forth a joint communique signed by both parties.

11. The personal and political safety of representatives from both sides must be guaranteed.

12. After each round of dialogue, all results and communiques must

be reported accurately in the national newspapers and on radio and television. And the location, time and other details of the next round of dialogue must be announced.

Concerning these demands, we issue the following declaration:

1. In order to insure that a dialogue is conducted as quickly as possible, we hope that the above demands will be answered before noon on May 3. The answer should be in the form of a written document with specific responses to specific demands and notation of the reasons for each response.

2. If we have not received an answer by noon of May 3, we reserve the right to continue our petitionary demonstrations on May 4.

3. We propose that the first round of dialogue be held at 8:30 a.m., May 4. The location could be at Beijing University.

4. A copy of this petition will be delivered to the Chinese People's Political Consultative Conference.

"China Will Not Sink Into Turmoil"

Zhao Ziyang's Speech at Asian Development Bank

On May 4, Zhao Ziyang met with delegates at the 22nd annual meeting of the Asian Development Bank in the Great Hall of the People. During the meeting, Zhao for the first time openly challenged the conservative position by such remarks as "China will not sink into turmoil,"—eight days before, the People's Daily *had already branded the student movement a "turmoil." Thus, while the students were demonstrating at Tiananmen Square outside the hall, Zhao clearly sent out a signal that a more conciliatory line should be taken to deal with the protesters. He called for soberness, reason, restraint, and order to solve the mounting crisis ignited by the student movement.*

However, since the downfall of Zhao, this speech has been officially branded a "turning point for the escalation of the turmoil." And Zhao had to pay a heavy political price for this speech, as well as his overall more conciliatory attitude toward the protestors. Excerpts of his speech are translated here.

All of you who have come to China probably know that recently some students have taken to the streets. Does this mean that China's political situation is not stable?

Here I want to emphasize that the basic slogans of the marching students are: "Support the Communist Party," "Support socialism," "Support the constitution," "Uphold the reforms," "Push forward democracy," and "Oppose corruption." I believe that this reflects the basic attitude of the majority of the marching students toward the Party and government—namely they are both satisfied and dissatisfied. They are by no means opposed to our basic system. What they want is that we eliminate the defects in our work. They are very satisfied with the accomplishments of the past ten years of reconstruction and reform, and with the progress and development of our country. But they are very dissatisfied with the mistakes we have made in our work. They want us to correct our mistakes and improve our work, which happened to be the stand of the Party and government as well. We also aim to affirm the accomplishments, correct our mistakes, and move further toward progress.

Are there people who have tried to use and are still using the students? China is such a big country. Of course this is difficult to avoid. There are always some people who want to see us in turmoil. There are always people who are ready to make use [of the student movement]. It is unimaginable that they are not going to make use of it. However, such people belong to a tiny minority, but we must always be on guard against them. I believe the majority of the students understand this point as well. At this point, some students in Beijing and some other cities are still demonstrating. But I firmly believe that the situation will gradually quiet down. China will not sink into turmoil. I have complete confidence in this.

[As to the questions raised by the students], I think we should solve them according to the rule of democracy and law. We should solve these problems through reform and in a reasonable and orderly way. If we analyze the specific situation, we will understand it more clearly. At present, the students' main dissatisfaction is with phenomena of embezzlement and corruption. This is a problem the Party and government have been trying to solve in recent years. But why do we still have so many people who are still dissatisfied and so strongly dissatisfied? There are two reasons for this: First, we lack a sound legal system and democratic supervision to the extent that some cases of corruption that certainly exist are not revealed and dealt with in a timely manner. Second, due to the lack of openness and transparency [Chinese term for *glasnost*], some rumors are either completely misrepresented, or unduly exaggerated, or purely fabricated. In fact, the majority of our Party and government office workers live on low salaries, and they do not have sources of income other than their fixed salaries, let alone special privileges accorded them by law. We do have some people who are engaged in violating the law, seeking special rights and special privileges. But there are not as many as rumored, and their cases are not as serious either. Of course the question of corruption has to be resolved, but that could be done only in the course of reform by improving the legal system and democratic supervision, and expanding transparency.

Since last year, we have made experiments in some urban and rural areas by opening up the working process of local governments, publicizing the results of such working process, encouraging the masses to supervise [government officials], and establishing supervision centers for people to report on the misconduct of government officials. In this way, we have combined the punishment of corruption with the construction of democracy and law. We are now gathering experience from such experiments, and we are going to apply them gradually at higher levels on a large scale.

[In terms of how to deal with the student demonstrations], I believe it also has to be solved according to the rule of democracy and law and in the atmosphere of reason and order. At present, we need to hold extensive and consultative dialogues with the students, with workers, with intellectuals, with various democratic parties, and with people in all fields. We must exchange ideas and promote understanding (between different sectors of the society) under the rule of democracy and law, and in the atmosphere of reason and order, and in this way, we will work together to solve the questions of common concern.

What is most needed now, however, is soberness, reason, restraint, and order. We must solve the problems according to the rule of democracy and law. The Party and government are ready to do so. I believe that the students and other individuals will also agree to work in this way. If everybody works in this way, then we can certainly achieve our goal of maintaining order and stability. I believe that this will mean a new unity on a higher level. On the basis of stability and unity, China's political and economic reforms and our socialist modernization construction will undoubtedly move forward more smoothly. I am very optimistic about China's political stability and the future of reforms. China's investment climate will continue to improve. I hope that my explanation of the situation will help in your understanding of China.

"May 16" Declaration

Intellectuals Speak Out

On May 16, 1989, three days after the students began a hunger strike, a group of well-known intellectuals, Yan Jiaqi, Su Shaozhi, Liu Zaifu, Bao Zunxin, Su Xiaokang, Lao Gui, and many others, wrote a statement in support of the student hunger strikers. Coincidentally, the statement, which has become known as the "May 16" Declaration, matched in date another historical statement—on May 16, 1966, the Party Central Committee issued a "'May 16' Notice," which declared the beginning of the Cultural Revolution. The recent declaration voiced the strongest demands for democracy ever expressed by Chinese intellectuals, some of whom are now on the government's wanted list after the June 4 crackdown. Following is a translation of the full text of the statement.

The "May 16 Notice" of 1966 undoubtedly symbolizes in the heart of the Chinese people dictatorship and darkness. Now, twenty-three years later, we have strongly felt the yearning for democracy and hopes for a bright future. History has finally reached a turning point. At present, a patriotic democracy movement, with the students in the vanguard, has spread throughout the country. Within less than a month, in Beijing and all over China, demonstrations have erupted, surging forward like great tidal waves. Hundreds of thousands of students have taken to the streets to denounce corruption, calling for democracy and the rule of law. Their call expresses the will of workers, peasants, soldiers, cadres, intellectuals and all working people of every field. This is a national awakening that has carried forward to new heights the spirit of the May Fourth Movement. This is a great historical opportunity that will determine the fate of China.

Since the Third Plenary Session of the Eleventh Congress of the Chinese Communist Party, China has embarked on a path of national renaissance and modernization. It is to be regretted, however, that the ineffectual efforts at the reform of political structure have brought severe setbacks to the initial successes of the economic reforms. Corruption grows worse by the day, social conflicts have grown ever sharper. The entire reform movement, in which the people have placed so much hope, thus now faces a crisis. China is at a crucial point. At this time when the fate of the people, of the country and of the ruling party is at stake, we intellectuals in or outside of China who have signed this statement on this day of May 16, 1989, do solemnly proclaim our stand and principles:

1. We feel that the Party and government have not been wise enough in dealing with the student movement. Not long ago, there were even signs of attempts by the authorities to deal with the students by force. History's lessons should not be forgotten. All attempts by the dictators to suppress the student movement with violence, whether it was the Beijing government in 1919, the Kuomintang of the '30s and '40s, or the Gang of Four in the later '70s, have all been recorded in China's history as pages of shame. History has proven that all those who try to suppress the student movement will come to no good end. Recently, the Party and government have started to show welcome signs of becoming more reasonable, and the situation has therefore improved a little. If the government would continue by following the principles of modern democratic processes, respecting the will of the people and joining the popular tide, China can emerge as a stable and democratic nation. Otherwise, a country that has been so full of hope can be driven into the abyss of a real civil turmoil.

2. If the present political crisis is to be handled according to democratic political principles, one unavoidable precondition is that the legality of the independent student organization which was born out of the democratic processes of the student movement must be accepted. Otherwise it would be in conflict with the constitution of the People's Republic of China which guarantees the freedom of assembly and association. The attempts once made by the government to brand the independent students union as illegal can only sharpen the conflicts and deepen the crisis.

3. The direct cause of the present political crisis is the widespread corruption, which the young students have firmly opposed during

the patriotic democratic movement. The biggest mistake of the past ten years of reform is not in the field of education, but rather in having neglected the reform of the political structure. [China's paramount leader Deng Xiaoping told a visiting foreign dignitary before the student movement that the biggest mistake of China's reform in the past decade has been the neglect of education.] It is because of bureaucracy, which has never really been dealt with, and the feudal-style special privileges which have been introduced and gained an unobstructed way into our economic life that corruption has developed into a vicious circle. This has not only swallowed the fruits of the economic reform but has shaken the people's faith in the Party and the government. The Party and government should draw profound lessons from this, and, according to the wishes of the people, push forward the reform of the political structure, do away with all special privileges, investigate and forbid "official profiteering," and uproot corruption.

4. During the student movement, the news media, as represented by the *People's Daily* and the Xinhua News Agency, has for a time withheld the true facts about the student movement and stripped the citizens of their right to know [of the important events]. The Shanghai Municipal Party Committee has fired Qin Benli, the chief editor of the *World Economic Herald*. These completely illegal acts are a gross violation of the constitution. Freedom of the press is an effective means to uproot corruption, maintain national stability and promote social development. Absolute powers that are unchecked and unsupervised will definitely lead to absolute corruption. Without freedom of the press, without independent newspapers, all hopes and promises about reform and the open policy will remain an empty sheet of paperwork.

5. It is wrong to brand this student movement as an anti-Party, anti-socialist political riot. The basic meaning of freedom of speech is to admit and protect the citizens' right to express different political views. Actually, ever since liberation [in 1949, when the People's Republic was founded], the nature of every political campaign launched by the authorities has been to suppress and strike blows at differing political views. A society that allows only one voice cannot be a stable society. The Party and government should draw profound lessons from all the past movements, such as the "Oppose Hu Feng Movement," the "Anti-Rightist

Campaign," the "Cultural Revolution," the campaign against "Spiritual Pollution," and the campaign against "bourgeois liberalization." They should, instead, open up communications with the people, with the students, the intellectuals, and together with them discuss the problems of the nation. Only in this way can a united and stable political situation really be established in China.

6. It is wrong to rant about the need to isolate "a handful of instigators" and "a small clique of bearded ones" who are allegedly the "behind-the-scenes plotters." All Chinese citizens, no matter what age, have equal political status, all have the political right to discuss and participate in political matters. Freedom, democracy and rule by law have never been bestowed upon anyone. All those who seek truth and love freedom should struggle tirelessly to make the guarantees in the constitution come true—freedom of thought, freedom of speech, freedom of the press, freedom to publish, freedom of assembly, freedom to hold public meetings and freedom to demonstrate.

We have come to a historic turning point. Our long-suffering nation cannot afford losing more opportunities and cannot turn back.

We Chinese intellectuals, who have a tradition of patriotism and are always concerned about the nation, should become conscious of our unshirkable historic duty. We should stand out and push forward the movement for democracy. *Let us struggle to build a politically democratic, economically developed modern state! Long live the people! Long live a free, democratic socialist motherland!*
Beijing, May 16, 1989

"May 17" Declaration

After the "'May 16' Declaration," Yan Jiaqi, Bao Zunxin and many other intellectuals felt disappointed at the government's reaction to the student hunger strikers. On May 16, Zhao Ziyang, general secretary of the Chinese Communist Party, told the visiting Soviet leader Mikhail Gorbachev that

Deng Xiaoping was still the one to make final decisions on major issues. Zhao's remark was unusual at the time because as the crisis in Tiananmen developed and his own moderate line failed, he took the step to separate himself from more conservative members of the Politburo. Zhao's statement had a major impact on the intellectuals who accused Deng of being the "emperor without the title." They issued yet another statement on May 17, which has come to be known as the "'May 17' Declaration."

Since the afternoon of May 16, more than 3,000 students have gone on a hunger strike at Tiananmen Square that has lasted over 100 hours. Over 700 of them have now fainted from it. This is an unprecedented tragedy in our nation's history. The students demand that the April 26 editorial of the *People's Daily* [which accused the students of creating turmoil] be retracted and a live dialogue between government officials and the students be conducted. As the sons and daughters of our nation are falling one after another, their justified demands are being ignored, which is the real reason that the hunger strike could not come to an end. Today, our nation's problem is that, because the dictator holds unlimited power, the government has lost its sense of responsibility and has lost its humanity. Such a government is not one of the republic, but one under the absolute power of a dictator.

Seventy-six years have passed since the Qing dynasty fell [the Qing dynasty is the last feudal dynasty in China that was ruled by an emperor]. Yet China continues to have an emperor, though without that title—an elderly doddery dictator. On the afternoon of May 17, Secretary Zhao Ziyang publicly declared that all major decisions have to be approved by this aging dictator. Without the approval of this dictator, the April 26 *People's Daily* editorial cannot be retracted. Now that the students have persisted in a hunger strike of over 100 hours, there is no other choice. The Chinese people can no longer wait for the dictator to admit his mistakes. Now it is up to the students, up to the people. Today, we declare before all China, before the whole world, that the 100-hour hunger strike of the students has won a great victory. The students have used their own actions to declare that this student movement is not a riot, but a great patriotic movement to finally and at last bury dictators in China, bury the system of monarchy. Let us all cheer for the victory of the hunger strike! Long live the spirit of nonviolent struggle!

Down with dictators! Dictators will come to no good end!

Li Peng's Conversation with Student Leaders

On May 18, five days after the students began a hunger strike, Chinese Premier Li Peng finally agreed to meet with student leaders. While it is still not clear what his real motives were in such a meeting, Li seemed to have one goal in mind—to persuade the students to return to campus. Due to his uncompromising manner, the meeting did not start well. In fact, it began with a shouting match between Li and Wu'er Kaixi, the brash student leader from Beijing Normal University who made his way to France after the June 4 crackdown. The conduct of the meeting was highly unusual in Chinese politics, and indeed, something rarely seen in the West—it was the first time ever an ordinary Chinese citizen openly shouted down a state leader face-to-face in a televised conversation.

Also present at the meeting were Li Tieying, Politburo member and Minister in charge of the State Education Commission, Yan Mingfu, member of the Secretariat of the Party Central Committee who held several other important posts before losing his job at the Secretariat after the June 4 crackdown: Chen Xitong, mayor of Beijing; Li Ximing, Politburo member and secretary of the Beijing Municipal Party Committee, and Wang Xuezhen, Party secretary of Beijing University and leaders from other universities.

The student leaders at the meeting included Wu'er Kaixi, Wang Dan, a history student at Beijing University; Xiong Yan, a law student at Beijing University; Wang Chaohua, a graduate student at the Chinese Academy of Social Sciences, and Wang Zhixin, a student at China University of Political Science and Law. All of them are now on the government wanted list of 21 student leaders.

Following are some excerpts from the conversation between Li Peng and the student leaders.

LI PENG *(China's Premier):* I'm glad to see you. Today, we will talk about only one question: how to get the fasting students out of their present plight.

The Party and government are deeply concerned and worried about the matter and their health. Let's solve this problem first and other matters can be discussed later. We have no other motives; we are simply concerned.

You are all young, no more than twenty-two or twenty-three years of age. My youngest son is older than you. I have three children. None of them engage in official profiteering. To us, you are like our own children.

WU'ER KAIXI *(Student leader from Beijing Normal University)*: Premier Li, if we go on like this, it seems we don't have enough time. We should enter into substantive talks as soon as possible. Now I want to make clear what we want to say. Just now you said we would discuss only one question, but the fact is that it was not you who invited us to be here; rather it was so many people in Tiananmen Square who asked you to come out and talk with us. So as to how many questions we should discuss, it is up to us to decide.

Fortunately, our [the students'] point of view is unanimous. Now there are many people in the square; you have probably known how many of them have fainted. I think the most important thing is to find a solution. Yesterday, we all listened to and read Comrade Zhao Ziyang's written speech. Why have no students left the square so far? We believe that it is not enough, far from enough. You know our conditions and the situation in the square.

WANG DAN *(Student leader from Beijing University)*: As to the situation in the square, I can make a brief introduction. So far more than 2,000 students have fainted. In order to make them stop the hunger strike and leave the square, our two demands must be completely met. We already talked with Minister Yan Mingfu [Yan is also minister in charge of the work of the United Front] about this question. The government must pay close attention to the will of the people and solve the problem as soon as possible. Therefore our opinion is very clear. The only way to let the hunger-striking students leave the square is to meet our two demands.

WU'ER KAIXI: I think I might call you Teacher Li because you are of such an advanced age and I feel I might do so. But the question now is not to persuade us to leave. We really hope to ask the students to leave the square. However, now in the square there is not such a thing as majority rules; in fact, it is that 99.9 percent of people must obey the will of the 0.1 percent of the people—if only one hunger striker refused to leave, then the other hundreds would never leave the square either.

WANG DAN: Yesterday we conducted a poll among more than 100 students. We asked them if we should leave the square after Comrade Yan Mingfu came to talk to the students in the square. The result was 99.9 percent of the students did not agree to leave. Here I want to once again reiterate our two demands: 1) to declare the current student movement as a patriotic democratic movement, and not a so-called turmoil; and 2) to conduct as soon as possible a real dialogue which will be telecast live. If the government could meet these two demands, we could go to the square to persuade them to leave. Otherwise, it will be hard for us to do so.

WU'ER KAIXI: As for these two points, I want to add that we have proposed an earlier rehabilitation of the student movement and denunciation of the April 26 *People's Daily* editorial. This means that first, we demand that the government not only affirm the student movement from the positive side, but also negate from the negative side the April 26 editorial, which labeled the movement as a turmoil. Up to now no one has ever said that the student movement is not a turmoil. Besides, the nature of this movement shall be defined. Then we may have several possibilities:

First, we think Comrade Zhao Ziyang or Comrade Li Peng —better be Comrade Zhao Ziyang—had better go to Tiananmen Square and talk directly with the students there. Secondly, the *People's Daily* should put out another editorial to negate its April 26 editorial, and to apologize to people all over the country and acknowledge the great significance of the current student movement. Only in this way could we try our best to persuade the students to switch from hunger strike to sit-in. And then under such circumstances we can go on with our effort to solve the problem. We may try our best, but we can't guarantee we can make it. But if this demand cannot be satisfied, it will be hard to predict how things will develop. As for the dialogue, it should be an open, equal, direct, and sincere one with representatives of the masses of students. The State Council has already said it wants to hold dialogue, but why can't we set these conditions? Here, open means a live television broadcast. This is openness in a real sense. And both Chinese and foreign reporters should be present. As for equal, it means the dialogue should be conducted between leaders who have the decision-making power and genuine student representatives who can influence the student movement and are directly elected by the students. This means direct and equal. During the dialogue, responses such as "I cannot answer this question" or "this is just my personal view" are unacceptable. One might give such a response if some questions we raise haven't been discussed at the meetings of the Politburo, but new meetings should be immediately convened to discuss such questions. We think this is the genuine attitude toward solving problems.

WANG DAN: We representatives here actually represent the fasting students in Tiananmen Square and assume the responsibility for the safety of their lives. So we hope every leader can make known his opinion on the demands we have raised. As initiators and organizers of the hunger strike, we are all worried about our fellow fasting students' lives. I assume every leader shares the same concern. Based on such thinking, we hope the two questions can be expounded as soon as possible.

WU'ER KAIXI: Do other students have other ideas—please say it quickly, because we don't have too much time.

XIONG YAN *(Student leader from Beijing University):* We believe, no matter whether the government or other sectors recognize it as a patriotic and democratic movement or not, history will surely do so. But why do we especially urge the government and other sectors to recognize it? Because it represents the people's wish: they want to see whether the government is really their own government. This is where the question stands. Secondly, as people who are fighting for communism, we all have a conscience and a sense of humanity. To solve the present crisis, questions such as face-saving and others must be excluded from any consideration. As long as it is a people's government, the people will still support it after it admits its mistakes. Third, we have complaints about Premier Li Peng, not because we have personal grievances against you. We do so because you are the premier of the republic.

WANG CHAOHUA *(A graduate student at the Chinese Academy of Social Sciences):* I agree with the student who just said that any decision that does not represent the will of the majority of the students will not help.

WANG XUEZHEN *(Party Secretary of Beijing University):* There are a lot of students from Beijing University who are now in Tiananmen

Square. As teachers and the elders, we feel very sad for the actions taken by the students. I think that all the students are patriotic, they want to push forward the political and economic reforms in our country. The students do not represent turmoil. As for this point, I hope the government will affirm it. Secondly, I hope the government leaders and the Party General Secretary go to Tiananmen Square to talk to the students. On the one hand, they could express their understanding for the students. After all, the government has expressed many times its determination to solve the problems of "official profiteering" and corruption. On the other hand, they should tell the students that their movement has not been branded a turmoil by anybody. I hope the government will cooperate with the students and persuade the hunger strikers to go back to campus. If the hunger strike continues, it will do no good to the health of the students. After all, China will have to depend on these youngsters to build the country and push forward a democratic political system.

WANG ZHIXIN *(A student at the China University of Political Science and Law):* We have been chanting the slogan of "democracy" and "science" for 70 years, but it has never materialized. Today we are chanting the same slogan again. I would like to offer another word to the government. When we began our petition on April 22, you didn't come out. We have staged a hunger strike from May 13 until now. There is an international practice that any government should respond when a hunger strike has lasted for seven days. Even such a country as South Africa can comply. One more question. How does the government feel now when people from all walks of life, even including kindergarten teachers, have joined the demonstration?

WANG CHAOHUA: I believe that the students are staging a democratic movement of their own accord to gain the rights stipulated by the constitution. This is the point that I wish to make clear. If it were only patriotic enthusiasm, anything might have happened with such enthusiasm. Otherwise, no one can explain the sober-mindedness, reason, restraint and good order in this very movement.

YAN MINGFU *(Minister in charge of works of the United Front):* In these past few days, I have had many contacts with the students. At this point, the only question that I am concerned with is to save the hunger strikers in the square. These kids now have very weak bodies and their lives are endangered. I think we should separate the two questions of the final resolution of the problems and the hunger strike. Those students who are not on hunger strike should protect the hunger striking students. I believe the problem could eventually be solved. However, we must send those students who have become very weak to the hospitals today. We should reach an agreement to separate the two questions. As I told Wu'er Kaixi and Wang Dan on the evening of May 13, the development of the situation has already gone beyond the good intentions of the organizers, who can no longer control and effectively influence the situation.

On May 16, I went to the square to exchange ideas with the students. At that point, I proposed three suggestions: 1) The students should leave the square immediately, and the hunger strikers must be sent to the hospital soon; 2) I declared on behalf of the Party Central Committee that there would be absolutely no reprisals against the students; 3) If you students do not believe in what I said, I could go with you to the schools before the meeting of the Standing Committee of the National People's Congress. I heard that the students discussed my proposal after I left. Some students agreed, but most of you disagreed. Under this situation, the Party leaders were ready to go to the square to see the students, but they were unable to enter the square because we did not get in touch with you. You may have already known this.

At present, more and more facts indicate that the three independent student organizations have less and less ability to control the situation. The situation now is not developing in the way you wished. We're all very concerned about how it will develop. Now the only thing you could effectively achieve is to decide that the hunger striking students leave the square. The Party Central Committee and the State Council do have the sincerity and determination to solve the questions you have raised. At this point, the most important thing that people are all concerned with are the lives of the students. We must pay close attention and be responsible for their lives.

LI PENG: Now let me say a few words. Since you all wish to talk about substantive questions, I'll first come to a concrete one. I suggest that the national and Beijing municipal Red Cross societies send all the fasting students safely to the hospitals. I hope that all the other students on the square will support and cooperate with them. This is my concrete suggestion. At the same time, I demand that the medical workers in all hospitals in Beijing, whether they belong to the Beijing municipality or to the central government departments, should go all out to take care of the hunger strikers and assure the absolute safety of their lives. Whatever common points or differences we have, the most important thing is to save their lives. In this regard, the government is duty-bound. Every student on the square should also cooperate for the sake of caring about your fellow students. What I want is not that the fasting students be brought to hospital only after they are critically ill. We must do it now. I have issued directives that all hospitals must try their best to prepare beds and necessary medical equipment for treating the students. The doctors and nurses have been toiling day and night taking care of the students. This morning, Ziyang, Qiao Shi, Qili and I went to visit some students in the hospitals.

Second, neither the government nor the Party has ever said that the students are creating turmoil. We have been affirming the students' patriotism, and many things you've done are right. Many questions you have raised are just the ones that the government hopes to deal with. Frankly speaking, you have actually helped the government to a certain degree in its efforts toward solving these problems. There are some problems which we have long been trying to solve but could not solve in a timely way because of many obstructions. Students have sharply raised questions about such problems, which will help the government remove the obstacles on its way ahead. I think this is positive. But, the development of the situation does not depend on your best intentions, desirable expectations, and patriotic enthusiasm. In fact, disorder has already appeared in Beijing and it is spreading across the whole country. I didn't mean at all to let the students bear the blame. But the actual situation is there. I can tell you that the transportation on the Beijing-Guangzhou Railway artery was blocked at Wuhan for three hours yesterday. Now many people who have no fixed jobs from other cities have come to Beijing in the name of the students. In the past few days, Beijing has basically been in a state of anarchy. But I want to reiterate it again that I have no intention of letting the students be blamed. I hope that you can think about it. What will come out of it if things go on like this?

The government of the People's Republic of China is one that is responsible to the whole nation. We cannot ignore the current situation. We must protect the students' lives, we must protect the factories, and the achievements of socialism as well as our capital. No matter whether you like this or not, I am glad to have such an opportunity to tell you. Turmoils have happened many times in Chinese history. At the beginning, many people did not intend to arouse turmoil but finally it happened.

Third, now there are some government functionaries, Beijing residents, workers, even people from some of the State Council departments who have taken to the street to show their support for the hunger strikers. But you should not misunderstand their intentions. They did so out of their concern about you, hoping that your health will not be harmed. But I don't totally approve some of their practices. If they try to persuade you to eat and drink, take care of your health and then persuade you to leave the square as soon as possible and later discuss your problems with the government, it will be completely correct. But quite a number of them are actually encouraging you to keep on striking. I cannot say what their motivation is, but I don't approve of such acts. As premier, I have to explicitly express my attitude.

I understand that you have raised two questions. As the premier of the government and a Party member, I do not intend to hide my points of view, but I am not going to talk about them today and I will discuss it at an appropriate time. Moreover, I have already stated my views. If you insist on squabbling over this issue today, I don't think it is appropriate. If you don't think you students present here can influence your companions on the square, I would like to have you pass on my urgings to the hunger strikers. I hope that they end the hunger strike as soon as possible and receive treatment in hospital at once. On behalf of the Party and government, I again express my cordial solicitude for them and sincerely hope that they will accept this simple, but urgent request from the government.

WU'ER KAIXI: Very sorry, just now I passed on a note to you. I want to remind you that, just now you were talking about us squabbling over our two demands. In fact, we students are only wishing to resolve the problem from a humanitarian position.

The other point is that the key to solving the problem lies not in persuading us present here to leave, but in persuading those out in the square to leave. I have made clear the conditions for their leaving. There is only one choice and this is an objective reality. If one student refuses to leave and continues the hunger strike, it will be extremely difficult for us to guarantee that the others will go. I also want Premier Li Peng and other leaders to consider the feasibility of leaving the problem to the Red Cross to handle.

I want to repeat once again what I have said. Let us stop squabbling and give a quick answer to our demands, because the students are still suffering from the hunger strike in the square. Otherwise, we will say that the government has no sincerity at all and it is unnecessary for us representatives to sit here any longer.

WANG DAN: If Premier Li thinks that (the student movement) will develop into a turmoil and thus render bad influence on the society, I would have to say on behalf of all the students that the government, rather than the students, should shoulder the blame.

"The Capital Is in Anarchy"

Li Peng's Speech at May 19 Meeting

At midnight on May 19–20, a meeting attended by all top Party, government and military leaders was conducted in the Great Hall of the People, which was a clear indication that the hard-liners had finally won a top level power struggle. During the meeting, which Zhao Ziyang refused to attend, Li Peng delivered a strongly-worded speech accusing a handful of people of taking the hunger strikers "hostage" for their own ulterior political purposes. The premier also called for resolute and powerful measures to curb what he called "turmoil." Several hours later, the measures proved to be "martial law," which was declared at 10 a.m. on May 20 by Li Peng. Following is a translation of some excerpts of Li Peng's speech.

Comrades,

According to a decision of the Standing Committee of the Politburo, the Party Central Committee and the State Council are now holding this meeting of the Party, government and military leaders working at the central government and Beijing municipal government. [The Politburo] urges every one of you to mobilize quickly and take resolute and powerful measures to curb turmoil, restore order, and maintain unity and stability so as to ensure the smooth progress of the reform, the open policy and socialist modernization.

Just now, the briefing by the Beijing Municipal Party Secretary Li Ximing showed that the capital is in a critical situation. The anarchic state is going from bad to worse, and laws and discipline are being violated. Before the beginning of May, the situation was beginning to cool down as a result of great efforts. But after that, the turmoil revived again. More and more students and other people were involved in demonstrations and many colleges and universities had come to a standstill. Traffic was jammed everywhere, Party and government offices were affected and public security was deteriorating. All this has seriously disturbed the normal order of production, work, study and everyday life of Beijing residents. Some activities on the agenda of the Sino-Soviet summit that attracted worldwide attention had to be canceled, greatly damaging China's international image and prestige.

Some of the students on a hunger strike at Tiananmen Square are continuing their fast. Their health is deteriorating and the lives of some are in imminent danger. In fact, a handful of people are using the hunger strikers as "hostages" to force the government to yield to their political demands. Do they still have a trace of basic humanism?

The Party and government have on the one hand taken every possible measure to treat and rescue the fasting students. On the other hand, they have held several dialogues with representatives of the fasting students and have earnestly promised to continue to listen to their opinions in the future, in the hope that the students would end their hunger strike immediately. But the dialogues did not yield results as expected. Representatives of the hunger striking students said that they could no longer control the situation on Tiananmen Square, which is packed with extremely excited crowds who keep shouting demagogic slogans. If we do not act quickly now to end this situation, and let it go on like this, there is no guarantee that the result which everyone does not want to see will not happen.

The situation in Beijing is still worsening, and has already affected many other cities around the country. In many places, more and more people are taking to the streets. In some places, local Party and government offices were attacked. There have been even such serious illegal activities as fighting, vandalizing, looting and burning. Recently, the trains on some trunk railways were blocked. Traffic was stopped. All this indicates that a nationwide turmoil cannot be avoided if action is not taken to stabilize the situation. Our nation's reform, open policy and the four modernizations are at stake. The future and fate of the People's Republic is already seriously threatened.

The Party and government have pointed out time and again that the students are kindhearted. And subjectively they do not want to create turmoil. They have patriotic enthusiasm, and they hope to promote democracy and punish corruption. All this is in line with the goals the Party and government have strived to achieve. Questions raised by the students have exerted positive influence on improving the work of the Party and government. But, demonstrations, protests, class boycotts, hunger strikes, and other forms of petition have upset social stability, and will not help solve the problems. On the contrary, the development of the situation has not followed the track of the young students' subjective wills, and has gone more and more against their wills.

It has become more and more clear that a tiny minority of people want to create turmoil and so to reach their political goal, which is to negate the leadership of the Chinese Communist Party and the socialist system. They have openly demanded the repudiation of such slogans as "combating bourgeois liberalization" in order to obtain the absolute freedom of viciously opposing the Four Cardinal Principles. They have spread a lot of rumors, attacking, slandering and scolding the main leaders of our Party and government. Now they have concentrated their attack on Comrade Deng Xiaoping, who has made great contributions to the reform and open policy. Their purpose is to overthrow the people's government elected by the National People's Congress and totally negate the people's democratic dictatorship. They stir up trouble everywhere, establish secret ties, set up illegal organizations and force the Party and government to recognize them. In doing so they attempted to lay a foundation to set up opposition factions and opposition parties in China. If they should succeed, the reform and opening to the outside world, democracy and legality, and socialist modernization will all come to nothing. China will suffer a historical setback. A hopeful China with a bright future will become one without hope and future.

One important purpose for us to take a clear-cut stand in opposing the turmoil and exposing the political conspiracy of a handful of people is to distinguish the masses of young students from the handful of people who incited the turmoil. Our restraint in dealing with the student unrest earlier stemmed from a wish not to hurt good people, especially the young students. However, the handful of behind-the-scenes people took our tolerance as weakness. They have continuously spread rumors and poisoned people's minds. As a result, the situation in the capital and many other places around the country has become more and more serious. Under these circumstances, we were forced to take decisive measures to put an end to the turmoil.

It must be stressed that even under such circumstances, we should still persist in protecting the patriotism of the students, make a clear distinction between them and the very few people who created the turmoil, and we will not penalize students for their radical words and actions in the student movement. Moreover, dialogues will continue between the Party and government on one hand and the students and people from all walks of life on the other, including dialogue with those students who participated in the demonstrations, class boycotts and hunger strike. Dialogues will be continued extensively at various levels, through various channels, and in various forms. We will also give definite answers to the reasonable demands of the students, and seriously listen to and take their reasonable criticisms and suggestions, such as punishing official profiteering, rooting out corruption, and overcoming bureaucracy, so as to improve the work of the Party and government.

Under extremely complicated conditions in this period, leaders, teachers and students of many universities have taken pains to try to prevent demonstrations and keep order for teaching and studying. Public security personnel and armed police have made great contributions in maintaining traffic, social order and security under extremely difficult conditions. Government offices, factories, shops, enterprises and institutions have persisted in production and work, taking pains to keep social life in order. For all this, the Party and goverment are grateful. People will not forget you.

Now, to check the turmoil and quickly restore order, I want to urgently appeal to you on behalf of the Party Central Committee and the State Council:

1. The fasting students who are still in Tiananmen Square should immediately end the hunger strike, leave the square and accept medical treatment so as to recover their health as soon as possible.

2. The students and various social circles should immediately stop all demonstrations, and from a humanitarian point of view stop the so-called "support" for the hunger strikers. No matter what your motives are, such "supports" can only push them to the death line.

"Sorry, we have come too late"

Zhao Ziyang's Farewell Speech at Tiananmen

In the early morning of May 19, General Secretary Zhao Ziyang made an unexpected appearance at Tiananmen Square. Having failed to convince the hard-liners not to use military force to deal with the students, Zhao knew that this might be his last chance to convey his personal opinion to the people. Although strongly opposed by the other members of the Standing Committee of the Polituro, Zhao not only went to Tiananmen Square, but also made a highly emotional speech, in which he once again revealed his own differences with aging conservatives. With tears in his eyes, Zhao apologized for coming too late and urged the students to stop the hunger strike and not to give up their lives so easily. As Zhao talked for about 20 minutes, he was surrounded by the students, who handed in their notebooks, shirts, or whatever was available to ask for Zhao's autograph, which he gave readily. Following are some excerpts from Zhao's speech.

Students, I want to say a few words to you. We're sorry we've come too late. It is right if you should blame us, and criticize us. But I am here now not to ask for your forgiveness. I just want to say that your bodies are very weak now. You have been on a hunger strike for seven days, you must not go on like this. If you continue refusing to eat, the effects on your health could be permanent. It can endanger your lives. What is most important now is that I hope you will stop your hunger strike as soon as possible. I know that you are on a hunger strike because you want the Party and government to give you satisfactory answers to your demands. But you have been on a hunger strike for seven days, do you really want to proceed to the eighth, the ninth, or the tenth day? Many problems could be solved eventually, and the channel for dialogue is still open, the door of dialogue will never be closed. But some problems need some time before they can be fully resolved. I feel that the substantive questions you have raised could eventually be solved, and we could eventually reach a consensus in solving these problems. But you should understand that in resolving any question, the situation is always complicated and more time is still needed.

With your hunger strike reaching the seventh day, you must not persist in the strike until satisfactory answers are given. It won't help. By that time it will be too late and you will never be able to make up for [the damage to your health]. You are still young and have a long way to go. You must live on in good health, live to the day when China finally realizes the Four Modernizations. You are not like us. We are getting old and it doesn't matter what happens to us. It has not been easy for the state and your parents to raise you and send you to college. You're only eighteen, nineteen or twenty years old. Are you going to give up your lives like this? Think about it, in a more rational way.

I have not come to hold a dialogue with you. I just want to urge you to think more rationally about what situation you are facing. You know that the Party and government are very worried about you. The entire society is worried, people in the whole city of Beijing are talking about you. Also you know that Beijing is the capital. The situation is getting worse every day. It cannot go on like this. You comrades all mean well, you are all for the good of our country, but if this situation continues and gets out of control, the consequences could be very serious.

I think that is what I want to tell you. If you stop your hunger strike, the government will not thereby close the doors to further dialogues. It will definitely not do that. We will continue to study the issues you have raised. It is true that we have been slow in solving some of the problems, but our views on some questions are gradually coming closer to each other. I have come today mainly to see you students and tell you what I feel. I hope you students and the organizers of the hunger strike will think about this question [of stopping the hunger strike] very calmly and coolly. It will be very hard to think clearly about this question like this when you're not in a rational state of mind. As young people, it is understandable that you are all bursting with passion. I know that. We all used to be young. We also have taken to the streets, some of us have even lain across railroad tracks to stop trains. At that time we also never thought about what would happen afterwards.

Students, please think about the question calmly. Many problems could be resolved gradually. I do hope that you will stop your hunger strike very soon. Thank you, comrades. [Zhao bowed to the students, who clapped enthusiastically.]

Yang Shangkun's Speech to Military Commanders

At a May 24 expanded meeting of the Central Military Commission, Yang Shangkun, China's president and vice chairman of the Central Military Commission, revealed that the decision to implement martial law in Beijing was first put forward by Deng Xiaoping and later supported by such old guards as Chen Yun, Li Xiannian, Peng Zhen, Bo Yibo and Wang Zhen, and strongly opposed by Party Secretary Zhao Ziyang. Yang's speech was supposed to be highly confidential, but its full text was pasted on the wall outside Zhongnanhai the very next day, indicating strong opposition to the declaration of martial law within the top leadership. The speech also revealed how Zhao Ziyang fell from power. Excerpts from the speech are translated as follows:

The Central Military Commission has decided to hold this emergency enlarged meeting and has invited the main leaders of various units to attend. We want to brief you on only one thing. At present, Beijing is in a chaotic situation. Although martial law has been declared, some martial law tasks are actually not carried out. Some martial law tasks have been obstructed. In order to avoid direct confrontation, troops have not moved ahead by force. After several days of work, most troops have now entered projected positions.

The situation was even more chaotic a few days ago. All vehicles that carry military plates could not be allowed to pass. How can you say that this is not turmoil? The situation in the capital is definitely a turmoil, and this turmoil is still not curbed. For over a month, the student movement has been wavering between a high and low point, with a general tendency of going to the high point.

Since the death of Comrade [Hu] Yaobang, the slogans on the streets have undergone several changes. At first, they demanded a rehabilitation for Comrade Yaobang. Then they began to chant such slogans as "Down with the Communist Party," "Down with the bureaucratic government," and "Down with corruption." At that time, there were not many people who chanted "Down with Deng Xiaoping." This happened only on some rare occasions. On April 26, the *People's Daily* published an editorial entitled "We Must Take a Clear-Cut Stand Against Turmoil." After that, the students changed their slogans to "Root out corruption," "Down with official profiteering," and "Support the correct leadership of the Communist Party." After May 4, however, there were suddenly comrades within the party who referred to the student unrest as patriotic and reasonable. This gave rise to another peak point in the student movement, which finally developed into a hunger strike. Comrade Li Ximing [Beijing Municipal Party Secretary] has made a report which detailed the actual situation. The report has been delivered by the Party Central Committee. Please read it yourself. And I'm not going to repeat it here.

The Party Central Committee has been trying to calm down people's emotions. But they have stirred up more and more trouble, to an extent that Beijing is now out of control. For a time, cities outside Beijing were relatively quiet, but now trouble has been stirred up all over, almost in every province and city. In a sense, every time we retreat one step, they will move forward one step. At present, they are concentrating on one slogan: "Down with Li Peng!" Their purpose was to overthrow the Communist Party and the current government.

Why has this happened? Why is Beijing out of control? Why do demonstrations take place all over the country? Why have they targeted the State Council? Not long ago, several respected old comrades—Chen Yun, Li Xiannian, Peng Zhen, [Deng] Xiaoping, Wang Zhen, and Sister Deng [Deng Yingchao, widow of the late premier Zhou Enlai]—were very much worried about the situation. They all felt that the nature (of the student movement) had changed since the students chanted "Down with Deng Xiaoping." Therefore it was decided that the April 26 *People's Daily* editorial be published. At that time, Comrade [Zhao] Ziyang was not in Beijing. He was in North Korea. The essence of Comrade Xiaoping's speech and the editorial was sent to Comrade Ziyang in a telegram. He sent back a telegram agreeing completely. But on the second day he returned to Beijing, he suggested that the tone of the editorial was not right. It was overstated. He felt that the editorial was a mistake and wanted it changed.

At that time, everyone was trying to convince him that for the sake of unity, we all had to speak on the basis of the editorial. Then he delivered several speeches. The first one was when he spoke at a meeting commemorating the 70th anniversary of the May Fourth Movement. Comrades Li Peng, Qiao Shi, Yilin, Ximing and I all insisted that he add one sentence—"Oppose bourgeois liberalization"—in the report. But he declined. Comrade Li Peng gave me a revised version of the speech. And I went to him [Zhao Ziyang] and said, "Several comrades made this suggestion. Will you please add this sentence?" He declined again.

It was especially after Comrade Ziyang's speech to the delegates of the Asian Development Bank meeting that Comrade Xiaoping knew that the situation was getting worse. I suggest you go back and read this speech very carefully. It was still understandable when he said that the students were patriotic. But he continued to say that we did have corruption in the Party, and thus was mouthing the same words as the students. In the speech, he did not even mention the April 26 *People's Daily* editorial. He did not say it was wrong, neither did he say it was right. Comrade Zhao Ziyang's speech was a turning point. It revealed all the differences of members of the Standing Committee of the Politburo in front of the students. As a result, the students stepped up their activities and began to chant slogans such as "Support Zhao Ziyang," "Overthrow Deng Xiaoping," and "Overthrow Li Peng."

During this period, the Politburo's Standing Committee held several meetings, insisting that the tone [of the editorial] could not be changed. But he [Zhao Ziyang] persisted in his own opinion. Later, Comrade Xiaoping called a meeting at his place. Comrade Ziyang was present, and so was I. Comrade Xiaoping put forth one question: "Retreat? Where do you think we can retreat?" I said that this would be the last breach in the dam. If we retreated, everything would collapse. Comrade Xiaoping said: "I know you have differing opinions among you. But we are not here now to judge which is right or wrong. We are not going to discuss this question today. We will only discuss whether to retreat or not." Comrade Xiaoping felt that we could not retreat. He said that the problem was right within the Party and that we must implement martial law. Several comrades in the

Standing Committee spoke, and I spoke too. We all felt that we could not retreat. At that meeting, Comrade Ziyang did not make his attitude clear. He said: "I cannot carry out this policy. I have difficulties [with it]." Comrade Xiaoping said: "The minority must obey the majority." Comrade Ziyang also agreed that there was a Party principle that the minority must obey the majority, and indicated that he would obey the majority.

That evening at eight o'clock, the Standing Committee met to make arrangements about what to do. I attended the meeting too. At this meeting, Comrade Ziyang said: "My assignment is finished by now. I cannot continue to function [as the party secretary], because I disagree with the majority of you. How can I act as the general secretary and carry out the policy with which I do not agree? I will only make it more difficult for you on the Standing Committee to work if I can't implement these policies. Therefore I resign." Then everybody was saying to him: "You should not talk about this issue now. When we had the meeting at Comrade Xiaoping's place, didn't you agree that the minority should obey the majority? You also said then that having a resolution was better than no resolution." I said, "Comrade Ziyang, your attitude is not right. Now we must maintain unity. How can you wash you hands of it at this time." He said he was not in good health and he had no interest in that arrangement [made by Deng].

Later he wrote a letter to the Politburo, the Standing Committee and Comrade Xiaoping, in which he said: "I cannot carry out the policy you have decided on. I still insist on my original opinion." His "original opinion" was that Comrade Xiaoping should admit that the April 26 *People's Daily* editorial was a mistake. For this, Comrade Xiaoping made a very important statement. He said, "Comrade Ziyang, your speech at the Asian Development Bank meeting on May 4 was a turning point. From that time on, the students have created even greater disturbance."

Comrade Ziyang also said in his letter that he would resign from his positions as the general secretary and vice chairman of the Central Military Commission. I criticized him for this. I said that he was wrong on five accounts. "First of all, if you, the general secretary, resign, how can we explain it to the people; secondly, how can we explain it to the whole party; thirdly, how can we explain it to the Politburo; fourthly, how can we explain it to the Standing Committee; finally and most importantly, you have always been saying that you would defend the prestige of Comrade Xiaoping. Now Comrade Xiaoping has made his decision, and you have agreed to it. Are you defending Comrade Xiaoping or attacking him?" By this, I think I have made a very frank statement.

In the end, he [Zhao] wrote me another letter, saying, "Comrade Shangkun, I respect your opinion. And I will not release this letter. But I still stick to my original opinion. Therefore I feel that it will be difficult to do my work. I cannot put this policy into effect." Later he called me on the phone. He wanted me to pass on a word to Comrade Xiaoping and ask him to admit that the April 26 *People's Daily* editorial was a mistake. I said that I could not do it. After that, he said he was sick. He wrote me a letter saying he felt dizzy and asking for sick leave. Right now he is at home and is indeed sick. The doctor says that he is really dizzy and lacks sufficient supply of blood to the heart.

Later, Comrades Chen Yun, Xiannian, Peng Zhen, and Wang Zhen all learned of this news. They said that they must go to Comrade Xiaoping to find a solution to the problem. That day, Comrade Xiaoping met with Chen Yun, Xiannian, Peng Zhen, Wang Zhen and me. Several members of the Standing Committee and some from the military were also present. Comrades Chen Yun, Xiannian and Peng Zhen all said that it was ridiculous [that Zhao wanted to resign]. They all endorsed Comrade Xiaoping's proposal for martial law. Without martial law, Beijing would sink further into anarchy. Comrade Ziyang did not attend this meeting. He asked for sick leave.

That day Comrade Xiaoping invited Comrades Chen Yun, Xiannian and Peng Zhen to discuss the problem. They all said that the problem was within the party. If there were not differing opinions within the party, if the party were in unity, there would not have been such chaotic situation as we see now. Beijing has already got out of control, therefore we must declare martial law. We must first of all maintain stability in Beijing, otherwise the problems in other provinces and cities could not be resolved. People are now lying on railway tracks, they are fighting, smashing, and looting. If this is not turmoil, then what is it? We have all come under siege.

Those comrades in Beijing have seen it clearly. On May 19, Comrade Ziyang went to Tiananmen Square to see the hunger striking students. Look at what he said there! People with some brain all felt that what he said was nonsense. First he said "We have come too late," and then began to cry. Secondly he said that "things are complicated. Many problems cannot be solved now, but they will eventually be solved. You are all young and have a long way to go. We are old and don't count much." He made such a low-spirited speech. It seems that he was mistreated and had a whole lot of grievances. Many cadres in Beijing who read the speech said that he had gone too far. He had no sense of regulation and discipline. That night, he was asked to give a speech at the meeting of cadres from the Party, government and army organs at the central and Beijing municipal levels. But he refused. Then he was asked to preside over the meeting, and he refused too. In the end, he did not even show up at the meeting. He was the general secretary. When he did not attend such an important meeting, the outsiders immediately knew that we had problems within ourselves.

Recently, four organizations—the Chinese Insitute for Economic Reform, the Development Institute of the State Council Research Center, the International Studies Institute of China International Trust and Investment Corporation, and the Beijing Youth Economic Association—pirated the name of People's Daily and published an "Extra," divulging the statement made by Comrade Zhao Ziyang. It contained a lot of rumors. It said that the five-point proposal of Comrade Ziyang had been overruled. This is completely untrue. He proposed that we use the means of democracy and law to solve the problems, and we all agreed. He proposed that we clean up companies, and we all agreed on this too.

Comrade Xiannian said that there are two commanding headquarters. We have to make clear which one is really in command. Therefore, if we do not get to the bottom of this very quickly, it will be very difficult to deal with. In people's minds, Comrade Ziyang is a reformer. In fact, all of the things he has reformed were designed by Comrade Xiaoping. The [economic] problems all appeared in the days when he was the premier. Comrade Xiaoping has said, "The problems started five years ago and became clear three years ago." [Yao Yilin interposed a remark: "When Comrade Li Peng made the Report on the Work of the Government, Comrade Ziyang did not agree with the section on self-criticism. In the end, he put all the blame for mistakes on Comrade Li Peng's head."] [Li Peng interposed a remark: "He did not admit that the problems were created over several years. He only admits the mistakes of the past year."]

Deng's Talk on Quelling Rebellion in Beijing

Following is a translation of some exerpts of a speech delivered by Deng Xiaoping, chairman of the Central Military Commission on June 9 in Beijing to commanders above the corps level of the martial law enforcement troops. The speech has since been studied by people throughout China, including students, as an "important speech."

You comrades have been working hard.

First of all, I'd like to express my heartfelt condolences to the comrades in the People's Liberation Army, the armed police and police who died in the struggle; and my sincere sympathy and solicitude to several thousand comrades in the army, the armed police and police who were wounded in the struggle, and I want to extend my sincere regards to all the army, armed police and police personnel who participated in the struggle.

I suggest that all of us stand and pay a silent tribute to the martyrs.

I'd like to take this opportunity to say a few words. This storm was bound to happen sooner or later. As determined by the international and domestic climate, it was bound to happen and was independent of man's will. It was just a matter of time and scale. It has turned out in our favor, for we still have a large group of veterans who have experienced many storms and have a thorough understanding of things. They were on the side of taking resolute action to counter the turmoil. Although some comrades may not understand this now, they will understand eventually and will support the decision of the Central Committee.

The April 26 editorial of the *People's Daily* classified the problem as turmoil. The word was appropriate, but some people objected to the word and tried to amend it. But what has happened shows that this verdict was right. It was also inevitable that the turmoil would develop into a counterrevolutionary rebellion. We still have a group of senior comrades who are alive, we still have the army, and we also have a group of core cadres who took part in the revolution at various times. That is why it was relatively easy for us to handle the present matter. The main difficulty in handling this matter lay in that we had never experienced such a situation before, in which a small minority of bad people mixed with so many young students and onlookers. We did not have a clear picture of the situation, and this prevented us from taking some actions that we should have taken earlier. It would have been difficult for us to arrive at a conclusion on the nature of the matter had we not had the support of so many senior comrades. Some comrades didn't understand this point. They thought it was simply a matter of how to treat the masses. Actually, what we faced was not just some ordinary people who were misguided, but also a rebellious clique and a large number of the dregs of society. The key point is that they wanted to overthrow our state and the Party. Failing to understand this means failing to understand the nature of the matter. I believe that after serious work we can win the support of the great majority of comrades within the Party.

The nature of the matter became clear soon after it erupted. They had two main slogans: to overthrow the Communist Party and topple the socialist system. Their goal was to establish a bourgeois republic entirely dependent on the West. Of course we accept people's demands for combating corruption. We are even ready to listen to some people with ulterior motives when they raise the slogan about fighting corruption. However, such slogans were just a front. Their real aim was to overthrow the Communist Party and topple the socialist system.

During the course of quelling the rebellion, many comrades of ours were injured or even sacrificed their lives. Some of their weapons were also taken from them by the rioters. Why? Because bad people mingled with the good, which made it difficult for us to take the firm measures that were necessary.

Handling this matter amounted to a severe political test for our army, and what happened shows that our People's Liberation Army passed muster. If tanks were used to roll over people, this would have created a confusion between right and wrong among the people nationwide. That is why I have to thank the PLA officers and men for using this approach to handle the rebellion.

The PLA losses were great, but this enabled us to win the support of the people and made those who can't tell right from wrong change their viewpoint. They can see what kind of people the PLA are, whether there was bloodshed at Tiananmen, and who were those that shed blood.

Once this question is made clear, we can take the initiative. Although it is very sad that so many comrades were sacrificed, if the event is analyzed objectively, people cannot but recognize that the PLA are the sons and brothers of the people. This will also help people to understand the measures we used in the course of the struggle. In the future, whenever the PLA faces problems and takes measures, it will gain the support of the people. By the way, I would say that in the future, we must make sure that our weapons are not taken away from us.

In a word, this was a test, and we passed. Even though there are not so many veteran comrades in the army and the soldiers are mostly little more than 18, 19 or 20 years of age, they are still true soldiers of the people. Facing danger, they did not forget the people, the teachings of the Party and the interest of the country. They kept a resolute stand in the face of death. They fully deserve the saying that they met death and sacrificed themselves with generosity and without fear.

When I talked about passing muster, I was referring to the fact that the army is still the people's army. This army retains the traditions of the old Red Army. What they crossed this time was genuinely a political barrier, a threshold of life and death. This is by no means easy. This shows that the people's army is truly a Great Wall of iron and steel of the Party and country. This shows that no matter how heavy the losses we suffer and no matter how generations change, this army of ours is forever an army under the leadership of the Party, forever the defender of the country, forever the defender of socialism, forever the defender of the public interest, and they are the most beloved of the people.

At the same time, we should never forget how cruel our enemies are. For them we should not have an iota of forgiveness.

The outbreak of the rebellion is worth thinking about. It prompts us to calmly think about the past and consider the future. Perhaps this bad thing will enable us to go ahead with reform and the open door policy at a more steady, better, even a faster pace. Also it will enable us to more speedily correct our mistakes and better develop our strong points. I cannot elaborate on this today. I just want to raise the subject here.

The first question is: Are the line, goals and policies laid down by the Third Plenum of the 11th Central Committee, including our "three-step" development strategy, correct? Is it the case that because this riot took place there are some questions about the correctness of the line, goals and policies we laid down? Are our goals "leftist"? Should we continue to use them for our struggle in the future? These significant questions should be given clear and definite answers.

We have already accomplished our first goal of doubling the gross national product. We plan to use 12 years to attain our second goal of doubling the GNP. In the 50 years after that, we hope to reach the level of a moderately developed country. A two-percent annual growth rate is sufficient. This is our strategic goal.

I don't believe that what we have arrived at is a "leftist" judgment. Nor have we set up an overly ambitious goal. So, in answering the first question, I should say that our strategic goal cannot be regarded as a failure so far. It will be an unbeatable achievement for a country with 1.1 billion people like ours to reach the level of a moderately developed nation after 61 years.

China is capable of realizing this goal. It cannot be said that our strategic goal is wrong because of the occurrence of this event.

The second question is this: Is the general conclusion of the 13th Party Congress of "one focus [refers to making economic development the nation's central task] and two basic points" correct? Are the two basic points—upholding the Four Cardinal Principles and persisting in the policy of reform and opening up—wrong?

In recent days I have pondered these two points. No, we haven't been wrong. There's nothing wrong with the Four Cardinal Principles. If there is anything amiss, it's that these principles haven't been thoroughly implemented; they haven't been used as the basic concept to educate the people, educate the students and educate all the cadres and Party members.

The crux of the current incident was basically the confrontation between the Four Cardinal Principles and bourgeois liberalization. It isn't that we have not talked about such things as the four cardinal principles, worked on political concepts, and opposed bourgeois liberalization and spiritual pollution. What we haven't done is maintain continuity in these talks. There has been no action and sometimes even hardly any talk.

The fault does not lie in the Four Cardinal Principles themselves, but in wavering in upholding these principles, and in the very poor work done to persist in political work and education.

In my Chinese People's Political Consultative Conference talk on New Year's day 1980, I talked about "four guarantees,"* one of which was the "enterprising spirit of hard struggle and plain living." Hard working is our tradition. Promoting plain living must be a major objective of education and this should be the keynote for the next 60 to 70 years. The more prosperous our country becomes, the more important it is to keep hold of the enterprising spirit. The promotion of this spirit and plain living will also be helpful for overcoming corruption.

After the People's Republic was founded we promoted plain living. Later on, when life became a little better, we promoted spending more, leading to wastage everywhere. This, in addition to lapses in theoretical work and an incomplete legal system, resulted in backsliding.

I once told foreigners that our worst omission of the past ten years was in education. What I meant was chiefly political education, and this doesn't apply to schools and students alone, but to the masses as a whole. And we have not said much about plain living and the enterprising spirit, about what kind of a country China is and how it is going to turn out. This is our biggest omission.

Is there anything wrong with the basic concept of reforms and opening up? No. Without reforms and opening up how could we have what we have today? There has been a fairly satisfactory rise in the standard of living, and it may be said that we have moved one stage further. The positive results of ten years of reforms must be properly assessed even though there have emerged such problems as inflation. Naturally, in reform and adopting the open policy, we run the risk of importing evil influences from the West and we have never underestimated such influences.

In the early 1980s, when we established special economic zones, I told our comrades in Guangdong Province that on the one hand they should persevere with reforms and opening up and on the other hand they should deal severely with economic crimes and carry out ideological and political education.

Looking back, it appears that there were obvious inadequacies; there hasn't been proper coordination. Being reminded of these

*The other three of the "four guarantees" are: It is necessary to: unswervingly implement the Party's political line; maintain a political situation of stability and unity; train a contingent of cadres who adhere to the socialist road and have professional expertise.

inadequacies will help us formulate future policies. Further, we must persist in the coordination between a planned economy and market regulation. There cannot be any change in this policy.

In the course of implementing this policy we can place more emphasis on planning in the adjustment period. At other times there can be a little more market regulation so as to allow more flexibility. The future policy should still be a marriage between the planned economy and market regulation.

What is important is that we should never change China back into a closed country. Such a policy would be most detrimental. We don't even have a good flow of information. Nowadays, are we not talking about the importance of information? Certainly, it is important. If one who is involved in management doesn't possess information, he is no better than a man whose nose is stuffed and whose ears and eyes are shut. Again, we should never go back to the old days of trampling the economy to death. I put forward this proposal for the consideration of the Standing Committee. This is also an urgent question, a question we'll have to deal with sooner or later.

In brief, this is what we have achieved in the past decade: Generally, our basic proposals, ranging from a developing strategy to policies, including reforms and opening up, are correct. If there is any inadequacy, then I should say our reforms and opening up have not proceeded adequately enough. The problems we face in implementing reforms are far greater than those we encounter in opening our country. In political reforms we can affirm one point: We have to adhere to the system of the National People's Congress and not the American system of the separation of three powers. The US berates us for suppressing students. But when they handled domestic student unrest and turmoil, didn't they send out police and troops to arrest people and cause bloodshed? They were suppressing students and the people, but we are putting down a counterrevolutionary rebellion. What qualifications do they have to criticize us? From now on, however, in handling such problems, we should see to it that when a trend occurs we should never allow it to spread.

What do we do from now on? I would say that we should continue, persist in implementing our set basic line, principles and policies. Except where there is a need to alter a word or phrase here and there, there should be no change in the basic line or basic policy. Now that I have raised this question, I would like you all to consider it seriously. As to how to implement these policies, such as in the areas of investment, the manipulation of capital, etc., I am in favor of putting the emphasis on capital industry and agriculture. In capital industry, this calls for attention to the supply of raw materials, transportation and energy; there should be more investment in this area for the next ten to 20 years, even if it involves heavy debts. In a way, this is also openness. Here, we need to be bold and to have made hardly any serious errors. We should work for more electricity, railway lines, highways and shipping. There's a lot we can do. As for steel, foreigners estimate we'll need some 120 million tons a year in the future. Now we turn out some 60 million tons, half of what we need. If we were to improve our existing facilities and increase production by 20 million tons we could reduce the amount of steel we need to import. Obtaining foreign loans to improve this area is also an aspect of reform and opening up. The question now confronting us is not whether the policies of reform and opening up are correct or not or whether we should continue with these policies. The question is how to carry out these policies, where do we go and which area should we concentrate on?

We have to firmly implement the series of policies formulated since the Third Plenary Session of the 11th Party Central Committee. We must conscientiously sum up our experiences, persevere in what is right, correct what is wrong, and do a bit more where we lag behind. In short, we should sum up the experiences of the present and look forward to the future.

That's all I have to say on this occasion.

Chen Xitong's Report to the National People's Congress

The following is the full text of the speech authorized by the State Council and delivered by Chen Xitong, mayor of Beijing and concurrently a State Councillor, at the Eighth Session of the Seventh National People's Congress Standing Committee on June 30.

Chairman, Vice-Chairman and Committee Members:
    During late spring and early summer, namely, from mid-April to

early June, of 1989, a tiny handful of people exploited student unrest to launch a planned, organized and premeditated political turmoil, which later developed into a counterrevolutionary rebellion in Beijing, the capital. Their purpose was to overthrow the leadership of the Chinese Communist Party and subvert the socialist People's Republic of China. The outbreak and development of the turmoil and the counterrevolutionary rebellion had profound international background and social basis at home. As Comrade Deng Xiaoping put it, "This storm was bound to happen sooner or later. As determined by the international and domestic climate, it was bound to happen and was independent of man's will." In this struggle involving the life and death of the Party and the state, Comrade Zhao Ziyang committed the serious mistake of supporting the turmoil and splitting the Party, and had the unshirkable responsibility for the shaping up and development of the turmoil. In the face of this very severe situation, the Party Central Committee made correct decisions and took a series of resolute measures, winning the firm support of the whole Party and people of all nationalities in the country. Represented by Comrade Deng Xiaoping, proletarian revolutionaries of the older generation played a very important role in winning the struggle. The Chinese People's Liberation Army, the armed police and the police made great contributions in checking the turmoil and quelling the counterrevolutionary rebellion. The vast numbers of workers, peasants, and intellectuals firmly opposed the turmoil and the rebellion, rallied closely around the Party Central Committee and displayed a very high political consciousness and a sense of responsibility as masters of the country. Now, entrusted by the State Council, I am making a report to the Standing Committee of the National People's Congress on the turmoil and the counterrevolutionary rebellion, mainly the happenings in Beijing, and the work of checking the turmoil and quelling the counterrevolutionary rebellion.

One. The turmoil was premeditated and prepared for a long time.

Some political forces in the West have always attempted to make the socialist countries, including China, give up the socialist road, eventually bring these countries under the rule of international monopoly capital and put them on the course of capitalism. This is their long-term, fundamental strategy. In recent years, they stepped up the implementation of this strategy by making use of some policy mistakes and temporary economic difficulties in socialist countries.

In our country, there was a tiny handful of people both inside and outside the Party who stubbornly clung to their position of bourgeois liberalization and went in for political conspiracy. Echoing the strategy of Western countries, they colluded with foreign forces, ganged up themselves at home and made ideological, public opinion and organizational preparations for years to stir up turmoils in China, overthrow the leadership by the Communist Party and subvert the socialist People's Republic. That is why the entire course of brewing, premeditating and launching the turmoil, including the use of varied means such as creating public opinion, distorting facts and spreading rumors, bore the salient feature of mutual support and coordination between a handful of people at home and abroad.

This report will mainly deal with the situation since the Third Plenary Session of the 13th Central Committee of the Chinese Communist Party. Last September, the Party Central Committee formulated the policy of improving the economic environment, straightening out the economic order and deepening the reform in an all-round way. This policy and the related measures won the support of the broad masses and students. The social order and political situation were basically stable. A good proof of this was the approval of Comrade Li Peng's government work report by an overwhelming majority (with a mere two votes against and four abstentions) at the National People's Congress in the spring of this year. Of course, the people and students raised many critical opinions against some mistakes committed by the Party and the government in their work, corruption among some government employees, unfair distribution and other social problems. At the same time, they made quite a few demands and proposals for promoting democracy, strengthening the legal system, deepening the reform and overcoming bureaucracy. These were normal phenomena. And the Party and government were also taking measures to solve them. At that time, however, there was indeed a tiny bunch of people in the Party and society who ganged up together and engaged in many very improper activities overtly and covertly.

What deserves special attention is that, after Comrade Zhao Ziyang's meeting with an American "ultra-liberal economist" on September 19 last year, some Hong Kong newspapers and journals, which were said to have close ties with Zhao Ziyang's "brain trust," gave enormous publicity to this and spread the political message that "Beijing is using Hongkong mass media to topple Deng and protect

Zhao." In his article entitled "Big Patriarch Should Retire" published in Hong Kong's *Economic Journal*, Li Yi (alias Qi Xin), editor-in-chief of the reactionary *Nineties* magazine, clamored for "removing the obstacle of super old man's politics" and "giving Zhao Ziyang enough power." Another article in the *Nineties* appealed to Zhao to be an "autocrat." Hongkong's *Emancipation* monthly also carried a lengthy article, saying that some people in Beijing had "overt or covert" relations with certain persons in Hongkong media circles, which "are sometimes dim and sometimes bright, just like a will-o'-the-wisp," and that such subtle relations now "have been newly proved by a drive of toppling Deng and protecting Zhao launched in the recent month." The article also said that "in terms of the hope of China turning capitalist, they settle on Zhao Ziyang." To coordinate with the drive to "topple Deng and protect Zhao," Beijing's *Economics Weekly* published a dialogue on the current situation between Yan Jiaqi (research fellow at the Institute of Political Science under the Chinese Academy of Social Sciences) who had close ties with Zhao Ziyang's former secretary Bao Tong, and another person. It attacked "the improvement of economic environment and the straightening out of economic order," saying that would lead to "stagnation." It also said that a big problem China was facing was "not to follow the old disastrous road of non-procedural change of power as in the case of Khrushchev and Liu Shaoqi." It is said that "non-procedural change of power as in the 'cultural revolution' will no longer be allowed in China." The essence of the dialogue was to whip up public opinion for covering up Zhao Ziyang's mistakes, keeping his position and power and pushing on bourgeois liberalization in an even more unbridled manner. This dialogue was reprinted in full or parts in Shanghai's *World Economic Herald,* Hong Kong's *Mirror* monthly and other newspapers and magazines at home and abroad.

Collaboration between forces at home and abroad intensified towards the end of last year and early this year. Political assemblies, joint petitions, big- and small-character posters and other activities emerged, expressing fully erroneous or even reactionary viewpoints. For instance, a big seminar "Future China and the World" was sponsored by the "Beijing University Future Studies Society" on December 7 last year. Jin Guantao, deputy chief editor of the *Toward the Future* book series and advisor to the society, said in his speech "attempts at socialism and their failure constitute one of the two major legacies of the 20th century." Ge Yang, chief editor of the fortnightly *New Observer*, immediately stood up to "provide evidence," in the name of "the eldest" among the participants and a Party member of dozens of years' standing, saying "Jin's negation of socialism is not harsh enough, but a bit too polite." On January 28 this year, Su Shaozhi (research fellow at the Institute of Marxism-Leninism-Mao Zedong Thought under the Chinese Academy of Social Sciences), Fang Lizhi and the like organized a so-called "neo-enlightenment salon" at the Dule Bookstore in Beijing, which was attended by more than 100 people, among them the Beijing-based American, French, and Italian correspondents as well as Chinese. Fang described this gathering as "smelling of strong gunpowder" and "taking a completely critical attitude to the authorities." He also said "what we need now is action" and professed to "take to the street after holding three sessions in a row." In early February, Fang Lizhi, Chen Jun (member of the reactionary organization Chinese Alliance for Democracy) and others sponsored a so-called "winter jasmine get-together of famed personalities" at the Friendship Hotel, where Fang made a speech primarily on the two major issues of "democracy" and "human rights," and Chen drew a parallel between the May Fourth Movement and the "democracy wall at Xidan." Fang expressed the "hope that entrepreneurs, as China's new rising force, will join force with the advanced intellectuals in the fight for democracy." At a press conference he gave for foreign correspondents on February 16, Chen Jun handed out Fang Lizhi's letter addressed to Deng Xiaoping and another letter from Chen himself and 32 others to the Standing Committee of the National People's Congress (NPC) and the Central Committee of the Chinese Communist Party (CPC), calling for amnesty and the release of Wei Jingsheng and other so-called "political prisoners" who had gravely violated the criminal law. On February 23, the Taiwan *United Daily News* carried an article headlined "Beginning of a Major Movement —a Mega-Shock." It said, "A declaration was issued in New York, and open letters surfaced in Beijing; as the thunder of spring rumbles across the Divine Land (China), waves for democracy are rising." On February 26, Zhang Xianyang (research fellow at the Institute of Marxism-Leninism-Mao Zedong Thought under the Chinese Academy of Social Sciences), Li Honglin (research fellow at the Fujian Academy of Social Sciences), Bao Zunxin (associate research fellow at the Institute of Chinese History under the Chinese Academy of Social Sciences), Ge Yang and 38 others, jointly wrote a letter to the CPC Central Committee, calling for the release of so-called "political prisoners."

Afterwards, a vast number of big- and small-character posters and assemblies came out on the campuses of some universities in Beijing, attacking the Communist Party and the socialist system. On March 1, for example, a big-character poster entitled "Denunciation of Deng Xiaoping—a letter to the nation" was put up at Qinghua University and Beijing University simultaneously. The poster uttered such nonsense as "the politics of the Communist Party consists of empty talk, coercive power, autocratic rule and arbitrary decision," and openly demanded "dismantling parties and abandoning the Four Cardinal Principles (adherence to the socialist road, to the people's democratic dictatorship, to the leadership by the Communist Party and to Marxism-Leninism and Mao Zedong Thought)." A small-character poster entitled "Deplore the Chinese" turned up in Beijing University of March 2, demanding the overthrow of "totalitarianism" and "autocracy." On March 3, there appeared in Qinghua University and other universities and colleges a "Letter to the Mass of Students" signed by the "Preparatory Committee of the China Democratic Youth Patriotic Association," urging students to join in the "turbulent current for 'democracy, freedom and human rights' under the leadership of the patriotic democratic fighter, Fang Lizhi." On the campuses of Beijing University and other schools of higher learning on March 29, there was extensive posting of Fang's article "China's disappointment and hope" written for the Hongkong *Ming Pao Daily News*. In the article, Fang claimed that socialism had "completely lost its attraction" and there was the need to form political "pressure groups" to carry out "reforms for political democracy and economic freedom." But what he termed as "reform" actually is a synonym of total Westernization. The big-character poster, "Call of the Times" that came out in Beijing University of April 6, questioned in a way of complete negation "whether there is any rationale now for socialism to exist" and "whether Marxism-Leninism fits the realities of China after all." On April 13, the Beijing Institute of Post and Telecommunications and some other schools received a "Message to the Nation's College Students" signed by the Guangxi University Students' Union, which called on students to "hold high the portrait of Hu Yaobang and the great banner of 'democracy, freedom, dignity and rule by law'" in celebration of the May Fourth Youth Day.

Meanwhile, so-called "democratic salon," "freedom forum" and various kinds of "seminars," "conferences" and "lectures" mushroomed in Beijing's institutions of higher learning. The "democratic salon" presided over by Wang Dan, a Beijing University student, sponsored 17 lectures in one year, indicative of its frequent activities. They invited Ren Wanding, head of the defunct illegal "Human Rights League," over to spread a lot of fallacies about the so-called "new-authoritarianism and democratic politics." At one point they held a seminar in front of the Statue of Cervantes, openly crying to "abolish the one-party system, force the Communist Party to step down and topple the present regime." They also invited Li Shuxian, the wife of Fang Lizhi, to be their "advisor." Li fanned the flames by urging them to "legalize the democratic salon," "hold meetings here frequently," and "abolish the Beijing Municipality's ten-article regulations on demonstrations."

All this prepared, in terms of ideology and organization, for the turmoil that ensued. A *Ming Pao Daily News* article commented: "The contact-building and petition-signing activities for human rights initiated by the elite of Chinese intellectuals exerted enormous influence on students. They had long ago planned a large-scale move on the 70th anniversary of the May Fourth Movement to express their dissatisfaction with the authorities. The sudden death of Hu Yaobang literally threw a match into a barrel of gunpowder." In short, as a result of the premeditation, organization and engineering by a small handful of people, a political situation already emerged in which "the rising wind forebodes a coming storm."

Two. Student unrest was exploited by organizers of the turmoil from the very beginning.

Comrade Hu Yaobang's death on April 15 prompted an early outbreak of the long-brewing student unrest and turmoil. The broad masses and students mourned Comrade Hu Yaobang and expressed their profound grief. Universities and colleges provided facilities for the mourning on the part of the students. However, a small number of people took advantage of this to oppose the leadership of the Communist Party and the socialist system under the pretext of "mourning." Student unrest was manipulated and exploited by a small handful of people from the very beginning and bore the nature of political turmoil.

This turmoil found expression first in the wanton attack and slanders against the Party and the government and the open call to overthrow the leadership of the Communist Party and subvert the present government as contained in the large quantity of big- and small-character posters, slogans, leaflets and elegiac couplets. Some of the posters on the campuses of Beijing University, Qinghua University and other schools abused the Communist Party as "a party of conspirators" and "an organization on the verge of collapse"; some attacked the older generation of revolutionaries as "decaying men administering affairs of the state" and "autocrats with a concentration of power"; some attacked by name the Chinese leaders one by one, saying that "the man who should not die has passed away while those who should die remain alive"; some called for "dissolving the incompetent government and overthrowing autocratic monarchy"; some demanded the "abolition of the Chinese Communist Party and adoption of the multi-party system" and "dissolving of party branches and removal of political workers in the mass organizations, armed forces, schools, and other units;" some issued a "declaration on private ownership," calling on people to "sound the death knell of public ownership at an early date and greet a new future for the Republic;" some went so far as to "invite the Kuomintang back to the mainland and establish two-party politics," etc. Many big- and small-character posters used disgusting language to slander Comrade Deng Xiaoping, clamoring "down with Deng Xiaoping."

This turmoil, from the very beginning, was manifested by a sharp conflict between bourgeois liberalization and the Four Cardinal Principles. Of the programatic slogans raised by the organizers of the turmoil at the time, either the "nine demands" first raised through Wang Dan, leader of an illegal student organization, in Tiananmen Square or the "seven demands" and "ten demands" raised later, there were two principal demands: one was to reappraise Comrade Hu Yaobang's merits and demerits; the other was to completely negate the fight against bourgeois liberalization and rehabilitate the so-called "wronged citizens" in the fight. The essence of the two demands was to gain absolute freedom in China to oppose the Four Cardinal Principles and realize capitalism.

Echoing these demands, some so-called "elitists" in academic circles, that is, the very small number of people stubbornly clinging to their position of bourgeois liberalization, organized a variety of forums during the period and indulged in unbridled propaganda through the press. Most outstanding among the activities was a forum sponsored by the *World Economic Herald* and the *New Observer* in

Beijing on April 19. The forum was chaired by Ge Yang and its participants included Yan Jiaqi, Su Shaozhi, Chen Ziming (director of the Beijing Institute of Socioeconomic Science), and Liu Ruishao (head of the Hongkong *Wen Wei Po's* Beijing office). Their main topics were also two: one was to "rehabilitate" Hu Yaobang; the other was to "reverse" the verdict on the fight against bourgeois liberalization. They expressed unequivocal support for the student demonstrations, saying that they saw from there "China's future and hope." Later, when the Shanghai Municipal Party Committee made the correct decision on straightening things out in the *World Economic Herald*, Comrade Zhao Ziyang, who consistently winked at bourgeois liberalization, refrained from backing the decision. Instead he criticized the Shanghai Municipal Party Committee for "making a mess of it" and "landing itself in a passive position."

This turmoil also found expression in the fact that, instigated and engineered by the small handful of people, many acts were crude violations of the constitution, laws and regulations of the People's Republic of China and gravely running counter to democracy and the legal system. They put up big-character posters en masse on the campuses in disregard of the fact that the provision in the constitution on "four big freedoms" (speaking out freely, airing views fully, holding great debates and writing big-character posters) had been abrogated; and turning a deaf ear to all persuasion they staged large-scale demonstrations day after day in disregard of the 10-article regulations on demonstrations issued by the Standing Committee of the Beijing Municipal People's Congress; late on the night of April 18 and 19, they assaulted Xinhuamen, headquarters of the Party Central Committee and the State Council, and shouted "down with the Communist Party," something which never occurred even during the Cultural Revolution; they violated the regulations for the management of Tiananmen Square and occupied the square by force several times, one consequence of which was that the memorial meeting for Comrade Hu Yaobang was almost interrupted on April 22; ignoring the relevant regulations of the Beijing Municipality and without registration, they formed an illegal organization, "Solidarity Student Union" (later changed into "Federation of Autonomous Student Unions in Universities and Colleges"), and "seized power" from the lawful student unions and postgraduate unions formed through democratic election; disregarding law and school discipline, they took by force school offices and broadcasting stations and did things as they wished, creating anarchy on the campuses.

Another important means that the small number of turmoil organizers and plotters used was to fabricate a spate of rumors to confuse people's minds and agitate the masses. At the beginning of the student unrest, they spread the rumor that "Li Peng scolded Hu Yaobang at a Political Bureau meeting and Hu died of anger." The rumor was meant to spearhead the attack at Comrade Li Peng. In fact, the meeting focused on the question of education. When Comrade Li Tieying, member of the Political Bureau, state councillor and minister in charge of the State Education Commission, was making an explanation of a relevant document, Comrade Hu Yaobang suffered a sudden heart attack. Hu was given emergency treatment right in the meeting room and was rushed to a hospital when his conditions allowed. There was definitely no such thing as Hu flying into a rage.

On the night of April 19, a foreign language student of Beijing Teachers' University was run down by a trolley-bus on her way back to school after attending a party. She died despite treatment. Some people spread the rumor that "a car of the Communist Party's armed police knocked a student down and killed her," which stirred up the emotions of some students who did not know the truth.

In the small hours of April 20, policemen whisked away those students who had blocked and assaulted Xinhuamen, and sent them back to Beijing University by bus. Some people concocted the rumor of "April 20 bloody incident," alleging that the "police beat people at Xinhuamen, not only students, but also workers, women and children," and that "more than 1,000 scientists and technicians fell in blood." This further agitated some people.

On April 22, when Li Peng and other leading comrades left the Great Hall of the People at the end of the memorial meeting for Comrade Hu Yaobang, some people perpetrated a fraud with the objective of working out an excuse for attacking Comrade Li Peng. First they started the rumor that "Premier Li Peng promised to come out at 12:45 and receive students in the square." Then they let three students kneel on the steps outside the east gate of the Great Hall of the People to hand in a "petition." After awhile they said, "Li Peng went back on his word and refused to receive us. He has deceived the students." This assertion fanned strong indignation among the tens of thousands of students in Tiananmen Square and almost led to a serious incident of assaulting the Great Hall of the People.

Rumor-mongering greatly sharpened students' antagonism toward the government. Using this antagonism, a very small number of people put up the slogan: "The government pays no heed to our peaceful petition. Let's make the matter known across the country and call for a nationwide class boycott." This led to the serious situation in which 60,000 university students boycotted class in Beijing and many students in other parts of China followed suit. The student unrest escalated and the turmoil expanded.

This turmoil was marked by another characteristic, that is, it was no longer confined to institutions of higher learning or the Beijing area; it spread to the whole of society and to all parts of China. After the memorial meeting for Comrade Hu Yaobang, a number of people went to contact middle schools, factories, shops and villages, made speeches in the streets, handed out leaflets, put up slogans and raised money, doing everything possible to make the situation worse. The slogan "Oppose the Chinese Communist Party" and the big-character poster "Long live class boycott and exam boycott" appeared in some middle schools. Leaflets "Unite with the workers and peasants, down with the despotic rule" were put up in some factories. Organizers and plotters of the turmoil advanced the slogan "Go to the south, the north, the east and the west" in a bid to establish ties throughout the country. Students from Beijing were seen in universities and colleges in Nanjing, Wuhan, Xian, Changsha, Shanghai and Harbin, while students from Tianjin, Hebei, Anhui and Zhejiang took part in demonstrations in Beijing. Criminal activities of beating, smashing, looting and burning took place in Changsha and Xi'an.

Political forces outside the Chinese mainland and in foreign countries had a hand in the turmoil from the very beginning. Hu Ping, Chen Jun and Liu Xiaobo, members of the Chinese Alliance for Democracy which is a reactionary organization groomed by the Kuomintang, wrote "An Open Letter" from New York to Chinese university students, urging them to "consolidate the organizational links established in the student unrest and strive to carry out activities effectively in the form of a strong mass body." The letter told the students to "effect a breakthrough by thoroughly negating the 1987 movement against liberalization," "strengthen contacts with the mass media," "increase contacts with various circles in society" and "enlist their support and participation in the movement." Wang Bingzhang and Tang Guangzhong, two leaders of the Chinese Alliance for Democracy, made a hasty flight from New York to Tokyo in an attempt to reach Beijing and have a direct hand in the turmoil.

A number of Chinese intellectuals residing abroad who advocate instituting the Western capitalist system in China invited Fang Lizhi to take the lead, and cabled from Columbia University a "Declaration on Promoting Democratic Politics on the Chinese Mainland," asserting that "the people must have the right to choose the ruling party" in a bid to incite people to overthrow the Communist Party.

Someone in the US, using the name of "Hong Yan," sent in by fax "ten pieces of opinions on revising the constitution," suggesting that deputies to the national and local people's congresses as well as judges in all courts should be elected from among candidates without party affiliation," in an attempt to keep the Communist Party completely out of the state organs of power and judicial organs.

Some members of the former *China Spring* journal residing in the United States hastily founded a China Democratic Party. They sent a "Letter addressed to the entire nation" to some universities in Beijing, inciting students to "demand that the conservative bureaucrats step down" and "urge the Chinese Communist Party to end its autocratic rule."

Reactionary political forces in Hongkong, Taiwan, the United States and other Western countries were also involved in the turmoil through various channels and by different means. Western news agencies showed unusual zeal. The Voice of America, in particular, aired news in three programs beamed to the Chinese mainland for a total of more than ten hours every day, spreading rumors, stirring up trouble and adding fuel to the turmoil.

Facts listed above show that we were confronted not with student unrest in its normal sense but with a planned, organized and premeditated political turmoil designed to negate the Communist Party leadership and the socialist system. It had clear-cut political ends and deviated from the orbit of democracy and legality, employing base political means to incite large numbers of students and other people who did not know the truth. If we failed to analyze and see the problem in essence, we would have committed grave mistakes and landed ourselves in an extremely passive position in the struggle.

Three. People's Daily *April 26 editorial was correct in determining the nature of the turmoil.*

From the death of Comrade Hu Yaobang on April 15 to the conclusion of the memorial service on April 22, Comrade Zhao Ziyang all along tolerated and connived at the increasingly evident signs of the turmoil during the period of the mourning, thus facilitating the formation and development of the turmoil. In the face of the increasingly grave situation, many comrades in the central leadership and Beijing municipality felt that the nature of the matter had changed, and repeatedly suggested to Comrade Zhao Ziyang that the central leadership should adopt a clear-cut policy and measures to quickly check the development of the situation. But, Zhao kept avoiding making a serious analysis and discussion on the nature of the matter. At the end of the memorial meeting for Comrade Hu Yaobang, comrades in the central leadership again suggested to Zhao that a meeting be held before his visit to the Democratic People's Republic of Korea on April 23. Instead of accepting this suggestion, Zhao went golfing as if nothing had happened. Owing to such an attitude, the Party and the government lost a chance to quell the turmoil.

On the afternoon of April 24, the Beijing Municipal Party Committee and people's government reported to Comrade Wan Li. At his proposal, members of the Standing Committee of the Political Bureau held a meeting that evening presided over by Comrade Li Peng, to analyze and study seriously the development of the situation. A consensus was reached that all signs at that time showed we were confronted with an anti-Party and anti-socialist political struggle conducted in a planned and organized way and manipulated and instigated by a small handful of people. The meeting decided that a group for quelling the turmoil be established in the central leadership, requiring at the same time the Beijing Municipal Party Committee and people's government to mobilize the masses fully, to win over the majority so as to isolate the minority and to strive to put down the turmoil and stabilize the situation as soon as possible.

In the following morning, Comrade Deng Xiaoping made an important speech, expressing his full agreement and support of the decision of the Political Bureau Standing Committee and making an incisive analysis of the nature of the turmoil. He pointed out sharply that this was not a case of ordinary student unrest, but a political turmoil aimed at negating the leadership of the Communist Party and the socialist system. Deng's speech greatly enhanced the understanding of the cadres and increased their confidence and courage in quelling the turmoil and stabilizing the overall situation.

The *People's Daily* editorial on April 26 embodied the decision of the Political Bureau Standing Committee and the spirit of Comrade Deng Xiaoping's speech, and pointed out the nature of the turmoil. At the same time, it made a clear distinction between the tiny handful of people who organized and plotted the turmoil and the vast number of students. The editorial made the overwhelming majority of the cadres feel reassured. It clarified the orientation of their activities, thus enabling them to carry out their work with a clear-cut stand.

After the editorial of the *People's Daily* was published, the Beijing Municipal Party Committee and people's government, under the direct leadership of the Chinese Communist Party's Central Committee and the State Council, convened in quick succession a variety of meetings inside and outside the Party to uphold the principle and unify their understanding, then proceeded to clear up rumors and reassure the public by any means, render support to the leadership, Party and Youth League members and student activists in educational institutions, encourage them to work boldly, and persuade those students who took part in demonstrations to change their course of actions, and actively conduct a variety of dialogues to win over the masses. The dialogues, whether conducted by the State Council spokesman Yuan Mu and other comrades with the students or by leaders of relevant central departments with the students and principal leaders of the Beijing Municipal Party Committee and people's government with the students, all achieved good results.

Meanwhile, earnest work was being carried out in the factories, villages, shops, primary and secondary schools and neighborhoods to stabilize the overall situation and prevent the turmoil from spreading to other sectors of society. Various provinces, municipalities and autonomous regions also did a good job in their respective localities according to the spirit of the editorial to prevent the influence of Beijing's situation from spreading to other parts of the country.

The clear-cut stand of the April 26 editorial forced the organizers and plotters of the turmoil to make an about-face in strategy. Before the publication of the editorial, large numbers of posters and slogans were against the Communist Party, socialism and the Four Cardinal Principles. After the publication of the editorial, the illegal Beijing Federation of Autonomous Student Unions in Universities and Colleges, issued on April 26 Bao Tong's "No. 1 Order of the New Student Federation" to change their strategy, urging students to "march to Tiananmen under the banner of supporting the Communist Party" on April 27. The designated slogans included "Support the Communist Party", "Support socialism" and "Safeguard the constitution." It also, at the suggestion of Fang Lizhi, changed the subversive slogans as "Down with the bureaucratic government,"

"Down with the corrupt government," "Down with the dictatorial rule," etc. into those like "Oppose bureaucracy, oppose corruption and oppose privilege," and other slogans that could win support from people of various circles.

The Japanese Jiji News Agency then dispatched from Beijing a news story entitled "Young Officials Form a Pro-Democracy Group," describing some figures in the so-called "Zhao Ziyang's brain trust" as "young officials of the Chinese Communist Party's Central Committee and the government," noting that they "made frequent contacts with representatives of the new autonomous student unions in Beijing's universities and colleges including Beijing University, Qinghua University, People's University and Beijing Normal University, which took part in the demonstrations, and offered advice to the students." It also said that during the mass demonstration on April 27, the students held "placards of 'Supporting socialism' and 'Supporting the leadership of the Communist Party' at the instruction of the same group."

Leaders of the student demonstrations originally planned to stage "a hundred-day demonstration and a student strike of indefinite duration." But the students lost such enthusiasm after the publication of the editorial.

Compared with the demonstration on April 27, the number of students taking part on May 4 dropped from over 30,000 to less than 20,000, and the onlookers also decreased by a big margin. After the May 4 demonstration, 80 percent of the students returned to class as a result of the work of the Party and administrative leaders of various universities and colleges. After the publication of the *People's Daily* April 26 editorial, the situation in other parts of the country also became stabilized quickly. It was evident that with some more work, the turmoil, instigated by a small handful of people making use of the student unrest, was likely to calm down. A host of facts showed that the *People's Daily* April 26 editorial was correct and played its role in stabilizing the situation in the capital and the whole country as well.

Four. Comrade Zhao Ziyang's speech on May 4 was the turning point in escalating the turmoil.

When the turmoil was about to subside, Comrade Zhao Ziyang, as General Secretary of the Chinese Communist Party, adopted a capricious attitude of going back on his words. At first, when members of the Political Bureau's Standing Committee solicited his opinion during his visit to Korea, he cabled back and explicitly expressed "full agreement with the policy decision made by Comrade Deng Xiaoping on handling the current turmoil." After he returned on April 30, he once again expressed at a meeting of the Political Bureau's Standing Committee his agreement with Comrade Deng Xiaoping's speech and the determination of the nature of the turmoil as made in the April 26 editorial, and maintained that the handling of the student unrest in the previous period was appropriate.

A few days later, however, when he met with representatives attending the annual meeting of the Asian Development Bank on the afternoon of May 4, he expressed a whole set of views diametrically opposed to the decision of the Political Bureau's Standing Committee, to Comrade Deng Xiaoping's speech and to the spirit of the editorial. Firstly, as the turmoil had already come to the surface, he said "there will be no big turmoil in China;" secondly, when a host of facts had proved that the real nature of the turmoil was the negation of the leadership of the Communist Party and the socialist system, he still insisted that "they are by no means opposed to our fundamental system. Rather they are asking us to correct mistakes in our work;" thirdly, although facts had shown that a tiny handful of people was making use of the student unrest to instigate turmoil, he merely said that it was "hardly avoidable" for "some people to take advantage of this," thus totally negating the correct judgment of the Party's Central Committee that a handful of people were creating turmoil.

This speech of Comrade Zhao Ziyang's was prepared by Bao Tong beforehand. Bao asked the Central Broadcasting Station and CCTV to broadcast the speech that very afternoon and repeat it for three days running. He also asked the *People's Daily* to frontpage the speech the following day and to carry a large number of positive responses from various sectors. Differing views were held up and not even allowed to appear in confidential materials. Comrade Zhao Ziyang's speech, publicized through the *People's Daily* and certain newspapers, created serious ideological confusion among the cadres and the masses and inflated the arrogance of the organizers and plotters of the turmoil.

The great difference between Comrade Zhao Ziyang's speech and the policy of the Party Central Committee not only evoked much comment at home but was also seen clearly by the media abroad. A

Reuter dispatch said that Zhao's remarks constituted a sharp contrast to the severe condemnation of students a week earlier and that it was a major revision of the previous week's judgment. An article in *Le Monde* on May 6 stated that it seemed that the Party chief (referring to Zhao Ziyang) remarkably turned the development of the situation to his advantage.

After the speech was thrown into the open, leading officials at various levels, the Party and Youth League members and the activists among the masses, particularly those working in universities and colleges—all became confused. They were at a loss what to do and many voiced their objection. Some asked, "There are two voices in the central leadership. Who is right and who is wrong? Whom are we supposed to follow?" Some queried, "We are required to maintain identical views with the central leadership, but with which one?" Others complained, "Zhao Ziyang plays the good guy at the top while we play the villains of the grassroots." Cadres in universities and colleges and student activists as a whole felt being "betrayed" and troubled from a laden heart, some even shed tears. Work at the universities and colleges completely stagnated.

At that time, the Beijing Municipal Party Committee and people's government were also in an agonizing situation. Although they knew opinions differed in the central leadership, they had to say against their will that the central leadership was unanimous and they only stressed different points. They had to ask the central leadership for instructions on many things, but Comrade Zhao Ziyang, as General Secretary, was reluctant to call a meeting. Under the strong demand of the Beijing Municipal Party Committee and people's government, a meeting was convened on May 8. But Zhao refused to hear the briefing of the Beijing authorities. At the meeting some comrades said Comrade Zhao Ziyang's speech on May 4 was not in accord with the spirit of the April 26 editorial. Zhao sternly retorted, "I'll be responsible for what was wrong in my speech." At another meeting, when someone said that comrades at the grassroots complained that they "had been betrayed," Comrade Zhao Ziyang rebuked, "Who betrayed you? People were betrayed only during the "Cultural Revolution." In those days, quite a few people echoing Hongkong and Taiwan newspapers, repeatedly attacked the comrades in Beijing Municipal Party Committee and the people's government who were working at the front lines. Hooligans yelled in the demonstrations: "The Beijing Municipal Party Committee is guilty of making false reports to deceive the central leadership." In face of the worsening situation, certain contemplated measures could not be implemented.

In contrast to the above, organizers and plotters of the turmoil were encouraged by Comrade Zhao Ziyang's speech. Yan Jiaqi, Cao Siyuan (director of the Research and Development Institute of the Stone Company) and others said that "things have turned for the better. It is necessary to mobilize the intellectuals to support Zhao Ziyang." Zhang Xianyang said: "Aren't we supposed to make use of the students? Zhao Ziyang is now doing just this."

Egged on by Comrade Zhao Ziyang and plotted by a few others, leaders of the Autonomous Student Unions of Beijing University and Beijing Normal University declared resumption of the class boycott that night. Many other universities followed suit and organized "pickets" to prevent students from going to the classroom.

After that, a new wave of demonstrations surged ahead. On May 9, several hundred journalists from more than 30 press units took to the streets and submitted a petition. About 10,000 students from a dozen universities including Beijing, Qinghua and People's universities, Beijing Normal University and the China University of Political Science and Law, staged a demonstration, supporting the journalists, distributing leaflets and calling for continued class boycott and a hunger strike.

Henceforth, the situation took an abrupt turn for the worse and the turmoil was pushed to a new height. Influenced by the situation in Beijing, the already calmed-down situation in other parts of China became tense again. Shortly after Comrade Zhao Ziyang's speech, a large number of student demonstrators assaulted the office buildings of the Shanxi Provincial Party Committee and Provincial Government in Taiyuan on May 9 and 10. They also assaulted the ongoing International Economic and Technological Cooperation Fair, the Import and Export Commodities Fair and the Folk Arts Festival. The above incidents exerted very bad influence both at home and abroad.

Five. The hunger strike was used as coercion to escalate the turmoil.

Good and honest people asked if the lack of understanding, consideration and concession on the part of the government had brought the students to make so much trouble?

Facts are just the opposite.

From the very beginning of the turmoil, the Party and government fully acknowledged the students' patriotism and their concern about the country and people. Their demands to promote democracy, promote reform, punish official profiteers and fight corruption were acknowledged as identical with the aspirations of the Party and government, which also expressed the hope of solving the problems through normal democratic and legal procedures.

But such good aspirations failed to win active response. The government proposed to increase understanding and reach consensus through dialogues of various channels, levels and forms.

The illegal student organization, however, put forward very strict conditions for terms of the dialogue. They demanded that their partners in the dialogues "must be people holding positions at or above the Standing Committee member of the Political Bureau of the Party Central Committee, vice-chairman of the NPC Standing Committee and vice-premier"; "a joint communique on every dialogue must be published and signed by both parties"; and dialogues should be "held in locations designated in turn by representatives of the government and students."

These were nothing like a dialogue, but stage-setting for political negotiations with the Party and government.

Especially after Comrade Zhao Ziyang's speech on May 4, a very small number of people took this as an opportunity, regarding the restraint on the part of the Party and government as a sign of weakness. They put forward harsher terms, adding increasing heat to the turmoil and escalating it.

Even under such circumstances, the Party and government still took the attitude of utmost tolerance and restraint, with the hope to continue to maintain the channels for the dialogue in order to educate the masses and win over the majority.

At two o'clock in the early morning of May 13, leaders of the Federation of Autonomous Student Unions in Universities and Colleges raised the demand for a dialogue, which was accepted two hours later by the General Office of the Party Central Committee and that of the State Council.

However, the students ate their own words and canceled the dialogue at daybreak. On the morning of May 13, the Bureau for Letters and Visits of the General Offices of the Party Central Committee, the State Council and the National People's Congress Standing Committee again notified them of the decision to hold the dialogue with students on May 15.

Despite their agreement, the students began their maneuvering regarding the number of participants in the dialogue.

After the government agreed to their first proposed list of 20 names, they demanded the number be raised to 200.

Without waiting for further discussion, they went on to condemn "the government's insincerity about dialogue." Only four hours after they were informed of the dialogue, they hastily made public the long-prepared "hunger strike declaration," launching a seven-day fast that involved more than 3,000 people and a long occupation of the Tiananmen Square afterward.

May 13 was chosen as the starting date of the hunger strike "to put pressure on them by way of Gorbachev's China visit," said Wang Dan, leader of the "federation."

The very small number of people who organized and plotted the turmoil used the fasting students as "hostages" and their lives as a ploy to blackmail the government by vile means, making the turmoil more serious.

During the student hunger strike, the Party and government maintained an attitude of utmost restraint and did everything they could in various areas. First of all, staff members of various universities and leading officials at all levels and even Party and state leaders went to Tiananmen Square to see the fasting students on many occasions and gave them ideological advice.

Secondly, efforts were made to help the Red Cross Society mobilize more than 100 ambulances and several hundred medical workers to keep watch at the fasting site day and night; 52 hospitals were asked to have some 2,000 beds ready so that students who suffered shock or illness because of the hunger strike could get first-aid and timely treatment.

Thirdly, all sorts of materials were provided to alleviate the sufferings of the fasting students and ensure their safety.

The Beijing Municipal Party Committee and people's government mobilized cadres, workers and vehicles to provide the fasting students with drinking water, edible salt and sugar via the Red Cross Society day and night.

The Municipal Environment Sanitation Bureau sent sprinklers and offered basins and towels for the fasting students.

Adequate supplies of medicine to prevent sunstroke, cold, and diarrhea were provided by pharmaceutical companies and distributed by the Red Cross Society.

The provisions department sent a large amount of soft drinks and bread to be used during emergency rescue of the students.

A total of 6,000 straw hats were provided by commercial units and 1,000 quilts were sent by the Beijing Military Area Command, in response to the city authorities' request, to protect the fasting students from heat in the day and cold at night.

To keep the hunger strike site clean, makeshift flush toilets were set up and sanitation workers cleaned the site at midnight. Before the torrential rain on May 18, 78 coaches from the public transport company and 400 thick boards from the materials bureau were sent to protect the fasting students from rain and dampness. No fasting student died in the seven-day hunger strike.

But all this failed to get any positive response. Facts told people time and time again that the very small number of organizers and plotters of the turmoil were determined to oppose us to the very end and that the problem could not be solved even with tolerance on 1,000 occasions and 10,000 concessions. It needs to be pointed out in particular that Comrade Zhao Ziyang failed to do what he should have when the situation quickly deteriorated, but instead stirred up the press with a wrong guidance for the public opinion, making the deteriorated situation more difficult to handle.

In his May 6 meeting with Comrades Hu Qili and Rui Xingwen, both then in charge of propaganda and ideological work in the Central Committee, Comrade Zhao Ziyang said, the press "has opened up a bit and there have been reports about the demonstrations. There is no big risk to open up a bit by reporting the demonstrations and increase the openness of news." He even said: "Confronted with the will of the people at home and the progressive trend worldwide, we could only guide our actions according to circumstances."

Here, he even described the adverse current against the Chinese Communist Party and socialism as "will of the people at home" and "progressive trend worldwide."

His instructions were passed on to major news media units in the capital the same day and many arrangements were made afterwards.

As a result, the *People's Daily* and many other national newspapers and periodicals adopted an attitude of full acknowledgement and active support to the demonstrations, sit-in and hunger strike, devoting lengthy coverage with no less exaggeration. Even some Hongkong newspapers expressed their surprise over this unique phenomenon.

Under the wrong guidance of the public opinion, the number of people who took to the streets to support the students increased day by day as their momentum grew since May 15. The number of people involved grew from tens of thousands to a hundred thousand and several hundred thousand in addition to the 200,000 students who came from other parts of the country to show their support for the fasting students.

For a time, it looked as if refusal to join in the demonstrations was "unpatriotic" and refusal to show support was equal to "indifference to the survival of the students."

Under such circumstances, the fasting students were put on the back of the tiger and found it difficult to get off. Many parents of the students and teachers wrote to or called leading organs, press organizations, radio and TV stations, asking them not to force the fasting students on to the path of death and show mercy in saving the children and stopping this kind of "killing by creating public opinion."

But this did not work. The students' hunger strike and the residents' demonstrations threw social order in Beijing into a mess and seriously disrupted the Sino-Soviet summit which was closely followed worldwide, forcing some changes on the agenda, with some activities even canceled.

Meanwhile, demonstrations in various major cities throughout China and even all provincial capitals registered a drastic increase in the number of people involved, while people also took to the streets in some small and medium-sized cities, producing a large scale of involvement and a serious disturbance never seen since the founding of the People's Republic.

In order to back up the students and add fuel to the flames of turmoil, some so-called "elitists" who took a stubborn stand for bourgeois liberalization threw away all disguises and came out to the front.

On the evening of May 13, the big-character poster "We can no longer remain silent," written by Yan Jiaqi, Su Shaozhi, Bao Zunxin and others appeared at Beijing University urging intellectuals to take part in the big demonstrations they had sponsored to support the students' hunger strike.

On May 14, "Urgent appeal for the current situation" was jointly made by 12 people including Yan Jiaqi, Bao Zunxin, Li Honglin, Dai Qing (reporter with the *Guangming Daily*), Yu Haocheng (former director of the Mass Publishing House), Li Zehou (research fellow at the Philosophy Institute of the Chinese Academy of Social Sciences), Su Xiaokang (lecturer at the Beijing Broadcasting Institute), Wen Yuankai (professor at the China University of Science and

Technology), and Liu Zaifu (president of the Literature Institute under the Chinese Academy of Social Sciences). They demanded that the turmoil be declared a "patriotic democratic movement" and the illegal student organization be declared legal, saying that they would also take part in the hunger strike if these demands were not met. This appeal was published on *Guangming Daily* and broadcast on the China Central Television. These people also went to Tiananmen Square many times to make speeches and agitate. They slandered our government as "incompetent," saying that through the fasting students, "China's bright future can be envisioned."

Then these people formed the illegal Beijing Union of Intellectuals and published the "'May 16' Declaration," threatening with counter-charges that "a promising China might be led into the abyss of real turmoil" if the government did not accept the political demands of the very small number of people.

As the situation became increasingly serious, Comrade Zhao Ziyang used the opportunity of meeting Gorbachev on May 16, deliberately directing the fire of criticism at Comrade Deng Xiaoping and making the situation even worse.

Right at the beginning of the meeting, he said: "Comrade Deng Xiaoping's helmsmanship is still needed for the most important issues. Since the 13th National Party Congress, we have always reported to Comrade Deng Xiaoping and asked for his advice while dealing with the most important issues." He also said that this was the first public disclosure of the "decision" by the Communist Party of China.

On the following day, Yan Jiaqi, Bao Zunxin and others published their most furious and vicious "'May 17' Declaration." They slandered by saying "Because the autocrat controls the unlimited power, the government has lost its own obligation and normal human feelings" and "despite Qing Dynasty's death 76 years ago, there is still an emperor in China though without such a title, a senile and fatuous autocrat." "General Secretary Zhao Ziyang declared publicly yesterday afternoon that all decisions in China must be approved by this decrepit autocrat." They said without any disguise in their hoarse voices, "Gerontocratic politics must end and the autocrat must resign."

Some newspapers and periodicals in Hongkong and Taiwan echoed their reactionary clamor. The Hongkong newspaper *Express* published an article on May 18 entitled "Down with Deng and Li but Not Zhao," saying, "Zhao Ziyang's speech was full of hints that the foul atmosphere at home now was caused by Deng Xiaoping's helmsmanship"; "at present the masses are eager to get rid of Deng and Li, while Zhao's role is almost open upon calling." It also added, *"It is a good news for Hongkong if Deng could be successfully ousted and China's reform embark on the path of legal rule with the realization of democracy."*

Against the backdrop of such screams, slogans smearing Comrade Deng Xiaoping and attacking Comrade Li Peng were all around. Some demanded "Deng Xiaoping step down" and "Li Peng step down to satisfy the people." Meanwhile slogans like "Support Zhao Ziyang," "Long live Zhao Ziyang" and "Promote Zhao Ziyang chairman of the Central Military Commission" could be seen and heard in the demonstrations and at Tiananmen Square.

Plotters of the turmoil attempted to use the chaos as an opportunity to seize power. They distributed leaflets, proclaiming the founding of the Preparatory Committee to the People's Conference of All Circles in Beijing to replace the Municipal People's Congress. A call was made to establish "Beijing regional government" to replace the legal Beijing Municipal People's Government. They attacked the State Council, which was formed in accordance with the law, as "pseudo-government." They also circulated rumors that the Ministry of Foreign Affairs and a dozen other ministries already "declared independence" from the State Council and that about 30 countries in the world broke diplomatic relations with our nation. After the rumor that "Deng Xiaoping has stepped down" was made, some went to demonstrations carrying a coffin, burned Comrade Xiaoping's effigy and set off firecrackers on Tiananmen Square to celebrate their "victory."

The situation in Beijing became increasingly serious, with anarchism viciously spreading and many areas sinking into complete chaos and white terror. If our Party and government did not take resolute measures under such circumstances, another vital chance would be missed and further irredeemable, great damages could be done. This would by no means be permitted by the broad masses of the people.

Six. The government had no alternative but to take the correct measure of declaring martial law in parts of Beijing.

To safeguard the social stability in the city of Beijing, to protect the safety of the lives and property of the citizens and ensure the normal functioning of the Party and government departments at the central level and of the Beijing Municipal Government, the State Council had no alternative but to declare martial law in parts of Beijing as empowered by Clause 16 of Article 89 of the Constitution of the People's Republic of China and at a time when police forces in Beijing were far too inadequate to maintain the normal production, work and living order. This was a resolute and correct decision.

The decision on taking resolute measures to stop the turmoil was announced at a meeting called by the central authorities and attended by cadres from the Party, government and military institutions in Beijing on May 19. Comrade Zhao Ziyang, persisting in his erroneous stand against the correct decision of the central authorities, neither agreed to speak at the meeting together with Comrade Li Peng, nor agreed to preside over the meeting. He even didn't agree to attend the meeting. By doing so, he openly revealed his attitude of separating himself from the Party before the whole Party, the whole country and the whole world.

Prior to this, members of the Standing Committee of the Political Bureau of the Party Central Committee met to discuss the issue of declaring martial law in parts of Beijing on May 17. On the same day, a few people who had access to top Party and state secrets gave the information away out of their counterrevolutionary political consideration. A person who worked at the side of Comrade Zhao Ziyang said to the leaders of the illegal student organization: "The troops are about to suppress you. All others have agreed. Zhao Ziyang was the only one who was against it. You must get prepared."

On the evening of May 17, Bao Tong summoned some people from the Political Structural Reform Research Center of the Party Central Committee for a meeting. After divulging the secret on declaring martial law, he made a "farewell speech" in which he warned the attendants not to reveal the schemes worked out at the meeting, saying that anyone who revealed them would be a "traitor," a "Judas."

On May 19, Gao Shan, deputy bureau director of this Political Structural Reform Research Center, hurried to the Economic Structural Reform Institute to pass on to those who were holding a meeting the so-called instructions from the "above." After that, the meeting, presided over by Chen Yizi, the institute director, drafted a "six-point statement on the current situation" in the name of the Economic Structural Reform Research Institute, the Development Institute of the China Rural Development Research Center under the State Council, the Institute on International Studies of the China International

Trust and Investment Corporation and the Beijing Association of Young Economists. The statement, which was broadcast at Tiananmen Square and distributed widely, demanded "publicizing of the inside story of the decision-making of the top leadership and the divergence of opinions" and "convening of a special session of the National People's Congress" and "a special congress of the Chinese Communist Party." It also urged the students on Tiananmen Square to "end their hunger strike as soon as possible," hinting that the government "would adopt an extreme action (military control)."

Soon after that, some people, who identified themselves as employees of the State Commission for Restructuring the Economy, went to Tiananmen Square to deliver a speech in which they said: "With deep grief and extreme anger, we now disclose a piece of absolutely true news—General Secretary Zhao Ziyang has been dismissed from the post." The speakers called on the workers, students and shopkeepers to carry out nationwide strikes and instigated the masses to "take immediate actions to fight a life-and-death struggle." The speech was soon printed in the form of *People's Daily* "extra" which was widely distributed. On the same evening, leaflets entitled "several suggestions on the tactics of the student movement" were found at the Beijing railway station and other public places. It said that "at present, hunger strike and dialogues should no longer be our means and demands. We should hold peaceful sit-ins and raise clear-cut new political demands and slogans: 1) Comrade Ziyang mustn't be removed; 2) A special National Congress of the Chinese Communist Party be convened immediately; 3) A special session of the National People's Congress be held immediately." It also said that people "shouldn't be terrified by the coming troops" and that "this attitude should be explained time and again to the students before their coming." Some leaders of the Autonomous Students Union of Beijing Universities and the Beijing Autonomous Workers Union, who had been arrested also confessed that at about four o'clock in the afternoon of May 19, someone, holding a piece of paper and identifying himself as a staff worker of a certain organization under the Party Central Committee, went to the "Tiananmen Square headquarters" and revealed the news that martial law was about to be declared.

As a result of the close collaboration between a small number of people who had access to top Party and state secrets and the organizers and schemers of the turmoil, the organizers made timely adjustments to their tactics. That night, 45 minutes before the meeting called by the central authorities and attended by cadres from the Party, government and military institutions in Beijing, they changed the hunger strike to a sit-in in a bid to give people the false impression that since the students had already ended their hunger strike it was not necessary for the government to declare martial law. By so doing they also gained time to organize people and coerce those who were in the dark to set up roadblocks at major crossroads to stop the advance of the troops and to continue to mislead public opinion and confuse people's minds. While cursing viciously Comrade Deng Xiaoping and other proletarian revolutionaries of the old generation, saying that "we don't need Deng Xiaoping's wisdom and experience," they lavished praises on Comrade Zhao Ziyang by saying that "the country is hopeless without Ziyang as the Party leader" and "give us back Ziyang." They also plotted to rally forces for greater turmoil, claiming that they were going to mobilize 200,000 people to occupy Tiananmen Square and to organize a citywide general strike on May 20. Concerting with Comrade Zhao Ziyang's three-day sick leave which started on May 19, they spread the word that a "new government" would be established in three days.

Under the extremely urgent circumstances, the Party Central Committee and the State Council decided resolutely to declare martial law in parts of Beijing, starting from 10 a.m., May 20, to prevent the situation from worsening and grasp the initiative to stop the turmoil so as to give support to the broad masses who were opposed to the turmoil and longed for stability. However, as the organizers and schemers of the turmoil had learnt of our decision before it was implemented, there were tremendous difficulties and obstacles to the troops' entry into the city.

On the eve of declaring the martial law and in the first two days after it was declared, all major crossroads were blocked up. More than 220 buses were taken away and used as roadblocks. Transportation came to a standstill. Troops to enforce martial law were not able to arrive at their designated places. The headquarters of the Party Central Committee and the State Council continued to be surrounded. Demagogic speeches could be heard anywhere on the street. Leaflets spreading rumors could be seen anywhere in the city. Demonstrations, each involving thousands of people, took place in succession and Beijing, our capital city, fell into total disorder and terror. In the following few days, the martial law troops managed to enter the city by different ways. Meanwhile, the armed police and security forces continued to perform their duties by overcoming tremendous difficulties. Urban and suburban districts organized workers, residents and government office workers, as many as 120,000 people altogether, to maintain social order. The outer suburban counties also sent out militiamen. The concerted efforts of the troops, police and civilians helped improve the transportation, production and living order in the capital and people felt much at ease. But the very small number of people never stopped for a single day their activities to create turmoil and never changed their goal of overthrowing the leadership of the Communist Party. Things were developing day by day toward a counterrevolutionary rebellion.

One of the major tactics of the organizers and schemers of the turmoil after martial law was declared was to continue to stay at Tiananmen Square. They wanted to turn the square into a "center of the student movement and the whole nation." Once the government made a decision, they planned to make "strong reaction" at the square and form an "anti-government united front." These people had been planning to stir up blood-shedding incidents on the square, believing that "the government would resort to suppression if the occupation of the square continues" and "blood can awaken people and split up the government."

To ensure that the situation on the square could be maintained, they used funds provided by reactionary forces both at home and abroad to improve their facilities and install advanced telecommunications devices, spending 100,000 yuan a day on an average. They even started illegal purchase of weapons. By using the tents provided by their Hongkong supporters they set up "villages of freedom" and launched a "democracy university" on the square, claiming they would turn the university into "the Huangpu military school of the new era." They erected a so-called goddess statue in front of the Monument to the People's Heroes. The statue was formerly named the Goddess of Freedom but was later renamed Goddess of Democracy, showing that they took American-style democracy and freedom as their spiritual pillar.

Fearing that the students who took part in sit-ins could not hold on, Liu Xiaobo and other behind-the-scene schemers went up to the front stage and performed a four-man farce of a 48-to-72 hour hunger strike so as to pep the students up. They said: "As long as the flags on the square are still up, we can continue our fight and spread it to the whole country until the government collapses."

Taking advantage of the restraint that the government and the troops still exercised after martial law was declared, the organizers and plotters of the turmoil continued to organize all kinds of illegal activities. Following the establishment of the Autonomous Students Union of Beijing Universities, the Beijing Autonomous Workers Union, the Fasting Contingent, the Tiananmen Square Headquarters and the Union of Capital's Intelligentsia, they set up more illegal organizations such as the Patriotic Joint Conference of People from All Walks of Life in the Capital for Upholding the Constitution, and the Autonomous Union of Beijing Residents. In the name of Research Institute for Restructuring the Economic System, the Development Institute of the China Rural Development Research Center under the State Council, and the Beijing Association of Young Economists, they openly sent telegrams to some of the troops in an attempt to incite defection. They were engaged in such underground activities to topple the government as organizing a special team in charge of molding public opinion and making preparations to launch an underground newspaper.

They organized their sworn followers in taking a secret oath, claiming "under no condition should we betray our conscience, yield to autocracy and bow to the emperor of China in the 1980s." Wan Runnan, general manager of Stone Company, listed the following six conditions for retreating from the Tiananmen Square when he called together some leaders of the Autonomous Students Union of Beijing Universities in the International Hotel: "To withdraw the troops, cancel the martial law, remove Li Peng, ask Deng Xiaoping and Yang Shangkun to quit and let Zhao Ziyang resume his post." During the meeting, they also planned to organize "a great march to claim victory at midnight." Moreover, as they believed that there was almost no hope of solving problems within the Party after Comrade Zhao Ziyang asked for sick leave, they pinned their hope on an emergency meeting by the Standing Committee of the National People's Congress.

Yan Jiaqi, Bao Zunxin and others sent a telegram to the leaders of the NPC Standing Committee, saying that "as the Constitution is being wantonly trampled by a few people, we hereby make an emergency appeal to hold an emergency meeting by the NPC Standing Committee immediately to solve the current critical problems."

Inspired by a certain member of the NPC Standing Committee,

the Stone Research Institute of Social Development issued an opinion-collecting letter on the suggestion to convene such an emergency meeting. After getting the signature of several members of the NPC Standing Committee, it sent urgent telegrams to the NPC Standing Committee members outside Beijing. Conspiratorially, they said nothing about their true purposes in those letters and telegrams in an attempt to deceive those comrades who did not know the truth. They even went so far as to usurp the names of those comrades to serve their ulterior motives.

After doing all this, Yan Jiaqi and Bao Zunxin published an article in Hongkong's *Ming Pao Daily News,* entitled "Solve China's Present Problems in a Democratic and Legal Way—also a Letter to Li Peng," which called on "every member of the NPC Standing Committee and every deputy to the NPC to cast a sacred vote to abolish martial law and dismiss Li Peng as premier."

Organizers and instigators of the turmoil also agitated and organized acts of violence in an unbridled fashion. They hooked up local hooligans, ruffians and criminals from other parts of the country, ex-convicts who did not turn over a new leaf, and people who have deep hatred of the Communist Party and the socialist system to knock together so-called Dare-to-Die Corps, Flying Tiger Teams, Volunteer Army and other terrorist organizations, threatening to detain and kidnap Party and state leaders and "seize state power by means of storming the Bastille." They distributed leaflets to stir up counterrevolutionary armed rebellion, advocating "a single spark can start a prairie fire" and calling for establishing "armed forces that might be called the people's army," for "uniting with various forces including the Kuomintang in Taiwan" and for "a clear-cut stand to oppose the Communist Party and its government and not sparing to sacrifice lives."

They declared they would settle accounts with the Party and the government after the event and even prepared a blacklist of cadres to be suppressed. The *Ming Pao Daily News* published a "dialogue" on June 2 between Liu Xiaobo, one of the organizers and planners, and "a mainland democratic movement leader," in which Liu said: "We must organize an armed force among the people to materialize Zhao Ziyang's comeback."

The activities of the instigators of the riots have strong financial backing. In addition to the materials worth some hundreds of thousands of yuan from the Stone Company and others, they got support from hostile forces overseas and other organizations and individuals. Some people from the United States, Britain and Hongkong offered them nearly 1 million US dollars and millions of Hongkong dollars. Part of the money was used for activities to sabotage the martial law enforcement. Anyone who took part in establishing obstacles to stop traffic and block army vehicles could get 30 yuan a day. Also they set high prices to buy off rioters to burn military vehicles and beat soldiers, promising to offer 3,000 yuan for burning one vehicle and more money for capturing or killing soldiers.

A high-ranking official from Taiwan launched a campaign to "send love to Tiananmen" and took the lead of donating 100,000 Taiwan dollars. A member of the Central Committee of the Kuomintang in Taiwan suggested that 100 million Taiwan dollars be donated to establish a "fund to support the mainland democratic movement." Some people of the Taiwan arts and cultural circles also launched "a campaign supporting the democratic movement on the mainland." A letter by the Autonomous Students Union of Beijing Universities to "Taiwan friends in art circles" said that "we heartily thank you and salute you for your material and spiritual support at this crucial moment."

All this shows that the turmoil planned, organized and premeditated by a few people could not be put down merely by making some concessions on the part of the government or just by issuing an order to impose martial law, contrary to the imagination of some kindhearted people.

They have made up their minds to unite with all hostile forces overseas and in foreign countries to launch a battle against us to the last. All one-sided good will would lead only to their unscrupulous attack against us—and the longer the time the greater the price.

Seven. How did a small minority of people manage to stir up the counter-revolutionary rebellion?

The Chinese People's Liberation Army undertakes not only the sacred duty of "strengthening national defense, resisting aggression and defending the motherland" but also the noble responsibility of "safeguarding the people's peaceful labor, participating in national reconstruction and working hard to serve the people," which are provided for in Article 29 of the Constitution of the People's Republic of China. It was exactly to carry out the tasks entrusted to them by the constitution that the troops entered the city proper and safeguarded social order.

After the announcement of martial law in some areas of the capital on May 20, the troops, despite repeated obstructions, were mobilized to march towards the city proper in accordance with a deployment plan and by different ways to take up appointed positions.

The handful of organizers and plotters of the rebellion were well aware that they would not be able to continue their illegal and counterrevolutionary activities and their conspiracy would come to nothing if the martial law troops took up positions in the center of Beijing. Therefore, they started to create trouble deliberately and did their best to aggravate the unrest, which eventually developed into a counterrevolutionary rebellion.

On June 1 the Public Security Bureau detained a few of the ringleaders of the illegal "Federation of Autonomous Workers' Unions." The agitators of the rebellion then took advantage of this opportunity to incite some people to surround and attack the offices of the Beijing Municipal Public Security Bureau, the Municipal Party Committee and Government, and the Ministry of Public Security.

On the evening of June 1 a police jeep on loan to the Chinese Central TV Station was involved in a traffic accident in which three people died. None of the victims was a student. This was deliberately distorted as a provocation by martial law troops. The conspirators attempted to seize the bodies and parade them in coffins, stirring up the people and making the atmosphere extremely tense. After this incitement and uproar they lit the fire of the counterrevolutionary rebellion.

In the small hours on June 3, while the martial law troops were heading for their positions according to schedule, agitators urged crowds to halt military and other motor vehicles, set up roadblocks, beat soldiers and loot trucks of materials at Jianguomen, Nanheyan, Xidan, Muxidi and other road crossings. Some 12 military vehicles were halted by crowds near Caogezhuang. Soldiers marching past the Yanjing Hotel were stopped and searched by rioters, and military vehicles parked in front of the Beijing Telegraph Office had their tires slashed and were surrounded with road dividers.

About dawn, military vehicles on the Yongdingmen Bridge were overturned, others at Muxidi had their tires slashed and some 400 soldiers in Chaoyangmen were stoned. In the Liubukou and Hengertiao areas, military vehicles and soldiers were surrounded by unruly crowds.

Around 7 a.m., some rioters swarmed over military vehicles which had been halted at Liubukou and snatched machine guns and ammunition. From Jianguomen to Dongdan and in the Tianqiao area, martial law troops were surrounded and beaten. On the Jianguomen flyover some soldiers were stripped and others severely beaten. Later in the morning, troops in the Hufangqiao area were beaten by rioters and some were blinded. The mob prevented some injured soldiers from reaching hospitals by deflating ambulance tires and the victims were dragged from the vehicles. From Hufang Road to Taoranting Park, 21 military vehicles were surrounded and halted. Policemen escorting the soldiers were beaten by the rioters.

From noon onward, many of the soldiers trapped by mobs and barricades at the southern end of the Fuyoujie, the northern end of the Zhengyilu, Xuanwumen, Hufangqiao, Muxidi and Dongsi cross-roads were injured and their equipment was taken away. At Liubukou policemen tried several times to recover a military truck loaded with arms and ammunition from an enraged mob but failed. They were then forced to use tear gas to disperse the rioters and recapture the dangerous cargo.

About the same time, mobs began to surround and assault buildings housing state organizations and establishments of vital importance, including the Great Hall of the People, the Propaganda Department of the CPC Central Committee and the Ministry of Radio, Film and Television, as well as the west and south gates of Zhongnanhai, the seat of the Party Central Committee and the State Council. Dozens of policemen and guards there were injured.

As the situation rapidly deteriorated, the instigators of the up-heaval became more vicious. At about 5 p.m., the ringleaders of the illegal "Beijing Federation of Autonomous Students Unions of Universities and Colleges" and "Federation of Autonomous Workers Unions" distributed knives, iron bars, chains and sharpened bamboo sticks, inciting the mobs to kill soldiers and members of the security forces. In a broadcast over loudspeakers in Tiananmen Square, the "Federation of Autonomous Workers Unions" urged the people "to take up arms and overthrow the government." It also broadcast how to make and use Molotov cocktails and how to wreck and burn military vehicles.

A group of rioters organized about 1,000 people to push down the wall of a construction site near Xidan and stole tools, reinforcing bars and bricks, ready for street fighting.

They planned to incite people to take to the streets the next day, a Sunday, to stage a violent rebellion in an attempt to overthrow the government and seize power at one stroke.

At this critical juncture, the Party Central Committee, the State Council and the Central Military Commission decided to order troops poised on the outskirts of the capital to enforce martial law and quell the counterrevolutionary rebellion.

Eight. How did the counterrevolutionary rebels injure and kill People's Liberation Armymen?

Since the enforcement of martial law in Beijing, the martial law troops heading for Beijing proper tried their best to avoid conflicts, exercising great restraint in accordance with instructions of the Party Central Committee. After the June 3 riot happened and before the troops entered the city, the Beijing municipal government and the headquarters of the martial law enforcement troops issued an emergency announcement at 6:30 p.m., which said, "All citizens must heighten their vigilance and keep off the streets and not go to Tiananmen Square as of the issuing of this notice. Workers should remain at their posts, and other citizens must stay at home to insure their security." The announcement was broadcast over and over again on TV and radio.

About 10 p.m. on June 3, most of the martial law troops heading for Beijing proper from various directions had been halted at barricades set up at the main crossroads. Even so, the troops were still quite restrained, while the counterrevolutionary rioters took advantage to beat and kill soldiers, to seize military materials and burn military vehicles.

From 10 p.m. to 11 p.m. the same day, at Cuiweilu, Gongzhufen, Muxidi and Xidan, 12 military vehicles were burned. Some people threw bricks at soldiers. And some rioters pushed trolleybuses to the crossroads, set them on fire and blocked the roads. When some fire engines got there, they were also smashed and burned.

Around 11 p.m. three military vehicles were wrecked and one jeep was overturned at Hufangqiao, and military vehicles on Andingmen overpass were surrounded. In Chongwenmen Street, a regiment of soldiers was surrounded, and on Jianguomen overpass, 30 military vehicles were halted by barricades, and another 300 military vehicles were halted to the west of the Beijing Coal Industrial School.

Trying to persuade the rioters to let them through, PLA men from warrant officers to generals were beaten up or kidnapped.

To avoid conflicts, the barricaded military vehicles in Nanyuan Sanyingmen made a detour. When they reached the southern gate of the Temple of Heaven, they were halted again and many of these vehicles were wrecked and burned. One military vehicle was halted in Zhushikou and a group of people swarmed over it. When a man looking like a cadre came up and tried to persuade them to leave it alone, he was severely beaten and no one knows whether he died or not.

Just after dawn on June 4, more military vehicles were burned. Several hundred military vehicles on dozens of road crossings in Tiantan Dongce Road, the northern gate of Temple of Heaven, the western exit of the subway in Qianmen, Qianmen Donglu, Fuyou Street, Liubukou, Xidan, Fuxingmen, Nanlishilu, Muxidi, Lianhuachi, Chegongzhuang, Donghuamen, Dongzhimen, Dabeiyao, Hujialou, Beidougezhuang and Jiugongxiang in Daxing County were attacked with Molotov cocktails. Some soldiers were burned to death, and some others were beaten to death. In some areas, several dozens of military vehicles were burning at the same time.

At the Shuangjing crossroad, more than 70 armored personnel carriers were surrounded and machine guns ripped from 20 of them.

From Jingyuan crossroad to Laoshan crematorium, more than 30 military vehicles were burning at the same time. Some rioters with iron bars and gasoline drums, were waiting on the crossroads to burn passing motor vehicles. And many military vehicles carrying food, bedding and clothing were hijacked.

Several mobs drove snatched armored personnel carriers along the Fuxingmen overpass area firing its guns. The "Federation of Autonomous Workers Unions" claimed in their own broadcast that they had taken away a military transceiver and a cipher code book.

The mobs also assaulted civilian installations and public buildings. Shop windows including those of the Yanshan Department Store in Xicheng District were broken. Pine trees in front of Tiananmen gate and the western part of Chairman Mao's Memorial Hall were burned. Some public buses, fire engines, ambulances and taxis were also wrecked and burned. Some people even drove a public bus loaded with gasoline drums towards the Tiananmen rostrum and attempted to set fire to it. They were stopped by martial law troops on the southern side of Golden Water Bridges.

The mobs also murdered soldiers in various bestial ways. About dawn on June 4, some mobs beat up soldiers with bottles and bricks at Dongdan crossroad. In Fuxingmen, a military vehicle was surrounded and 12 soldiers were dragged off the vehicle. They were searched and severely beaten. Many of them were badly injured. In

Liubukou, four soldiers were surrounded and beaten up, and some were beaten to death. In the Guangqumen area, three soldiers were severely beaten. One was rescued by some bystanders and the other two have not been found yet. In Xixingsheng lane of the Xicheng District, more than 20 armed policemen were beaten up by mobs; some were badly injured, and the others' whereabouts are unknown. In Huguosi, a military vehicle was halted, and soldiers on it were beaten up and detained as hostages. Submachine guns were snatched. A truck full of bricks drove from Dongjiao Minxiang to Tiananmen Square, and people on the truck shouted "if you are really Chinese, attack the soldiers."

After dawn, a police ambulance carrying eight injured soldiers to a hospital was halted by mobs. They beat a soldier to death and shouted that they would do the same to the other seven. In front of a bicycle shop in Qianmen Street, three soldiers were severely beaten by hooligans, who threatened anyone who tried to rescue them. On Changan Avenue a military vehicle broke down suddenly, and was attacked right away by about 200 rioters. The driver was killed inside the cab. About 30 meters to the east of Xidan crossroad, another soldier was beaten to death. Then the mob poured gasoline over his body and set fire to it. In Fuchengmen, another soldier's body was hung over the overpass after he had been savagely killed. In Chongwenmen, a soldier was thrown from the overpass and burned alive. Near the Capital Cinema on West Changan Avenue, an officer was beaten to death, disembowelled and had his eyes plucked out. His body was then strung up on a burning bus.

In the several days of the rebellion, more than 1,280 military vehicles, police cars and public buses were wrecked, burned or otherwise damaged. Of the vehicles, over 1,000 were military vehicles, more than 60 were armored personnel carriers and about 30 were police cars. More than 120 public buses were destroyed as well as more than 70 other kinds of motor vehicles. During the same period, arms and ammunition were stolen. More than 6,000 martial law soldiers, armed police and public security officers were injured and the death toll reach several dozens. They sacrificed their blood and even their precious lives to defend the motherland, the constitution and the people. The people will remember their contributions.

Such heavy losses are eloquent testimony to the restraint and tolerance shown by the martial law troops. The PLA is an army led by the Chinese Communist Party and serves the people wholeheartedly. They are ruthless to the enemy but kind to the people. They were able to defeat the eight million Kuomintang troops armed by US imperialism during the war years and able to defeat US imperialism which was armed to the teeth, and to effectively safeguard the sacred territory and territorial waters and air space of our country. So why did they suffer such great casualties in quelling the counterrevolutionary rebellion? Why were they beaten and even killed, even when they had weapons in their hands. It is just as Comrade Deng Xiaoping pointed out: "It was because bad people mingled with the good, which made it difficult for us to take the firm measures that were necessary." It also showed that the PLA loves the people and is unwilling to injure civilians by accident.

The fact that they met death and sacrificed themselves with generosity and without fear fully embodies the nature of the PLA. Otherwise how could there be such a great number of casualties and losses? Doesn't this reflect that the army defends the people at the cost of its own life?

In order to quell the counterrevolutionary rebellion and to avoid more losses, the martial law troops, having suffered heavy casualties and been driven beyond forbearance, were forced to fire in the air to open the way forward after repeated warnings.

During the counterattack, some rioters were killed. Because there were numerous bystanders, some were knocked down by vehicles, some were trampled on or were hit by stray bullets. Some were wounded or killed by ruffians who had seized rifles.

According to the information we have so far gathered, more than 3,000 civilians were wounded and over 200, including 36 college students, died during the riot. Among the non-military casualties were rioters who deserved the punishment, people accidentally injured, and doctors and other people who were carrying out various duties on the spot. The government will do its best to deal with the problems arising from the deaths of the latter two kinds of people.

Due to a rumor spread by the Voice of America and some people who deliberately wished to spread rumors, people talked about a "Tiananmen bloodbath" and "thousands of people massacred." The facts are that after the martial law troops reached Tiananmen Square at 1:30 a.m., the Beijing municipal government and the martial law headquarters issued an emergency notice, which stated: "A serious counterrevolutionary rebellion occurred in the capital this evening" and "all citizens and students in Tiananmen Square should leave immediately to ensure that martial law troops will be able to implement their tasks." The notice was broadcast repeatedly for three hours through loudspeakers. The sit-in students gathered around the Monument to the People's Heroes in the southern part of the square. At around 3 a.m., they sent representatives to the troops to express their desire to withdraw from the square voluntarily and this was welcomed by the troops.

At 4:30 a.m., the martial law headquarters broadcast the following notice: "It is time to clear the square and the martial law headquarters accepts the request of the students to be allowed to withdraw." At the same time, another notice on quickly restoring normal order to the square was issued by the municipal government and the headquarters and broadcast. After hearing this, the several thousand students organized hand-in-hand pickets and started to leave the square in an orderly manner, carrying their own banners and streamers.

At about 5 a.m. the troops vacated a wide corridor in the southeastern part of the square to insure the smooth and safe departure of the students. At the same time, a few students who refused to leave were forced to leave by martial law troops. By 5:30 a.m., the clearing operation of the square had been completed.

During the whole operation no one, including the students who refused but were forced to leave, died. Tales of "rivers of blood" in Tiananmen Square and the rumor-mongers themselves "escaping from underneath piles of corpses" are sheer nonsense. The counterrevolutionary rebellion was put down with Tiananmen Square returning to the hands of the people and all martial law enforcement troops taking up their assigned positions.

During the quelling of the counterrevolutionary rebellion, the PLA, the armed police and the public security police fought valiantly and performed immortal feats. And many people gave first-aid to the wounded and rescued besieged soldiers, rendering their cooperation and support to the martial law enforcement troops.

Due to the turmoil and the counterrevolutionary rebellion. Beijing has suffered heavy losses in its economy, and losses in other fields can not be counted with money. Workers, peasants and intellectuals are now working hard to retrieve the losses. Now, order in the capital has fundamentally returned to normal and the situation throughout China is also tending to become calm, which shows that the correct decision made by the Party Central Committee has benefited the Chinese people of all nationalities. Yet, the unrest and the rebellion are not completely over, as a handful of counterrevolutionary rioters refuse to recognize defeat and still indulge in sabotage, and even dream of staging a comeback.

In order to achieve thorough victory, we should mobilize the people completely, strengthen the people's democratic dictatorship and spare no effort to ferret out the counterrevolutionary rioters. We should uncover instigators and rebellious conspirators, and punish the organizers and schemers of the unrest and the counterrevolutionary rebellion, that is, those who obstinately stuck to the path of bourgeois liberalization and conspired to instigate rebellion, those who colluded with overseas and other foreign hostile forces, those who provided illegal organizations with top secrets of the Party and state, and those who committed the atrocities of beating, smashing, grabbing and burning during the disturbances. We should make a clear distinction between two different types of contradictions and deal with them accordingly, through resolute, hard and painstaking work. We must educate and unite people as much as possible and focus the crackdown on a handful of principal culprits and diehards who refuse to repent. On this basis, we will retrieve all the losses suffered in the unrest and the counterrevolutionary rebellion as soon as possible. For this, we must rely on the people, try to increase production, practice strict economy and struggle arduously.

Chairman, vice chairmen and Standing Committee members, our country's just struggle to quell the unrest and the counterrevolutionary rebellion has won the understanding and support of governments and people of many countries. We extend our wholehearted gratitude for this. However, there are also some countries, mainly the US and some West European countries, which have distorted the facts, spread slanderous rumors and even uttered so-called condemnations and imposed sanctions on our country to set off an anti-China wave and wantonly interfere in our country's internal affairs. We deeply regret this. As for the outside pressures, our government and people have never submitted to such things, not this time nor any time. The rumors will be cleared away and the truth and facts will come out.

Our country will unswervingly take economic construction as the central task and persist in the Four Cardinal Principles and in economic reform and opening up to the outside world. Our country will, as always, adhere to our independent foreign policy of peace, continue to develop friendly relations with all countries in the world on the basis of the Five Principles of Peaceful Coexistence, and make our contributions to the safeguarding of world peace and the promotion of world development.

The Chinese Ambassador's Version

The Chinese Ambassador to the United States, Han Xu, made the following remarks on June 24 to a group in West Palm Beach, Florida.

The world has been watching closely the unfolding of events in China in recent months and the unfortunate trends in China-US relations. The inevitable questions on everyone's minds are: What happened in China? And, as a result, where are China-US relations headed?

There is a pervasive sense of pessimism, frustration and even hopelessness. People are concerned that China will once again fall back to its old days of isolation and that ties between our two countries are beyond repair. I believe otherwise.

My government believes that it confronted a serious insurrection in Beijing. My government has stated that a mob led by a small number of people prevented the normal conduct of the affairs of state.

For example, demonstrators marred the important visit of the Soviet President, Mikhail Gorbachev. And after a protracted period of patience, with considerable advance warning, military forces dispersed the mob.

There was, I regret to say, loss of life on both sides. I wonder whether any other government confronting such an unprecedented challenge would have handled the situation any better than mine did.

I know that most of you would describe the events differently than my government does. This is understandable. I am afraid the media have not been able to present the complete picture—namely, the very important historical context.

Let me sketch for you the broader political and economic situation that confronts my government, and indicate what its objectives are. With that background, I think it becomes possible to understand why my government places so much emphasis upon the maintenance of order and unity and why it must respond vigorously to signs of chaos and turmoil.

During the past decade, the Chinese people have been engaged in what may be the most important social experiment in the contemporary world—namely, to reform China's economy and open the country to the outside world.

No government faces similar challenges. China is a diverse land with many ethnic nationalities. It has a population of 1.1 billion, fully 22 percent of the world total, yet it has only 7 percent of the world's arable land to feed its population. Out of this population, 800 million are rural and, for the most part, still use hand tools to make a living.

Many industries are several decades or even a century behind present-day standards. Vast areas are still underdeveloped and impoverished. Nearly one-fourth of the population is illiterate or semi-illiterate.

All this predetermines that China's road to reform will inevitably be pitted with potholes and full of risks and uncertainties. Therefore, the maintenance of order and stability is a primary task of governance.

Today, with emotions running high, it is easy for people to overlook one thing: Against tremendous odds, the Chinese government and people have accomplished the unthinkable. In a world trapped in widening economic gaps, hunger and poverty, China is able to provide a decent living for almost a quarter of the world's population.

Its gross national product and per capita income literally doubled in a decade. Increasing prosperity has become a reality for several hundred million Chinese peasants.

A vigorous experiment has been carried out to reform the rigid economic management system. A whole new class of enterprising private businessmen has emerged, instilling vitality into the economy. For the first time in its modern history, China is wide open to the outside world on an unprecedented scale.

China has gone much further than any other socialist country in this bold experiment. And this is what I want to tell you: Despite what has happened in Beijing in the past few months, all this will continue in China.

Then why the unrest? The causes are complex and many. The transition from the old economic structure to the new gives rise to a degree of market chaos. Some corrupt officials and speculators have taken advantage of the situation.

The resulting income disparity has caused much complaint. An overheated economy plagued by ever greater demand eventually touched off runaway inflation. And the rapid spread of television has created rising expectations that cannot be met.

The ensuing frustration has proved incendiary. There are also people who wish to copy alien political institutions and introduce them to China overnight. In short, China now manifests all the social tensions that are generated by rapid economic development.

As the situation in Beijing has returned to normal, the government is engaged in a soul-searching review to draw lessons, both positive and negative, so as to insure the further progress of the reform.

Two things have emerged clearly. First, despite demonstrations and riots, both the government and the people remain united in their consensus view that the ongoing reform and opening up to the outside world must be sustained.

Experiences of the past decade have eloquently shown that reverting to the old way of doing things will lead China nowhere. This is the most important message; to miss this point is to miss the whole picture.

Secondly, China's reform, both political and economic, can succeed only if it proceeds gradually, in an orderly, evolutionary way. Asking for radical change overnight or imposing unrealistic demands can only hinder the reform.

I come to the final issue: relations between our two countries. No one wants to see our relations suffer as a result of the recent developments in China. I suspect that a similar tragedy occurring in many other capitals would not have provoked the same outpouring of American emotions.

I welcome this. If reflects the special nature of Chinese-American relations. It shows that the American people care about China and about our relations.

Is there any basis for the restoration and advancement of China-US relations? The answer is yes.

Neither of the two countries pose a security threat to the fundamental interests of the other. The confrontation that once existed between us shows that animosity can only hurt both. It cannot and must not be accepted as an alternative for our relations.

Our common interests far outweigh our differences. The most important one is a fundamental belief in maintaining world peace and stability. Anyone can see that China-US rapprochement has contributed significantly to peace and stability in Asia and the Pacific.

Mutually beneficial economic ties have served as the engine

pulling our relations forward. Our trade has grown at an annual rate of 20 percent. The US has become China's number two foreign trade partner, while China has jumped to the 13th biggest trade partner of the US. It has become one of the fastest growing export markets of the United States.

There is much talk of imposing further economic sanctions against China. Such sanctions must be firmly rejected. They hurt the US as much as China. The only effect on China is to push it back into the isolation of the old days.

The important thing is not to interfere in China's internal affairs, particularly when it is in difficulty. Do not make things more difficult. The principle of mutual noninterference, a cornerstone of China-US relations, must be strictly observed.

I appreciate the Bush Administration's resistance to further sanctions and I hope that the Congress will show more restraint. Let's be guided by the forces of history and reason from this time forward.

Appendix Two

Eyewitness Accounts

"Blame Me if You Want!"

Hunger Striker Hou Dejian's Eyewitness Account

Hou Dejian, a pop singer and composer from Taiwan, was one of four non-student hunger strikers in Tiananmen Square when troops moved in to clear the students out of the square. Hou, who defected to mainland China in 1983, is so popular in China that almost everybody knows him and his song "The Dragon's Descendants." On the night of June 3–4, he was in the square with the other three hunger strikers. When the danger of military suppression became imminent, the four fasting people made the decision to get the students out of the square safely. For this, Hou went to talk with an army commander named Ji Xinguo and urged the troops to give the students time to leave.

After June 4, Hou went into hiding in the Australian Embassy in Beijing, where he stayed for about 70 days. On August 16, he left the embassy after the government promised that he would not be arrested. In an interview with a Hongkong newspaper, Sing Tao Daily, Hou said he felt that the reason he was not arrested was that he was a "Taiwan compatriot." On August 17, the day after Hou left the embassy, he appeared on Chinese television recounting what happened in the Square on the night of June 3–4, and contradicting those other eyewitness accounts which claimed thousands were killed in the square. At one point, he insisted that he did not see students being shot dead or crushed by tanks in the square. However, he did see more than a dozen soldiers rush to the third tier of the monument and fire on the loudspeakers, an action also described by Chai Ling, one of the top student leaders.

During his stay in the embassy, Hou wrote an account of the events of June 3–4 which was later published in overseas Chinese newspapers and in part by the People's Daily. *He gives details on how the decision was made*

239

to withdraw from the square, how he negotiated with the army, and how the students reacted to his proposal to leave the square. As we read his recollections over and over, we strongly felt that Hou was honest in presenting his version of what happened in the square on that deadly night and that the information he has provided was largely reliable. Thus we are compelled to translate and publish the full text of Hou's article, which appears to be the single most authoritative eyewitness account of what occurred in the square itself.

Within the three hours after midnight on June 4, Tiananmen Square was ruled by a strong atmosphere of death and sacrifice. The Command Post was leading all the students in an oath, swearing to live or die with the square. "Our heads may be chopped off; our blood may be shed," they said, "but the people's square cannot be abandoned." Hearing this, I walked out of the tent housing us four hunger strikers to take the same oath, shouting in a loud voice slogans such as "Down with Li Peng's pseudo-government!"

Since the morning of June 3, we had been getting news that soldiers had opened fire, and many students, workers and citizens had fallen down. People had also shown us blood-stained clothes and bullets. However, we still could not imagine that soldiers with semi-automatic rifles would fire recklessly on the peaceful and non-violent sitting-in students in the square. It was even harder for us to believe that tanks would run in full speed and crush the people in the way. There were even some angry but naive and optimistic people who believed that soldiers would at most clear them away with tear gas, rubber bullets and clubs. They were even prepared to confront the army with sticks.

It had been more than a month (since the student occupation of Tiananmen Square). At this point, the students had been largely tired out from the adverse hygiene, living and resting conditions in the square. Therefore, it was really hard for them to think about the situation calmly, and even harder to make decisions rationally under the increasingly stressful atmosphere. Rumors were spreading quickly in the square. Some were saying that the 38th Army had staged a rebellion; others were calling for the people to destroy the tanks' caterpillar tracks with quilts; and some were even saying that troops had already withdrawn. The only things that were truly believable, however, were the flames of bullets and signal flares flying from western Changan Avenue toward the east, as well as the screaming from the people and the blood-stained clothes from the wounded and dead.

Liu Xiaobo, Zhou Duo, Gao Xin and I were still on a hunger strike in our tent on the third tier (the highest one) of the Monument to the People's Heroes. At one point, the pickets outside the tent passed on to us a note which said that as long as one of them was still alive, they would not let a single policeman enter our tent. On behalf of us four, Xiaobo wrote a note in return, saying we would live or die with the pickets. We all signed. The note was then taken away by a picket and was read loudly. The students responded to it with a burst of applause. Several foreign journalists who were still staying near the monument would pass by the tent from time to time. Every time they passed by, we said hello, we hugged, we expressed good wishes, and we told each other to take care, as if we were doing this for the very last time.

At around 3 a.m. on June 4, the atmosphere of terror reached its peak point. Almost no one in the square was still able to think about the situation calmly and rationally. Although no one was weeping because of fear, I clearly felt that the calmness shown on many faces was forced. In fact, even the four of us hunger strikers in our thirties were not able to control ourselves and our feelings were fluctuating with the changes of atmosphere in the square. Gao Xin and Zhou Duo could not bear seeing it any longer. They decided to get the students out of the square alive, and came to Xiaobo and me to ask for our opinions. Xiaobo was the only one who insisted on staying. But he had to, and he did, give in, because the three of us all agreed to leave.

As we were still struggling to make a final resolute decision, there came Chai Ling's excited yet weak voice, which showed an obvious lack of self-control. She was talking to the people in the square through the loudspeakers positioned near the command post. She told them that the final moment was coming, and those who wanted to leave could do so, while those who wanted to stay would live or die with the square. The four of us immediately realized the danger of such words. At this point, they could only serve to shake the already fearful yet unified will of the people in the square. If many people did begin to leave, the square could easily fall into chaos. More dangerously, such chaos, if it happened, was bound to give the soldiers reasons to kill. The obvious result would be that not only those who wanted to stay would surely die, but those choosing to leave might not be able to leave alive as well. It was within the second [we heard Chai Ling's words] that we decided to persuade all the people in the square to withdraw peacefully.

The decision was made, yet it didn't mean that we could definitely make it. In the west side of the square, the gunfire from the direction of the Great Hall of the People was getting closer and closer. From time to time, tear gas was fired onto us and exploded less than 50 yards from the monument. And around the monument, there were still about 20,000 people. How could they listen to our advice? How could those who had taken our advice influence those who had already written down their wills? These were all big questions. Only by acting together could we expect the best result. But we could not just grab the megaphone and shout "withdraw!" Because by doing so, it would not only be the least convincing, but also sound humiliating to the other people. Worse still, those being humiliated could easily tend to act in extremity. Therefore procedure became a most important technical problem.

The first step would be to lay down all the things on the Monument that looked like weapons. However, as pouring rainfall always comes when the roof is leaking, when the four of us under the protection of some pickets came down the third tier to the command post at the northeast corner of the monument, the loudspeakers were broken. So we asked some student leaders to follow us to a nearby tent and told them our intention. Chai Ling did not make any comment. Since we could not force her to agree to leave, we decided to act under the name of the four of us and call on the students, urging them to withdraw. The student leaders raised two questions: firstly, if they left, they would not have lived up to the expectations of the students and citizens who had already died; and secondly, they were worried about the reprisal that was bound to follow. And we convinced them on both accounts. But Chai Ling came up with the rumor that Zhao Ziyang and Yan Mingfu had hoped that the students would hang on till daylight, because by then they would be able to bring the troops under control. The four of us immediately dismissed this idea. After all, we should not sacrifice so many young lives just for such a rumor.

Fortunately, there was another low-power amplifier on the monument. Fortunately by this time the students were clustered around the monument. A male student—perhaps Li Lu or Feng Congde—with firm and calm voice showed remarkable self-restraint under such extreme condition. He tried to use his steady voice to calm down the others. It was also he who led the four of us back to the top of the monument, grabbed the microphone from a student who was reading a broadcast message, and introduced us to the students. Then we were able to begin our first step—to persuade everyone to lay down whatever in hand that looked like weapons by emphasizing the ideal of peaceful and nonviolent protest.

It was fairly easy to gain the cooperation of the students. Several student leaders and pickets who supported our position secretly told us that on the monument there were a machine gun, two semi-automatic rifles, a pistol and a case of incendiary bombs which the students had made with beer bottles.

The machine gun was guarded by some workers and was covered with quilts. It was set up on the third tier of the monument in the southwest corner. The workers who guarded it all had steel bars in hand and were ready to defend themselves if anyone would try to intrude. Seeing a crowd of us coming close, they were immediately on the alert. I held in my arms a man about 20 years of age and told him that I was Hou Dejian. He called me "Brother Hou" and then burst into tears. He told me that he was among the first and foremost workers who supported the students. Many of his comrades had died in blocking army vehicles and protecting the students. He himself was severely beaten, with wounds all over his body. I held him tightly and cried too. After many years, this was the first time that I cried, but I found no tears in my eyes. I dragged him into the hunger strikers' tent on the north side of the monument. Two other people followed in. Gao Xin and Xiaobo were still with the other workers, trying to win their support while Zhou Duo and I were in the tent talking to this man. Finally we unveiled our plan to peacefully withdraw from the square. We argued that if the soldiers found this machine gun in our possession, then all of us had to die and be labeled violent rioters. The young man was finally convinced by us and let us go and take the machine gun. We then went to another red tent to collect another unloaded assault rifle. The man who was guarding the rifle was a medium-sized worker in good shape. After the workers handed in the weapons, we all held each other and cried, and this time, I found that I had tears in my eyes.

After collecting the guns, Xiaobo immediately went to see the reporters. He smashed the guns while the reporters took pictures. Xiaobo also reiterated that our movement was a peaceful and nonviolent one. At this point, the students on the top tier of the monument began to throw away things such as sticks down to the bottom.

After smashing the weapons, the four of us gathered in the tent, discussing what our next step would be. At this time, two doctors from the Red Cross came into our tent with some good ideas. They suggested that we take the ambulance and go with them to negotiate with the troops. In this way, we hoped that we could obtain from the troops the promise and time for the students to leave peacefully. The suggestion was immediately accepted and I volunteered to go, because, I told them, I was the best choice. Since my face was familiar to them and everybody knew me, it would be safe if I went and I could also be easily accepted by the troops for this reason. I asked Zhou Duo to come with me. Zhou Duo was a suave man who always spoke slowly but very convincingly, so I chose him, while Xiaobo and Gao Xin would stay at the monument. They could on the one hand continue to collect weapons, on the other hand, they could try to make the rest of the people calm down.

In order to let the army feel that we could truly represent the people in the square, we decided to ask Chai Ling to go with us. But Chai Ling declined. She said she could not leave the square because she was the chief commander. It was already 3:30 a.m., and we could not find any other student who would be suitable to go. So we decided to go alone. Gao Xin and I and the two doctors from the Red Cross rushed down the monument on the west side and stopped an ambulance. Several pickets were worried about us. They had sworn to protect us, so they got on the ambulance as well. We drove to the north of the square. When we arrived at the northeastern corner, we saw thousands of troops along Changan Avenue taking the assault position. The ambulance came to an abrupt halt. We rushed down and ran toward the troops. At that point, there was nobody near the place where the ambulance parked, and we had no idea how long the troops had been waiting there. In any event, when they saw us running over, they all began to load their guns and shouted at us, ordering us to stop. We stopped and the doctors hurried to show their identity. They told the soldiers that I was Hou Dejian, and that I wanted to talk to their commander. The furious soldiers calmed down a bit and I could hear them snickering about my name. I didn't know what they were saying exactly, but I felt that they were not hostile.

The commander was standing not far from us. Knowing our

intention, he came up to us with four or five soldiers. He appeared to be normal, like the kind of three-star high level military commanders I had seen before. He was in his forties, and his once fit and strong body was beginning to gain weight. When we shook hands, he was very calm, and I couldn't find even a trace of anxiety in him. His hand was very thick, soft and warm. I felt that he was serious in listening to our request. At first, he was a bit severe, not terribly fierce though. He demanded that we should first stop the hunger strike. Zhou Duo and I told him that we had already done so. After that, his attitude softened a bit and remained so till the end. As to our request, he said he had to report it to the headquarters.

It was barely five minutes after the commander headed back to the troops when the lights in the square were suddenly extinguished. I did not look at my watch. I had no idea whether this was the signal that the troops would begin to clear out the square, or it was just a routine practice of turning off the light at five o'clock every morning. All I knew was that we were extremely frightened. At this point, the soldiers were getting furious again. They began to load their machine guns and shouted loudly. Some became so impatient that they continuously trampled the smashed bottles on the ground. Some were throwing the bottles with all their might to the empty edge of the square. The four of us were standing in the vast and empty northeast corner of the square and were very conspicuous. We dared not move in any direction. At this point, the doctors appeared to be calm. They told us not to move, and at the same time raised their hands, asking the commander to hurry up. About three minutes later, the commander came back to us again. He told us that the headquarters had agreed to our request and that the safest route of withdrawal was in the southeast corner of the square. Under our inquiries, the commander told us that he his name was Ji, and that he was the political commissar of the army. I can't remember his code number now, but anyway, we needed this information to convince the students. During our negotiation, Commissar Ji seemed to have said that if we could successfully persuade the students to leave the square, we would make an enormous contribution. Personally, I think he was sincere in saying so.

Once the army promised us time to leave, we rushed back to the monument as fast as we could. I grabbed the microphone and shouted to the students. I can't remember what I said exactly, but it was something like this: "Without your agreement, I have presumptuously negotiated with the army. I did this because personally I think enough blood has been shed. We cannot allow more people to die. I know that none of you in the square is afraid of death. I also believe that all of you who are still here represent the best hope of the Chinese nation. However, if we all die here like this, that would be the gravest crime we could commit against our state and our nation. The cause of democracy is by no means achievable in a short time. The student movement, the democracy movement participated in by people in all fields has so far achieved a great success. We have already won the victory. Now I plead to each and every one of you to live well for our country. I urge you to live on for our nation, and for the cause of democracy."

While I was talking, gunfire and the explosion of tear gas came closer and closer to the monument from the west side of the square. Every once in a while after I finished a sentence, I was scolded by people at the bottom of the monument. I couldn't hear exactly what they said, but I believed they were accusing me of surrender. I shouted loudly through the microphone: "Please blame me for this if you want. Please blame the four of us. As long as you can leave the square safely, you can do to us whatever you want."

I continued to say, "We will withdraw from the southeast corner of the square. It is my suggestion that we leave, and it is up to you to decide what to do. But in any case, I urge you to act in unison. The four of us will leave only after we see that each and every one of you has safely left. To insure the safety of the workers and residents, we should act together in a unified manner. As for the question of reprisal, it is going to happen anyway. It doesn't make any difference if we stay or leave. If such reprisal takes place, the four of us will be the first to be caught. It will be particularly hard for me to hide anywhere because I have a face that everyone will immediately recognize."

After I finished, Zhou Duo took the microphone and continued the shouting. What he said was more logical and in better order, but the content was basically the same. Then Xiaobo grabbed the microphone, saying he agreed with what we had said. He also said something new. As a result, the atmosphere began to change a little bit. However, at this point, the gunfire became more intense and was getting closer. I saw large numbers of soldiers approaching us from south of the square. I began to worry that this would damage the students' confidence in the army's promise, so I immediately went with Zhou Duo and two doctors toward the northeastern corner of the square, urging the troops to show restraint and give us more time.

At this point, the troops in the north were on the move too. We ran into Commissar Ji in the center of the square. Ji became more severe this time. He said that he had heard our broadcast, but time was up and that they had to finish their task before the given time. He said if we couldn't take the students out, we had better leave ourselves. But we told him that the four of us had to leave after all the students left, and that if we were afraid of death, we would have left the square long ago. Perhaps irritated by my words, a soldier standing beside Ji flushed and opened his eyes wide. He seemed to be utterly discomfited and furiously shouted at us. He couldn't wait to point his gun at us. Seeing this, we knew that we had nothing else to say, so we rushed back to the monument.

As we were running, we shouted to the students: "Leave quickly! "Go to the southeast corner!" By then, many people had already begun to withdraw. When I reached the second tier of the monument, I saw more than a dozen soldiers rushing to the third tier and firing furiously on the loudspeakers. Gunfire was everywhere. Several soldiers were pushing the students from behind. I raised my hand and signaled them to point their guns into the air. Some of them did so. They shouted my name and asked me to leave quickly. They seemed to be earnest. But there were also some soldiers who were very fierce. I couldn't tell how many of them belonged to which category, because under such circumstances, no one can really control himself and be calm and normal.

I stood on the first tier of the monument and saw the students slowly moving toward the southeast corner of the square. With banners in hands, they were in good order. Suddenly I saw one group stopped. I shouted at them: "Go, be quick!" Then I heard them shouting in unison at me: "Let's go together!" I waved at them and got off the steps on the east side of the monument with Zhou Duo under the protection of two pickets who had been following me all the time. We turned to the north of the monument.

The crowds in the north were still sitting on the ground, showing no sign of moving. I became really anxious. I rushed to the north while Zhou Duo went to the northeast. We dragged up everyone we saw and pushed them out to the southeast. Meanwhile, I was shouting: "You can put the blame on me, scold me, whatever!" At this point, nobody was still scolding me. The students on the ground shook my hands, unable to say a word. My voice became more furious and hoarse. I shouted with all the strength I had: "What's the use for you to die here? Will it get anywhere if I die here?" At this point, I couldn't think of other words to say. Some students began to stand up. While crying, they said: "Teacher Hou, we will not blame you. We thank you." I could not stand it any more and burst out crying loudly, while at the same time trying to drag up those who were still sitting on the ground. When the last group of students stood up, a team of soldiers were closing in on us like a human wall. They were barely five yards from us. The students had all stood up. Perhaps it was because the soldiers had approached too quickly, we in the last group to leave looked like water in a fat bottle with a tight neck. It was so crowded that we could hardly move our feet. I was held up by two pickets on both sides, which could just enable me to stand up. I felt that I was going to collapse and was about to suffer from shock. By then I had not eaten anything for two days, and I had just been running back and forth and shouting. At this point, I could no longer hold on. Moving with the crowds, I had difficulty breathing.

Suddenly our team began to move over from the northwest side of the monument. Many people were shouting: "Don't beat! Don't beat!" Squeezed in the middle of the crowd, I saw from over people's heads several plainclothes who looked like riot police waving thick sticks and indiscriminately beating the students. Some students were wounded on the head, and blood began to flow. The team then moved toward the northeast where a line of people stumbled over an iron fence and fell. People following them could not stop in time and fell over them. Two or three layers of people tumbled together. The picket on my left was in the second layer. We tried to pull him back, but he dragged me and made me tread over his body. As a result, I did not fall with the other people. It was a real mess.

Shortly after I squeezed my way out, I heard Xiaobo calling me. He had already left with the first groups, and had come back to look for the other three of us. At this point, the picket and I could hardly move on, so he came over and supported us. In this way, we went to the Red Cross emergency center near the west gate of the History Museum. It was not until then I realized that I had only collapsed, while the picket who had supported me had broken his leg. I looked back to the square and saw that tanks were already there. By the side of one tank, about ten students were carrying three wounded who had blood all over. More wounded people were taken to the emergency center. Xiaobo helped me lie on a camp bed. Beside me, some people were crying. A female student took off her red coat to cover me. Ten minutes later, Xiaobo told me that the students had all left the square and reached the outer Qianmen Avenue. The emergency center was surrounded by soldiers. Before I had time to think about where to go, several doctors came over and signaled me to lie down. They pulled up a coat to cover my head. The doctors told me to rest at ease and not to move. For one and a half hours I lay on the camp bed like this. By the time we arrived at the hospital, it was almost eight o'clock in the morning.

What Happened at Tiananmen?

A Widely Published Student's Account, Possibly Spurious

The following account was supposedly given by a 20-year old student at Qinghua University. It was first published by a Hongkong newspaper, Wen Wei Po, and a translation was published in the New York Times, the Washington Post, and the San Francisco Examiner in the United States. This article gave details of how the soldiers beat and machine-gunned the students around the Monument to the People's Heroes and has become the major source of many other reports on what happened in Tiananmen Square on the night of June 3–4. However, as pointed out by Nicholas Kristof, the Beijing correspondent for the New York Times, the article is highly questionable on many points. We have discussed Kristof's article questioning this student account in the text, so such discussion is not repeated here.

What is worth mentioning, though, is that this account contradicts Chai Ling's version as well. Firstly, while the Wen Wei Po article claimed that soldiers machine gunned the students at the bottom of the monument, Chai Ling, the student leader who claimed to be "the most qualified person to comment on the events of June 4," did not say so, although she did say that "soldiers with assault rifles rushed to the third tier of the monument." Secondly, the Wen Wei Po article said the students surrendered those weapons in their possession to the troops but the latter refused to accept them, while Chai Ling said they "returned the weapons to the Public Security Bureau and got their receipts."

Moreover, as we read the Wen Wei Po *article in Chinese, we could not avoid the feeling that it resembled more a neatly written report by a professional journalist than an eyewitness account from a frightened 20-year-old student. It is hard to believe that someone who had experienced such a terrifying incident only hours before—the author used "last night," which indicated that the article was written on June 4—could present such a well-organized and logical account. In a pamphlet published later by* Wen Wei Po, *this same article was reprinted to substantiate* Wen Wei Po's *own version of the events, which at one point said that two armored personnel carriers sped down the two sides of the square after midnight—which has been mentioned by other reports. However, when the "student account" said: "After midnight, namely after those two armored personnel carriers sped down the two sides of the square," we have every reason to doubt that the "student account" was truly a student account. Did the student read the* Wen Wei Po *pamphlet before he gave the account? Impossible. The pamphlet was published on June 12, while the account was given only hours after the incident. However, if he or she did see the pamphlet, it would only further discredit the account.*

Nevertheless, since this article was one of the major sources of many other reports on the incident at Tiananmen, especially that soldiers beat and machine gunned students around the monument, we have included it here for its historical interest.

I am a student at Qinghua University, and I'm 20 years old. Last night, I was sitting on the steps of the Monument to the People's Heroes and I witnessed the whole course of how the army opened fire on us sit-in students and civilians.

Several of my schoolmates have already been shot to death, and my clothes are still soaked with their blood. As a survivor, and an eyewitness, I would like to expose to all the peace-loving people around the world the whole course of the massacre.

Frankly speaking, by yesterday afternoon, we had already heard that the army would carry out the order to crack down. An anonymous phone call—to a public phone in a nearby alley—which was answered by a student leader, had come around 4 p.m. The caller told us definitely that the army was going to clear out the square by force. Alerted by the news, we had an emergency meeting and decided to take some measures to defuse the confrontation and avoid a bloodbath.

At that time, we had in our possession 23 assault rifles and some explosives, taken from soldiers two days before during confrontations [between the army and the civilians]. The Autonomous Students Association of Beijing Universities conducted a meeting and decided that to demonstrate our original intention to promote democracy through nonviolence, we would immediately surrender these weapons to the martial law enforcement troops. So yesterday evening, we made contact with the army under the portrait of Chairman Mao at the main gate of Tiananmen. An officer told us that the troops were under orders from superiors not to receive the weapons. The negotiations turned out to be fruitless. Thus at 1 a.m., when the situation became extremely volatile, the students destroyed the guns on the steps of the monument, and dismantled the bombs by pouring out the gasoline. We wanted to avoid any chance that they would be used by criminals, or by the authorities as "evidence" that the students had heartlessly killed soldiers.

Afterward, the Autonomous Students Association made a broadcast notice, telling everyone that the situation was extremely dangerous and that bloodshed seemed unavoidable, and urging students and civilians in the vicinity of the square to leave. However, some 40,000 to 50,000 students and about 10,000 civilians insisted on staying. I was one of them.

When I recall the atmosphere at that time, I could only say it was incredibly tense. For the students, this was the first time they ever faced such dangers. It would be a lie to say that we were not afraid, but we were mentally prepared and determined. Of course there were students who did not believe that the army would use deadly force. In a sense, we were motivated by a powerful sense of purpose. We believed that it would be worth sacrificing our lives for the sake of democracy and progress in China.

After midnight, namely after those two armored personnel carriers sped down the sides of the square from Qianmen, the situation became even more dangerous. The government-run loudspeakers repeatedly announced a "notification." Thick formations of soldiers in steel helmets were moving into the square from all sides. In the dark, we could see machine guns placed on the roof of the History Museum.

By then, all the students had retreated to the four sides of the Monument to the People's Heroes. I calculated it carefully in my heart: among the students, two thirds of them were men, and one third were women; one third of them were from Beijing, and most of them were from outside Beijing.

At 4 a.m., the lights on the square were suddenly extinguished.

Through the loudspeaker, we once again heard orders to "clear out." I felt a wave of anxiety in my mind and one voice kept saying over and over, "The moment has come. . . ."

By that time, Hou Dejian and other hunger strikers began to negotiate with the army for a peaceful withdrawal of the students. But just as we were about to leave, at 4:40 a.m., a barrage of red flares shot into the sky, and the lights in the square were immediately turned on again. I saw the front of the square was full of soldiers. From the east gate of the Great Hall of the People, a squadron of soldiers rushed out, dressed in camouflage, carrying assault rifles, and wearing helmets and gas masks. By the way, something has to be pointed out here before I continue. At around 6 p.m. of June 3, we held a negotiation with a regiment of soldiers at the west gate of the Great Hall of the People. Their commander told us that they were only the follow-up troops and he guaranteed that they would not fire on the students. However, he said that the troops that would eventually confront the students would be from Sichuan Province.

The soldiers that had just rushed out of the Great Hall were perhaps from Sichuan. The first thing they did was to erect 10 or more machine guns right in front of the monument. The soldiers took a prone position, with their backs to the Gate of Heavenly Peace. As soon as the placements were ready, a large number of soldiers and armed police appeared. They all held in their hands electric cattle prods and rubber truncheons, and some special-purpose weapons that I had never seen. They charged at us, breaking apart the formation in which we were sitting, beating us with all their might. Our ranks were broken into two groups, and they forced their way through in the middle to the third tier of the monument. I saw about 50 students who were so badly beaten that blood completely covered their faces. At that time, armored personnel carriers and more soldiers who had been waiting on the square closed in on us, and we were completely surrounded by rows of armored personnel carriers, leaving only a small gap in the direction of the museum.

Moreover, the soldiers and armed police who had reached the third tier smashed all of our broadcasting and printing equipment and forced the students down to the bottom. However, we remained seated all the time, holding hands, singing the "Internationale" and shouting "The People's Army must not hurt the people!" But the students sitting on the third tier could not resist the kicking and clubbing of so many attackers and were finally forced down.

As soon as the students in the third tier reached the ground, machine guns erupted. Some soldiers opened fire from a kneeling position, their bullets flying over our heads, but the gunners splayed on the ground were shooting right at our chests and heads. Given such a situation, we could only retreat back to the top of the monument, and as soon as we left the ground, the machine guns stopped. However, the soldiers on the top beat us and forced us down. Then the machine guns started again.

At this time, the workers and civilians who had formed a death squad were deeply irritated. They took up bottles, sticks and anything that could be used as weapons, and rushed across to fight the soldiers. At this moment, the Autonomous Students Association ordered the students to retreat to the outside of the square. It was barely five o'clock.

Then large numbers of students tried to get out through the gap left by the armored personnel carriers. But even this exit was sealed off. Over thirty armored personnel carriers came crushing into the crowd. Some students died under the wheels, and even the flagpole in front of the monument was knocked down. As this happened, the whole square was plunged into disorder.

I never thought that the students could be so courageous. One group went to try to turn over the vehicles, but were repulsed by the bullets. Then a second group, stepping over the bodies of those in front, rushed at the vehicles again. Finally we managed to topple one of them and made ourselves an exit. Three thousand students, myself included, rushed out amid flying bullets to the History Museum. By this time, only about one thousand students survived.

As we arrived at the museum, we saw large numbers of civilians. We joined forces there and began to run north toward the Gate of Heavenly Peace. Seeing flashes of gunfire from the trees ahead, we turned and ran south toward Qianmen.

Tears streamed down my face as I ran. I saw a second group of students trying to escape under machine gun fire, many of them falling. We all cried, and crying, we ran. Just as our group reached Qianmen, we were met by a large contingent of soldiers, all running from the direction of Zhubaoshi. When we met, they didn't shoot, but began beating us madly with huge wooden clubs.

At this point, a large number of citizens rushed to the scene from Qianmen and started fighting ferociously with the soldiers. They did this to protect us as we tried to break through in the direction of the railway station. The soldiers pursued us. By 5 a.m., the gunfire in the square was dying away. Later I ran into a friend at the

International Red Cross. He told me that by 5 a.m., anyone who could manage to escape had done so. The machine gun fire lasted for about 20 minutes.

The most unforgettable thing is that a Qinghua University friend of mine from Jiangsu Province was bleeding heavily but still running with us until he could no longer keep up. He fell against my shoulder, saying, "Can you help me?" I was already supporting two weak woman students so I couldn't get to him right away. He fell on the ground and the crowd trampled him. . . . He must have died. You see, I still have the stains of his blood on my back.

I will never be able to forget how the students helped each other. When some students were shot down, others would rush to the save the wounded and carry away the bodies. Some female students tore off their clothes to bandage wounds until they had nothing more to take off.

After we reached the train station, two other students and I went back to the square at 6:30 a.m. We saw many, many civilians near Qianmen, and we followed a huge crowd to the Mao Zedong Mausoleum. There, armored personnel carriers and a wall of soldiers blocked the way, so we couldn't go any further. We climbed up the trees on the side of the road, and we saw that soldiers were collecting corpses in big plastic bags on the square, one corpse in one bag. The bodies were piled on top of each other and covered with canvas.

There I ran into a student from my department. He was among those who escaped with the second group. He told me that the death toll was enormous. Soldiers had prevented the Red Cross ambulances from getting to the wounded students and civilians in the square. I went with this student to the emergency center of the International Red Cross near Hepingmen immediately, and we saw many wounded being sent here by tricycles. The doctors told us that an ambulance had caught on fire after soldiers fired on it in the square. Here we met with students who escaped with the second, third and fourth groups. They told us that many wounded students had been left in the square.

At around 7:20 a.m., I went back to the square again to find out more. I talked to some elderly people who said that on the sidewalks around the square, the dead bodies were bunched together. The soldiers had draped the area from the sight of the people with canvas sheets. They also said that many military trucks had come in and carried the wounded off to an unknown destination.

At about 7:30 a.m., the soldiers in the square suddenly fired tear gas on the crowds in my direction. Large numbers of soldiers rushed to the crowds. At this time, we once again ran in the direction of the train station. On the way to the station, we saw students who had left the square with the first and second groups. They were all crying.

The Autonomous Students Association asked us students from Beijing to send the students from outside Beijing to the train station. I took some of them to the waiting room, but we were told that there would be no trains that day. So we got out of the train station and were met with crowds of civilians. They told us that they would like to take the students home. Many civilians were very sad. They were all crying.

As to how many people died altogether, I don't really know. But I firmly believe that one day, people will know.

Am I pessimistic? No, I'm not. Because I have seen the will of the people. I have seen the hope of China. Some of my friends died. Even more are now bleeding. I am a survivor, and I know how to live my life from now on. I will never forget those students who had lost their lives. I also know for sure that all decent people in the world will understand and support us.

"If I Had a Gun, I Would Have Killed Soldiers"

Eyewitness Account of Yang Jianli

Yang Jianli, a doctoral candidate in the Mathematics Department of the University of California at Berkeley, was sent back to Beijing in late May to hand over donations to the students at Tiananmen Square. On June 3–4, he witnessed the killing of students and innocent civilians by Chinese army. After June 4, Yang managed to return to the US to continue his study at Berkeley. In a speech given to Chinese students there, he reported on what he saw during the Beijing crackdown. Following is a translation of excerpts from that speech.

In the early hours of June 3, I was sleeping in a dormitory building at Beijing Normal University. Suddenly, the students' shouting awoke me. For the first time since I arrived in Beijing, I felt the atmosphere was really tense. Wu'er Kaixi was announcing through the loudspeaker that troops had entered the city. He urged all the students to go to defend Tiananmen Square.

I hurried down out of the building. There, over 300 students had gathered, ready to run to Tiananmen Square. Among them were some female students, 17 or 18 years of age. A lot of young faculty and graduate students rode their bicycles to the square, and I went with them. We divided into small contingents of a dozen of so people, marching while shouting: "Troops have entered the city! Tiananmen Square has been surrounded!"

Alerted by our shouting, thousands of citizens got out of bed and poured onto the streets. People used their tricycles to block the road, and many military vehicles came to a halt as a result. At this point, the soldiers were unarmed and did not wear uniforms. They all had white shirts and green pants. The big buses that carried the soldiers did not have registration plates on. In Xidan [one of the major intersections with Changan Avenue west of the square], we worked with the citizens to block these buses, and found on them not only machine guns and assault rifles with bayonets, but also large numbers of bullets, leather belts, clubs, daggers and several bags of kitchen knives. People became really angry, and took the weapons to the top of the buses to exhibit.

We then went westward to Muxidi. We were told that a police car had run into four people when it sped down the street at 120 kilometers per hour. Again the police car had no plate on. We found in it clubs and daggers, and this really irritated the people. Several people including myself were on the scene for about four or five hours to keep it intact. However, when day broke, the *People's Daily*, the Central People's Broadcasting Station and the China Central Television all attributed the incident to an ordinary car accident. They even identified the plate number and the driver, but the fact is the car had no plate at all. I was talking with some students about the incident, and we all felt that a brutal crackdown was imminent. Why were there several bags of kitchen knives on the buses? When did they keep weapons in them? We believed that if they succeeded in their intention, they could complete the task of clearing out the square. Otherwise, they could put the blame on the students and citizens.

By the afternoon of June 3, our speculation proved to be true, because the martial law enforcement troops began to announce through loudspeakers, saying, "This morning, a counterrevolutionary rebellion took place (in Beijing). Some students and ruffians seized military vehicles, beat and insulted the soldiers. . . . " They also threatened that the troops would "use whatever means to quell the counterrevolutionary rebellion."

In the afternoon of June 3, the army began to crack down on the students and civilians with tear gas and clubs near Liubukou [not far from the square]. With some young faculty and graduate students, I rushed to the scene by bike. We all brought wet towels with us. After we got there, we saw several wounded students being carried away with tricycles. Their bodies were covered with blood. I also saw a student whose face was injured by the tear gas. Wounded students were carried away one after another, some female students from Beijing University died because of too much loss of blood. Seeing this, we all shouted slogans, begging the soldiers not to beat the students.

Enraged by the beating of the students, some workers from the Autonomous Workers Association took up big iron bars and charged the soldiers. "You have beaten the students, we will beat you," they said. The soldiers could not resist such forces with their clubs, so they retreated.

It was already 1 a.m. when we returned to Xidan. At that point, confrontation had begun for quite some time. Many military vehicles had already been burned by the enraged citizens, and casualties among the students and civilians were very high. At this time, tanks and other military vehicles were rumbling toward us, and people courageously surged ahead to block them. From time to time, the soldiers fired tear gas at us, so we retreated, and fought back again. In this place alone, we repeated such retreat-and-attack for seven or eight times, and the casualties were mounting.

After the soldiers got in the vehicles, they were on their way again. Slowly, some students including myself moved toward them, trying to figure out if they would really fire on us. They didn't, and we were able to get close to one vehicle, and began talking to the soldiers. We told them: "You should not kill the students, you should not kill the people. You have all seen it, so many people have been killed. . . . " We were trying to use the common human feeling to move them. Then somebody began to sing the "Internationale," and everybody joined in. We were singing and crying, begging the soldiers not to open fire. But those "sons and brothers of the people" [a Chinese term for soldiers in the People's Liberation Army] were not to be moved. Guns in hand, they all stared at us, showing no other feeling but provocation. At this point, people's grief was replaced by anger. They stopped begging and began calling for revenge. Someone was shouting: "Down with the fascists! Down with the Yang [Shangkun] family! Down with Deng Xiaoping!" Then another person shouted: "Attack!"

Hearing this, people in the back began to surge ahead, while in the army vehicle, a commander took out a pistol and fired into the crowd. One bullet hit the head of the student standing right next to me. For the first time in my life, I saw someone so close to me being shot to death. I saw him fall onto the ground, making no sound.

Facing live ammunition, people began to retreat. Moments later, when the soldiers stopped shooting, people went back to take that student's dead body away. Then the tanks were on the move again, one after another.

However, the deadly shooting did not frighten the students and citizens to death. We seized every chance to block the army vehicles. The spirit of defiance was high. I saw a person who has truly impressed me. At first, I thought he was an American student, but on a second look, he was a Uygur student from the Central Institute of Minority Nationalities. He desperately rushed ahead. He had been blocking the army vehicles with his schoolmates in Muxidi and had followed the troops to Fuyoujie. His blue T-shirt was soaked in blood. His eyes were blood red, tears being dried for long. With a hoarse voice, he shouted to the soldiers: "You have killed more than 120 people in Muxidi. Four of my best friends died in my arms. Fire on me, I don't care any more." Several citizens went to drag him away, telling him not to give up his life like that. At this point, the gunfire was erupting again, sounding like fire crackers. Hearing the gunfire, we all sprawled on the ground, rolling backward. Moments later, I heard someone shouting "Get out of the way, quick!" Some wounded people were then carried away. Shortly afterwards, a jeep ran toward us from between two trucks. The citizens had already been enraged, swearing, "We will kill every soldier we meet." Thus when the army commander showed up, people got even more angry. Over a hundred people rushed toward the jeep, breaking glasses and shouting slogans. But only five seconds later, soldiers on a truck 30 meters away from the jeep opened fire. Dozens of people were killed on the site. The citizens rushed to take the bodies away.

Seeing this tragic scene, an old man in his sixties who was walking his bicycle down the street shouted at the soldiers, calling them "fascists." Then I saw with my own eyes an officer take out his pistol and shoot the old man, who fell immediately on the ground.

At around 1 a.m., we began to hear machine gun fire near the Gate of Heavenly Peace. By five o'clock, gunfire became more intense—not assault rifles, but machine guns.

I was very much worried about the situation in the square. Many of my friends were there. We rode our bicycles and arrived at Qianmen Avenue [which is south of the square] by dawn. In the dim dawn light, we saw students marching ahead with banners in hand. They were helping each other, some of them had been wounded in the leg, some in the head. They were crying and shouting slogans. Countless citizens stood along the street, clasping the students' hands as if they were welcoming wounded heroes back from the battlefields. The scene was very moving and solemn. I shook hands with the students while crying. They were saying, "Some day we will come back to Tiananmen Square."

We rode our bicycles and slowly followed the students on the way back to campus. But soon we found ourselves heading back on Changan Avenue. Just as the first row of students was about to arrive at the avenue, four tanks were running from the square at full speed toward us. We began to retreat, hoping to avoid going on to the avenue. At this point, the lead tank was crazily running into the retreating students. A student who had been riding a bicycle with me was hit by the tank and fell against the fence. But the tank did not give up and continued to run ahead. That student was crushed. The other tanks followed and did the same thing. After they left, a large number of bodies were seen on the ground. I was very close to the scene and saw all this with my own eyes. Tears streamed down my face and I felt like my whole body was burning. At this point, the students and citizens were not just crying, they were wailing. Some people went to the scene, hoping to collect the bodies. But the soldiers on the second tank fired four tear gas cannisters into the crowd, and two people were instantly wounded. After this tank passed by, people went back again, but the soldiers on the next tanks began to shoot, and four or five more people were killed. There was a Red Cross emergency center nearby. Ambulances were running back and forth. Tricycles and bicycles were all used to carry the wounded to the emergency center.

It was light already. The students were crying while retreating.

There was a citizen in his late forties who was carrying two student bodies on a tricycle. I went close and found that the bodies had all become flat. Their mouths were about half foot long, and their eyes were open. It was too horrible to look at. Many students wanted to go back to Changan Avenue to fight but were dragged back by the citizens. The citizens lined up on both sides of the street to meet the students coming back from the square. Everyone was crying, shouting "revenge, revenge!" I cannot use words to describe the deep-rooted hatred felt by the people, and the moving and tragic scene.

When we arrived at the dormitory buildings of the PLA's General Staff Department, we saw slogans at the gate saying, "Support the Party Central Committee! Support the State Council!" I went up with other students and burned the signs. We also smashed the gate. At that point, I hated it so much that I felt I could do anything. If I had a gun, I would have gone to kill the soldiers.

"Everyone Was Crying"

Beijing Journal: Letter from a Citizen

Shortly after June 4, an editor for an official Chinese publication wrote a letter to her friends abroad to "expose the truth of the Beijing massacre on June 3–4." The editor, who is a Communist Party member, lives near Muxidi, where the heaviest casualties took place. She details in this letter what she experienced before and during the crackdown and conveys a message of how ordinary Beijing residents reacted to the use of force by the government. It should be kept in mind, however, that due to the strongly emotional nature of the event, any personal account may be too emotionally charged to be objective. In this letter, we have found that the author was on the one hand eager to give out the facts. On the other hand, she was more than ready to jump to conclusions that may be incorrect or unfair. In any event, this letter was originally written in Chinese and was taken out of China by the writer's foreign friends. In order to protect her and the people mentioned in the letter, pseudomyns have been used.

My Dear Friend,

I'm writing to you, with tears in my eyes, to expose the truth of the Beijing massacre on June 3–4—an unprecedented event in world history. As a Communist Party member, I was shocked and saddened by the fascist atrocities conducted by a communist government. Like all the Beijing residents, I have not closed my eyes for two days and nights. Everyone was crying. In the early morning of June 3, my son and I were about to go to school and office as usual. When we got to the No. 21 bus stop, we heard people saying, "There is no bus again today. There is a car accident by Muxidi. . . . " I didn't wait for them to finish and told my son that I would take him to school by bike. Muxidi is the place we had to pass by.

Even before we reached Muxidi, we were met with crowds of people. We saw two military vehicles—one had just been unloaded, the other was loaded with unloaded assault rifles and combat food. Several people were standing on top of the vehicles and showed to others the assault rifles, steel helmets and the food. People were watching and taking pictures. These days I have been taking my camera with me all the time, so I took some quick shots and continued to squeeze my way through the crowds. When we arrived at a place near the Inpatient Department of Fuxing Hospital, we saw a military jeep on the sidewalk together with two bicycles and a tricycle, which had been hit and crushed. Many foreign journalists were on the scene, shooting pictures. People were shouting, "Blood must atone for blood."

Since I had to take my son to school, we left. At around 10 a.m., I went with some colleagues to Xidan [a major intersection on Changan Avenue]. From afar we could see several buses clustered in the crossroad, with crowds of people on the top. We also climbed up. From there we saw two more military vehicles below the Telex and Telegraph Building. A machine gun was set up on one of them. Underneath the gun, there were two assault rifles.

By this time, the road to Tiananmen Square had been completely blocked by huge crowds. We didn't go any further, and we came back to the office, planning to go to the square by some side roads in the evening.

It happened to be Saturday. At 3 p.m., I took my son back home. Soon my husband came back. No matter how I argued, he would not let me go to the Square. He ordered me to babysit our son, and he himself went to the square with some friends.

From 7 to 9 p.m., the television repeatedly broadcast a "notice" from the martial law enforcement troops, asking people not to go onto the streets, otherwise they should be responsible for whatever happened to them. Hearing this, I began to feel that they really would use force this time. Bloodshed may not be avoided. I gave my husband a wet gauze mask. But what happened was totally beyond my imagination. The communist government and the "People's Army" did not use only clubs and tear gas, but live ammunition. If I had not seen it with my own eyes, I would never have believed this.

In Wukesong and Gongzhufen [both intersections with Changan Avenue west of the square], innocent citizens and students stood on the streets, hand in hand, trying to block the troops from entering the city. But it never occurred to them that, with clatters of machine guns and rumbling of engines, tanks would run over their heads. In an instant, the place where tanks had passed by became a mixture of soil and flesh. Frightened, people began to run, in all directions. Those awakened from the shock hurried to lie down; the stupid ones stood up and ran again, and those who ran slowly were shot by machine guns. Blood was flowing like a river.

All hospitals were full of bodies, dead and wounded. My apartment is not far from the Railway Hospital, so I went with some neighbors to give a hand. Every two minutes, a body would be taken in. Altogether more than 200. The hospital was soon packed and it couldn't accept more.

Since the troops used explosive bullets, doctors had to dig out whole pieces of flesh in order to get the bullets out. There were four operation rooms in this hospital. All the doctors living nearby were sent here. Those living too far away couldn't come anyway. In the hallway, blood was flowing like a river. Everyone was saying, had they not witnessed it, nobody would have believed that the Communists could be so brutal. In my neighborhood, a seven-year old boy was killed. Another young man in his twenties was shot in the thigh. In the neighborhood where many Xinhua News Agency staff lived, three people died and nine were wounded. More people died in the Design Institute of Nonferrous Metal, which was just opposite the Military Museum near Muxidi. It was now midnight, and people at Tiananmen Square still did not know what had happened. My husband came home at 9 p.m., my brother at 8 a.m. the next morning, and my friend Xiao Ming left the square at 12 midnight. The following are their accounts of what happened in the square, since I didn't go.

Before midnight, people at Tiananmen Square were singing the "Internationale" and taking solemn oaths. Many students and citizens wrote their wills. The government run loudspeakers repeatedly announced "An Open Letter to Beijing Citizens," urging people to leave. Many people did so, while several thousand stayed.

It was a solemn and tragic scene. From afar, the clatter of machine guns and rumbling of tanks could be heard. Facing the imminent danger, Hou Dejian [a pop singer from Taiwan] and some other hunger strikers went to negotiate with the army for a peaceful withdrawal of the students. The army agreed and promised half an hour for the students to leave. By doing so, Hou Dejian did save a lot of students. Most of the students agreed to leave, so they left, hand-in-hand, singing the "Internationale." Among them was Xiao Zhou, my collegue who had graduated from the Central Academy of Fine Arts. He was really lucky to come back safely. Some students were not so lucky. A group mainly consisting of students from Beijing University, Qinghua University, Beijing Normal University and students from other provinces, left the square and retreated westward from Qianmen. They made a grave mistake by going back to Chan-gan Avenue from Liubukou, because just as they turned into Chan-gan Avenue, tanks followed them. And my brother saw it with his own eyes that dozens of students were crushed by the tanks. Later the students had to follow some small alleys, but were pursued by gunfire. Many people climbed out alive from the piles of dead.

The next day, on June 5, I saw a female student near Muxidi. She was mentally deranged. She couldn't speak, and her body was covered with blood. She was actually not even wounded, but she knew only to wave her arms and hands aimlessly, walking like a drunkard. Many people came over to help her, asking her to go home. But she couldn't understand. Poor little girl!

Under the machine gun fire, the Beijing citizens began to fight back. They resorted to burning tanks and other military vehicles and had developed a way to do so. There were many traffic posts on the streets consisting of iron bars and reinforced concrete. After the tanks ran over them, the concrete was crushed and the iron bars became the weapons. When tanks came close, people inserted iron bars in the caterpillar tracks, and the tanks would come to a stop. The citizens would then flock up, pour gasoline on them and burn them. Some soldiers were burned to death. Others who managed to come out were beaten to death. Both sides were red-eyed with killing. My father was right. He said it would always be the ordinary folks who suffered the most. The soldiers were just ordinary people too, once they took off their uniforms.

Last night (June 5), there were rumors that troops had begun to fight each other. For instance there is still a division of soldiers staying in the Military Museum. Some people said that the division chief pledged not to fire on the people. He ordered his soldiers to stay in the Museum. Yesterday afternoon, three rows of tanks came from Tiananmen Square, with their machine guns aiming at the museum, where the soldiers all sprawled on the ground. The two sides remained facing each other for several minutes. Soldiers in the tanks fired into the air and left. My sister who lives in the building opposite the museum saw clearly with a telescope that the soldiers in the museum stood up only after the tanks left.

The situation is really tense. I heard that in the broadcast station building, people were not allowed to talk with each other. Soldiers were stationed in the corridor. The announcer of Radio Beijing was truly great. Shortly after he told the whole world about the Beijing massacre, he was arrested. Du Xian and Xue Fei [both were anchors for the Central China Televion who have now been removed from the anchor post] dressed in black on TV. Now many people on the streets wore black clothes. [Black is the color of mourning in many parts of China, although traditionally the Chinese used white to show respect for the dead.]

[The above was written on June 6.]

Since the letter could not be mailed out, I want to write some more. This morning I took a big risk by going to the office. Some colleagues living close to the office building were very surprised to see me, because I live in the most dangerous area—near the Military Museum. I found that everybody, including those "most revolutionary" such as Lao Wang, my boss, was enraged by the massacre. I used to hate him a lot, but today I even found him to be lovely, because he shared the same hatred.

I really don't know where China is going. Everybody is hoping for a coup, as if only a coup can save us ordinary people. This morning people were saying the 27th Army were most responsible for the killing. Most other armies did not kill people. Some say half of the 27th Army soldiers have died, so they want revenge. But the Beijing residents want revenge too; they are swearing that they will not let even one soldier from the 27th Army leave the city alive. Many wives were killed while seeking revenge for their husbands.

The heaviest casualties took place near Muxidi and the Military Museum. Some people now have guns in their possession. In the morning of June 4, several dozen soldiers were surrounded by the people and forced to throw away their guns. They took off their uniforms and are now under protection of the Beijing Railway Bureau. Now the Beijing citizens would beat any soldiers they saw.

The television is now talking nonsense. Many people say that they would have crushed their TV sets if they had not bought them with their own money.

[The above was written on June 8].

Today the situation turned a little better. I went out on to the streets and saw soldiers were cleaning the streets. There was no gunfire. But I still shuddered at seeing them. The television has broadcast the government version of the events between June 3–7. They only showed how soldiers were brutally killed. I think the killed soldiers are just as miserable. Those who had really killed the innocent might not have been killed by the citizens, and the dead soldiers might not have killed the innocent. Of course more innocent citizens were, and those citizens who did kill the soldiers and burn tanks might not have been caught. Anyway, this is how things happened. Those who suffered just had the back luck. For me, this is not the end of it. It is just the beginning of the crackdown. When everything calms down, they [the government] will come to every unit to check out everybody. It has been like this in Chinese history before. Ordinary people always take the hit. Leaving aside the many people being killed, the damage to the economy is enormous, and may not be recovered with us buying state bonds for another ten years. China is poor in the first place, and now with this disaster, our days will be more difficult.

June 9, 1989

"I'm Chai Ling. I'm Still Alive"

Following is a translation of some excerpts from a tape recording reportedly made by Chai Ling, one of the top student leaders. While her assessment of the death toll on Tiananmen Square is obviously exaggerated, the account gives a vivid sense of the mood of the students during the last days of their occupation of the square.

I am Chai Ling. I'm still alive. I am the chief commander of the Tiananmen Square Command Post. At 4 p.m. of June 8, I made this tape recording.

I think I am the most qualified person to comment on the events of June 4. In order to let the whole world know the truth, I have the responsibility to expose the whole course of the event.

In fact, even before the massacre, we had already got the signals that troops would move in to crack down on us students. At 10:30 p.m. of June 2, a speeding police vehicle ran into four people, killing three of them. This was the first signal. The second signal came when some soldiers tossed away their guns to the students, which strongly alerted us. We returned the guns to the Public Security Bureau and got their receipts. Then came the third signal. At around 1:10 p.m. of June 3, a number of armed police began beating students and civilians outside Xinhuamen near Liubukuo. One student climbed onto a motor vehicle and pleaded to the police, asking them not to beat the people. "People's Army loves the people; and people's police loves the people too," shouted the student. But the police climbed up the vehicle and fiercely kicked the student in the stomach, saying "who loves people like you!"

At that time, the Tiananmen Square Command Post had a broadcasting station. I had been staying there all the time and received emergency reports from many students. Li Lu and Feng Congde got similar reports from various channels. [Li is a student leader now on the government's wanted list. He escaped China after June 4. Feng is Chai Ling's husband who is also on the list.]

At around seven or eight o'clock, we held a press conference to tell our situation to the Chinese reporters in the square. There were only one or two foreign reporters present; we heard that the hotels where they stayed were watched by armed police. During the press conference, our command post raised the slogan: "Down with the Li Peng government!"

The situation began to worsen after eight o'clock. At 9 p.m., all the students in Tiananmen Square stood up. We raised our right hands and took an oath: "I will defend Tiananmen Square with my young life. My head may be chopped off, my blood may be shed, but the people's square cannot be abandoned. With our young life, we are willing to fight till the last minute."

At ten o'clock, the "Democracy University" was formally opened, with Zhang Deli, deputy commander of the Tiananmen Square

Command Post, as the president. We chose the place around the "Goddess of Democracy" as the classroom.

At that time, the situation was very tense. Soldiers of the 27th Army had already begun to kill people on Changan Avenue, where rivers of blood were flowing. The soldiers machine-gunned and bayoneted the students and civilians on the streets. Corpses were everywhere. Those students who ran back to the square from Changan Avenue had blood on their hands and all over their bodies. We held them in our arms.

After 10:30 p.m., the command post told everyone in the square to remain calm. We emphasized that the students' patriotic democracy movement had developed into a patriotic movement participated in by people from all professions and that the principle we had persisted in was peace. Many workers and civilians said that since the army had done such brutal things, we students should take up weapons to defend ourselves. However, we told them that we would insist on peace, and the highest principle of peace was to sacrifice.

After listening to our broadcast message, the students slowly walked out of their tents, quietly sat there (in the square), waiting for the slaughterers' knives. We were conducting a war between love and hatred, not a battle of weapons. If we had carried such things as sticks, "weapons" that are not really weapons, to fight those crazed soldiers with machine guns, that would have been the greatest tragedy. What we were waiting for was sacrifice.

Then the loudspeakers broadcast (the song) "The Dragon's Descendants." All the students joined in the singing, their eyes filled with tears. Everyone was grasping someone else, hands holding other hands. Everyone knew that the last moment in their lives was about to come.

There was a young student, Wang Li. He was only 15 years of age. But he had already written his will. A 15-year old boy was already considering death. Oh, Republic, you must remember—remember those kids who had fought for you!

In the small hours of June 4, the command post decided to give up the sit-in petition. We urged the students to leave, but they did not want to. The students were sitting (around the monument to the People's Heroes) quietly. Those in the front row were the most resolute. They were ready to die. I told them an old story. I said there were once a colony of ants numbering about 1.1 billion. One day, the mountain caught fire. Some of these ants had to go down the mountain and get help for the entire colony. As a result, they were burned to death, but many more lived. We all know that only our sacrifice could be exchanged for the new life of the Republic. . . . [heavy sobs and crying]. The students sang the "Internationale," their hands tightly clasped together.

Later, the four fasting compatriots—Hou Dejian, Liu Xiaobo, Zhou Duo and Gao Xin—began to persuade the students to leave. They said "you should not sacrifice like this. You must live on." They then went to negotiate with the martial law enforcement troops, telling them that the students were willing to withdraw and demanding that the troops guarantee their safety. The troops agreed. However, before we had time to tell the students this decision, soldiers with assault rifles had already rushed to the third tier of the monument. Most of the students began to leave. We were crying, but the civilians told us not to cry. We answered them: "We will return!" Even at this time, some students still had faith in the government. They stayed, thinking that the army would at most arrest them. But who knew that tanks would run over them. Those students still sleeping in their tents were crushed into flesh pie. It was said that 200 people were killed. Others said 4,000 people died in the square. At this point, it is still hard to have complete statistics of the death toll. However, all the workers—at least 20 or 30 of them—from the Autonomous Workers Union who were in the outskirts of the square were killed. After all, they had been prepared to die there to protect the students.

Later we were told that after the students left, tanks and armored personnel carriers crushed the tents. [The soldiers] then poured gasoline over the tents and cremated them together with the students' bodies. They then washed everything away with water. Those butchers! They wanted to cover up the truth of the massacre by leaving not a trace in the square.

The Goddess of Democracy, the symbol of the democracy movement, was run over by them and turned into rubble. We walked hand-in-hand onto the streets. When we passed the Mao Zedong Memorial Hall, we saw large numbers of soldiers running quickly toward the square along with tanks and armored personnel carriers.

After we passed Liubukou, we were walking along Changan Avenue, which by then had become a road of blood. However, we could not see even one corpse. People on the streets told us that the slaughterers who machine-gunned civilians in the front were followed by soldiers who piled the bodies of those being gunned down onto buses or tricycles. Those who still had a breath were choked to death.

We were all irritated and wanted to go back to the square to launch another sit-in protest. But the civilians pleaded with us not to make more sacrifices. "Machine guns had been set up in the square," so we were told. So we continued to walk westward to Xidan and turned north after passing the Xicheng District. We were coming close to our schools. We saw that all the people had tears in their eyes. A woman told us that at 2 a.m., she was blocking tanks [on the street], when she saw a little girl crushed into flesh pie by a tank.

On the way back to school, we saw slogans on some office buildings saying "Support the correct decision of the Party Central Committee!" The students furiously ripped them down. The broadcast stations were clamoring, "This is a counterrevolutionary riot, and order in the capital must be maintained."

Were we students rioters? Every Chinese who has some conscience, hold your hands to your heart and think about it. When we held hands, stood shoulder to shoulder, sat quietly beneath the monument, and met the executioners' butcher blades, were we rioters? How despotic have these fascists become! They are shamelessly telling the greatest lies in the world.

When we finally arrived at the campus of Beijing University, the university had prepared beds for those students from outside Beijing. We had returned alive. But more students stayed in the square, in the Avenue of Eternal Peace. They will never return. They are still young, but they will never come back.

Fellow countrymen! This is a callous, crazed, and illegal regime. After the bloodbath at Tiananmen, the massacre is bound to occur throughout the entire nation. This is a dark era, but dawn will appear from the darkness. A democratic republic is bound to be born. The key moment for the life and death of our nation has arrived. My fellow countrymen, awake!

Down with the fascists!

Chronology

April 15   Hu Yaobang, the former general secretary of the Chinese Communist Party died. Several hours later, big-character posters appeared on the campus of Beijing University, mourning the death of Hu and suggesting that "the wrong man died."

April 16   More posters appeared at Beijing University and other universities in Beijing. Many students placed wreaths under the Monument to the People's Heroes in Tiananmen Square to mourn the death of Hu.

April 18   6,000 students marched from Beijing University to Tiananmen Square early in the morning. Later more students launched a sit-in in front of the Great Hall of the People.

April 19   Students began a sit-in demonstration in front of Zhongnanhai, headquarters of the Chinese Communist Party and residential compound of many top Chinese leaders. About 300 students attempted to break in the gate and threw bottles and shoes at security guards, according to official reports.

April 20   The Chinese Communist Party announced that Hu's memorial service would be held on April 22. Student demonstrations spread to other cities such as Shanghai, Nanjing, Wuhan, Hefei, etc.

April 21   The Beijing municipal government declared that Tiananmen Square would be closed off during Hu's memorial service the next day. 100,000 students challenged this decision by gathering in the square on the night of April 21, making it impossible for the government to clear them out.

271

April 22   Hu's official memorial service, attended by almost all top leaders, was held in the Great Hall of the People, while outside the hall, over 100,000 students gathered to commemorate Hu in their own way. After the service, three student representatives were allowed to cross the police line to present a petition. They knelt down on the steps to the hall for a long time, but no official came out of the hall to receive the document.

April 23   A newly-established independent students union of Beijing universities called on the students to begin a class boycott and sent students to the streets to brief the general population on their movement. Class boycott formally began on many campuses in Beijing.

April 24   Zhao Ziyang left for North Korea for a previously-scheduled state visit.

April 25   Deng Xiaoping called a secret Politburo meeting in the absence of Zhao, and made two decisions: 1) to write a strongly-worded editorial for *People's Daily* to denounce the students for creating chaos; and 2) to crack down on the student protestors by using whatever force necessary.

April 26   The *People's Daily* published a harsh editorial accusing the students of creating turmoil. In Shanghai, the editor of the *World Economic Herald*, Qin Benli, was fired by the Shanghai Party Committee for publishing an article commemorating Hu Yaobang, in which a group of intellectuals criticized the sacking of Hu two years earlier.

April 27   In defiance of the *People's Daily* editorial, 500,000 students broke police barricades and marched to Tiananmen Square, forcing the government to agree to a dialogue with the students.

April 29   First official dialogue was held between Yuan Mu, the spokesman of the State Council and forty-five student representatives from sixteen Beijing universities. But the Autonomous Students Association of Beijing Universities did not accept it as a "real dialogue," because student delegates were chosen by the official students union rather than the Autonomous Association.

May 2	The students handed in a petition, demanding substantive dialogue with the government. The petition also had the tone of an ultimatum, because the students demanded that the government reply before noon of May 3; otherwise, they would take to the streets on May 4.
May 3	Yuan Mu held a press conference where he rejected the student demands and called the Autonomous Students Association of Beijing Universities illegal. He also claimed that the students were instigated by some "black hands," including the China Alliance for Democracy, a New York-based organization which the Chinese government had declared "reactionary."
May 4	20,000 students marched to Tiananmen Square and decided to resume attending classes the next day. Among the marchers were over 200 journalists who demanded that "newspapers should tell the truth," and that Qin Benli be returned to his post as editor of *World Economic Herald*. On the same day, Zhao Ziyang talked to the Asian Development Bank meeting and said that China would not sink into chaos. This was the first time the leadership made a conciliatory gesture toward student movement.
May 5	Students resumed attending classes in Beijing's major universities.
May 6	Zhao Ziyang told Hu Qili and Rui Xinwen, both in charge of propaganda, that "there is no risk for the press to open up a bit by reporting the student demonstrations and increasing the openness of news. Students handed in another petition to the National People's Congress, the State Council, and Party Central Committee, demanding "sincere and constructive dialogue regarding the current student movement, deepening political and economic reforms, and pushing forward democracy and the rule of law."
May 8	Zhao Ziyang told visiting Turkish dignitaries that China would "not only persistently carry out economic reform, but also further push forward political reform." In stressing political reform, Zhao was seemingly gaining control of the situation.

May 9   A petition carrying 1,013 signatures of journalists was handed in to the All China Journalists Association. The petition marked the first time in PRC's history that journalists openly demanded a dialogue on press reform with Party leaders in charge of propaganda work.

May 10   About 10,000 students demonstrated on bicycles demanding freedom of the press. They stopped by several major news agencies such as the Central Broadcasting Station, Xinhua News Agency, *People's Daily*, and *Guangming Daily*, urging them to "tell the truth."

May 11   Students at Beijing University decided to invite Gorbachev to give a speech at Beijing University when he arrived in Beijing on May 15.

May 12   The Autonomous Students Association of Beijing Universities made a decision to dramatize their action by launching a hunger strike at Tiananmen Square. Student leaders began enlisting hunger strikers at Beijing University and Beijing Normal University and dozens of other schools in Beijing. The turnout was low at the beginning. Only 150 students signed up for the strike at Beijing University.

May 13   About 400 students began a hunger strike at Tiananmen. Their two demands included 1) the April 26 *People's Daily* editorial be retracted; and 2) a sincere televised dialogue with Party leaders be held.

May 14   Hunger strike continued with more students joining in. Twelve prominent intellectuals went to Tiananmen Square to show their support but at the same time asked the students to leave the square so that their actions would not affect the Gorbachev visit scheduled for the next day.

May 15   Gorbachev arrived in Beijing for a historic visit. Because of the student occupation of Tiananmen Square, the welcoming ceremony was held at the airport. Chinese intellectuals held demonstrations at the square to show support for the hunger strikers.

May 16   Deng Xiaoping met with Gorbachev, but what should have been a personal triumph for Deng was over-shadowed by hunger strikers at Tiananmen Square. That same afternoon, Zhao Ziyang told Gorbachev that all major decisions in China had to be made by Deng Xiaoping, who was still the nation's "helmsman." In the meantime, a group of intellectuals released a "May 16 Declaration" which expressed strong support for the students.

May 17   "May 17 Declaration" was signed by dozens of intellectuals attacking Deng Xiaoping as the "last emperor without the title." Zhao Ziyang delivered a written speech on behalf of all the members of the Standing Committee of the Politburo urging the students to stop the hunger strike and leave the square and at the same time promising that "there would not be reprisals whatsoever against the participating students." Meanwhile, over one million people from government organizations and other units launched an unprecedented demonstration to show support for the students.

May 18   Another day of demonstrations, with more than one million people participating. Early in the morning, Zhao Ziyang, Li Peng, Qiao Shi and Hu Qili went to hospitals to visit students who had collapsed from lack of food. In the afternoon, Li Peng met with student leaders for about an hour in a discussion broadcast live on Chinese television. It turned out to be a tense confrontation between the premier and the defiant students, who accused Li Peng of "coming too late."

May 19   Early in the morning, Zhao Ziyang went to Tiananmen Square to talk to the students. With tears in his eyes, he apologized for "coming too late" and urged the students to stop the hunger strike. At 9 p.m., the students called off the hunger strike and turned it into a sit-in. At 12:30 a.m., Li Peng and Yang Shangkun delivered harsh speeches at a meeting attended by top Party and military officials, from which Zhao Ziyang was absent. Li accused "a handful of people with ulterior motives" of "taking hostage of student hunger strikers" to create turmoil. He threatened that "resolute measures" would be taken if the students did not leave the square.

May 20 Reacting to Li Peng's harsh speech, 200,000 students at Tiananmen Square declared that they would all resume the hunger strike. At 10 a.m., martial law was declared. Troops were brought to Beijing to clear out the protesters. Hundreds of thousands Beijing citizens went to all major intersections to block the troops. At 11 a.m., satellite transmission to foreign countries was stopped.

May 21 More than 30 members of the Standing Committee of the National People's Congress appealed to the NPC to convene an urgent meeting to lift martial law and dismiss Li Peng as premier. The appeal was supported by Zhao Ziyang. Nie Rongzheng and Xu Xiangqian, the only two remaining marshals, told visiting students that the troops were not brought in to attack the students, but to "restore order."

May 22 Over 10,000 intellectuals marched in Beijing to protest the declaration of martial law and Li Peng's speech. Wan Li, chairman of the National People's Congress Standing Committee, said in Toronto that "the patriotic enthusiasm should be protected."

May 23 Martial law enforcement troops were ordered to retreat. Over one million people took to the streets in protest against martial law. Satellite transmission to foreign countries was resumed and stopped twenty-four hours later.

May 24 Wan Li cut short his visit to the United States and returned to China after meeting with President Bush. Yang Shangkun delivered a confidential speech to top military commanders listing Zhao Ziyang's "mistakes."

May 25 Wan Li landed in Shanghai for "health reasons." Without his return to Beijing, an emergency meeting of the NPC Standing Committee was bound to be aborted. Students at Tiananmen Square voted on whether to leave or stay in the square, and they decided to stay.

May 26 Chen Yun delivered a speech to the Chinese Communist Party Central Advisory Committee and showed strong support for Li Peng and Yang Shangkun's speeches.

May 27 Li Xiannian spoke at the Chinese People's Political Consultative Conference to support Li Peng and Yang Shangkun's speeches. Wan Li delivered a written speech in Shanghai expressing support for Li Peng and Yang Shangkun.

May 28 Students at the square decided to stay in the square until June 20, when the projected meeting of the National People's Congress would convene. In a vote in which 228 schools participated, most of them from outside Beijing, and each allotted one vote, 160 chose to stay, while the rest voted to leave.

May 29 Peng Zhen talked to leaders of various democratic parties, saying the students had good motives, but used the wrong method to express themselves.

May 30 A statue—"the Goddess of Democracy"—was erected at Tiananmen Square, attracting more students back to the square. Three leaders of an independent workers organization were detained by the Public Security Bureau.

May 31 The three workers were released. A pro-government parade of peasants and soldiers took place in the suburbs of Beijing. Wan Li returned to Beijing from Shanghai.

June 1 Children's Day. Many parents brought their children to the square. Government officials blamed the student occupation of the square for preventing official activities celebrating the holiday.

June 2 Three people died in a car accident involving a police jeep. Angry citizens vowed to take to the streets the next day carrying the bodies of the dead.

June 3 Tens of thousands of soldiers marched to the city and were stopped near Beijing Hotel. In white shirts and green pants, the soldiers were unarmed. Massacre began in the evening when troops forced their way through the streets to Tiananmen Square, firing indiscriminately at civilians. Hundreds, perhaps thousands, of Beijing citizens and students died. At midnight, troops approached Tiananmen Square, while most students left the square under an agreement with the army, some were reported killed or crushed near and around the Monument to the People's Hero. The government had finally regained Tiananmen Square, which at this point was occupied by tanks and heavily armed soldiers. The seven-week pro-democracy movement came to a halt.

June 4   Gunshots continued in Beijing. In other parts of the world, government leaders condemned Chinese authorities for the use of force in quelling the protest.

Index

CHINA'S UNFINISHED REVOLUTION:
Problems and Prospects Since Mao
by James M. Ethridge

"An excellent primer. . .for people seeking to understand China's political and economic changes in recent years."
> Lyn Pan, FAR EASTERN ECONOMIC REVIEW

"An extremely useful guide for anyone . . . seeking to understand what's going on in China today against the background of the reform policies. . .written in a wonderfully lucid and lively manner, using anecdotes, concrete examples and even jokes to blaze a clear trail through what in other hands might be a thicket of ideological verbiage and concepts. . ."
> BEIJING REVIEW

From the founding of the Peoples Republic in 1949 to the student democracy movement of 1989, China remains a land confusing to most Americans.

Faced with the enormously complex task of modernization, how does the world's most populous nation manage its 1.1 billion people?

Ideologically, economically and socially, explanations of the reforms, plans and programs of the last 40 years of China's tumultuous history are clearly and concisely offered.

Packed with facts, figures and analyses of key political business and economic trends, CHINA'S UNFINISHED REVOLUTION is an essential reference for understanding modern China.

Also includes:
  ★ a mini-encyclopedia of concepts, events, slogans and miscellaneous features of Chinese life
  ★ a chronology of events since 1949

China Books

Cloth $24.95
illustrated with cartoons

ISBN 0-8351-2196-8
Send for our mail-order catalog.